How Labour Built Neoliberalism

Studies in Critical Social Sciences

Series Editor

David Fasenfest (*Wayne State University*)

Editorial Board

Eduardo Bonilla-Silva (*Duke University*)
Chris Chase-Dunn (*University of California-Riverside*)
William Carroll (*University of Victoria*)
Raewyn Connell (*University of Sydney*)
Kimberle W. Crenshaw (*University of California, LA,* and *Columbia University*)
Raju Das (*York University*)
Heidi Gottfried (*Wayne State University*)
Karin Gottschall (*University of Bremen*)
Alfredo Saad-Filho (*University of London*)
Chizuko Ueno (*University of Tokyo*)
Sylvia Walby (*Lancaster University*)

VOLUME 126

The titles published in this series are listed at *brill.com/scss*

How Labour Built Neoliberalism

Australia's Accord, the Labour Movement and the Neoliberal Project

By

Elizabeth Humphrys

BRILL

LEIDEN | BOSTON

Cover illustration: Australian Prime Minister Bob Hawke and British Prime Minister Margaret Thatcher -- at 10 Downing Street, London in 1986. With kind permission of Fox Photos/Hulton Archive/Getty Images.

Library of Congress Cataloging-in-Publication Data

Names: Humphrys, Elizabeth, author.
Title: How labour built neoliberalism : Australia's accord, the labour movement and the neoliberal project / by Elizabeth Humphrys.
Description: Leiden ; Boston : Brill, 2019. | Series: Studies in critical social sciences, ISSN 1573-4234 ; VOLUME 126 | "This book draws on my Ph.D., which I completed in the Department of Political Economy at the University of Sydney"-- Author's acknowledgments. | Includes bibliographical references and index.
Identifiers: LCCN 2018038577 (print) | LCCN 2018044459 (ebook) | ISBN 9789004383463 (E-Book) | ISBN 9789004349001 (hardback)
Subjects: LCSH: Australia--Economic conditions--1945- | Labor movement--Australia. | Neoliberalism--Australia. | Australian Labor Party. | Australian Council of Trade Unions. | Australia--Politics and government--1945-
Classification: LCC HC605 (ebook) | LCC HC605 .H775 2019 (print) | DDC 320.51/30994--dc23
LC record available at https://lccn.loc.gov/2018038577

Typeface for the Latin, Greek, and Cyrillic scripts: "Brill". See and download: brill.com/brill-typeface.

ISSN 1573-4234
ISBN 978-90-04-34900-1 (hardback)
ISBN 978-90-04-38346-3 (e-book)

This book is printed on acid-free paper and produced in a sustainable manner.

Contents

Acknowledgements

I acknowledge the assistance of the Noel Butlin Archives at the Australian National University, and the University of Melbourne Archives. For permission to access collections, I thank the Australian Council of Trade Unions (ACTU), the Victorian Trades Hall Council (VTHC) and the National and Victorian Branches of the Australian Manufacturing Workers' Union (AMWU). For access to other materials, I thank the Bob Hawke Prime Ministerial Library, the National Archives of Australia, the University of Sydney Library, Frank Stilwell, Paul Frijters and Robert Gregory. In 2013, I received the University of Sydney & WZB Fellowship at the Berlin Social Science Research Centre and I thank John Keane. I thank Dieter Plehwe for his support and friendship while I was in Berlin, and in the years following. I am also grateful to the Varuna National Writers' House for two residencies. Thank you to Lisa Adkins and the participants in the Neoliberalism's Complexities workshop at the University of Newcastle (Sydney Campus) in December 2017, as their presentations and feedback on my paper provided excellent motivation for revisions on the final chapter of this book. Thank you to Peter Thomas, Colin Barker, Jenny Haines, Humphrey McQueen and, more sadly, Frans Timmerman (1947–2014) and John Kaye (1955–2016) for advice during my research. I acknowledge the assistance of Kieran Latty in creating Figure 6.2, Margie Tubbs for proofreading and Amy Thomas for the index.

My colleagues at the University of Technology Sydney have provided incredible support while I was writing this book: thank you to Chris Ho, Liz Giuffre, Sarah Attfield, Lucy Fiske, Ben Abraham, Devleena Ghosh and Maryanne Dever. This book draws on my Ph.D., which I completed in the Department of Political Economy at the University of Sydney. I thank Gareth Bryant and Adam Morton in particular. My Ph.D. supervisor, Damien Cahill, and associate supervisor, Bill Dunn, were unfailingly generous. I am particularly indebted to Damien for his guidance, astuteness and for our friendship over many years. This book also benefitted from the thoughtful feedback provided by my Ph.D. examiners, and I thank Alfredo Saad-Filho, Andreas Bieler and Carol Johnson. Thank you to David Fasenfest, Jennifer Obdam and Judy Pereira for their thoughtful guidance and the opportunity to publish in this series.

Finally, thank you to my friends and family for their support. Thank you to Tadeusz Tietze for everything he did that made the Ph.D., which this book draws on, possible. Thank you to Frank Humphrys, Susan Humphrys, Fiona Collison, Luke Humphrys, Rachael Humphrys, Katerina Kraenzel-Paneras, Martin Kraenzel, Clinton Hill, Claire Parfitt, Eve Vincent, Jessica Whyte, Ihab Shalbek, Inger Mewburn, Tom Barnes, Rory Dufficy, Elena Gomez, Zoe Bowman, Frances Lockie and Devina Potter.

Illustrations

Figures

Tables

Abbreviations

ABS	Australian Bureau of Statistics
ACTU	Australian Council of Trade Unions
AFAP	Australian Federation of Air Pilots
ALAC	Australian Labor Advisory Council
ALP	Australian Labor Party
AMC	Australian Manufacturing Council
AMFSU	Amalgamated Metals Foundry and Shipwrights' Union
AMIEU	Amalgamated Meat Industry Employees' Union
AMWSU	Amalgamated Metal Workers' and Shipwrights' Union
AMWU	Amalgamated Metal Workers' Union (see Appendix A)
AMWU	Australian Manufacturing Workers' Union (see Appendix A)
ANZCERTA	Australia & New Zealand Closer Economic Relations Trade Agreement
AWU	Australian Workers' Union
BLF	Builders Labourers' Federation
BWIU	Building Workers' Industrial Union
CPA	Communist Party of Australia
CPI	Consumer Price Index
EPAC	Economic Planning Advisory Council
ETU	Electrical Trades Union
FCA	Federated Confectioners' Association
GDP	Gross Domestic Product
GST	Goods and Services Tax
IRC	Industrial Relations Commission
MTIA	Metal Trades Industry Association
NFF	National Farmers Federation
NSW	New South Wales
NUM	National Union of Mineworkers (UK)
NYC	New York City
NZ	New Zealand
OECD	The Organisation for Economic Co-operation and Development
PJT	Prices Justification Tribunal
PSA	Prices Surveillance Authority
SEP	Structural Efficiency Principle of the Accord
SPA	Socialist Party of Australia
TDC	Trade Development Council
TUC	British Trades Union Congress
UK	United Kingdom

US	United States of America
VBEF	Vehicle Builders' Employees Federation
VTHC	Victorian Trades Hall Council

CHAPTER 1

Introduction

> [L]aissez-faire … is a deliberate policy, conscious of its own ends, and not the spontaneous, automatic expression of economic facts. … [It] is a political programme, designed to change—in so far as it is victorious—a State's leading personnel, and to change the economic programme of the State itself—in other words the distribution of the national income …
>
> ANTONIO GRAMSCI, *Prison Notebooks*; Q13 §18

Neoliberalism is not the natural expression of economic truths, and its implementation required significant political, economic and social transformation. Public policy was recast, national and international finance systems were transformed, and the state and civil society were reorganised to facilitate a new phase of capitalism. Key to achieving these outcomes, in each country neoliberalism was implemented, was the curtailing of trade union power. This book investigates how neoliberalism was constructed in Australia, and in particular the role of organised labour in that process. The analysis focuses on the 1983–1996 social contract known as the Accord, signed between the Australian Labor Party (ALP) and the Australian Council of Trade Unions (ACTU).

The construction of neoliberalism in Australia, and the role of trade unions within that, is not simply an issue of historical interest to be argued about in the halls of the academy. The twentieth century was, ultimately, bookended by the formation and decline of organised labour in most advanced capitalist countries—and in many locations trade union organisation is in crisis. In Australia, union membership is at a historic low and sits at levels not seen since before the Great Depression. In the early 1980s when the Accord was adopted, trade union density was over 50 per cent. Today density languishes below 15 per cent, and it is under 10 per cent in the private sector. The strength of trade unions has waned so significantly that some ask the difficult question of whether it can recover to previous levels. The lack of workers' power is also, at times, a problem for capital, and in an astonishing recent statement the head of the Australian Reserve Bank called directly on workers to demand higher wages given their miserable longer-term growth was undermining accumulation (Greber 2017). Despite the discrediting of neoliberalism as a doctrine in the wake of the 2008 global economic downturn, there has been little revitalisation of labour organisation and militancy.

 | DOI:10.1163/9789004383463_002

The relationship between neoliberalism and the decline of labour organisation demands a candid reflection on how trade unions confronted—and at times facilitated—the advance of neoliberalism. This book examines how the trade union movement in Australia was integrated into a national project of economic restructuring, and one ultimately not in the interest of labour.

Alongside the sluggish and uneven economic environment in the wake of the 2008 crisis, a political crisis has also become clearer. Popular detachment from, distrust of, and contempt for political elites and their activities has grown over the last several decades. How this political crisis— the rise of anti-politics—relates to the development of neoliberalism has focussed the attention of scholars who seek to understand and explain events as diverse as Brexit, the election of Donald Trump, and the popular dissent of the Spanish 15M movement. If we are to understand the current political conjuncture, it is crucial we more deeply appreciate the role of organised labour and traditional reformist parties of the left—social democratic and labourist—in the construction of neoliberalism. Clarity on the roots of neoliberalism is central to understanding the growing detachment from politics felt by many citizens, particularly working-class communities and those who—only a few generations ago—would have filled the ranks of trade unions.

This book's key argument is that academic and popular understandings of how neoliberalism was constructed accept a particular narrative, one that explains neoliberal transformation based on the ascendancy of the New Right and the coercive implementation of economic reform. This narrative treats the experience under Ronald Reagan in the United States (US) and under Margaret Thatcher in the United Kingdom (UK) as exemplars. Although recent scholarship has emphasised the geographic variegation of neoliberalism—its '*systemic* production of geoinstitutional differentiation' (Brenner, Peck, and Theodore 2010, 184)—this dominant account of neoliberalism's origins and trajectory persists. Four elements of the prevailing narrative are subjected to critique in this book. First, the account claims that the origins of neoliberalism are to be found in the vanguard projects in Chile under Pinochet; in the 1975–1981 New York City Council fiscal crisis; under Margaret Thatcher in the UK (1979–1990); and under Ronald Reagan in the US (1981–1989). Second, that the geographically specific vanguard projects represent original types or templates, from which neoliberalism was later exported elsewhere. Third, that social democratic parties were not significant to neoliberalism's vanguard phase, instead implementing neoliberal projects at a later point and in a moderated form. And finally, that neoliberalism is a state-led coercive project imposed on trade unions and the labour movement more broadly, in which labour was the object or victim of change. I argue this origin story has been inappropriately universalised, and does not fit the experience in other locations that underwent neoliberal transformation in the same period. Further, the narrative obscures the complexity of the development of neoliberalism in the narrative's heartlands of the UK and US.

In this book, I engage in a reconsideration of the dominant story critical scholars and left commentators attach to the construction of neoliberalism through a detailed analysis of the experience in Australia. The development of vanguard neoliberalism in Australia runs directly counter to the prevailing narrative. In Australia, neoliberalism was constructed at the same time the ALP government and the trade unions were engaged in a wide-ranging 13-year social contract. The implementation of the agreement simultaneously deepened Australia's existing corporatism and advanced neoliberalism within a highly structured economic framework. Further, as a vigorous partner in a social contract, organised labour actively constructed and contributed to the formation of hegemonic neoliberalism. The organised labour movement was not, therefore, *only* an object or victim of the neoliberal project.

So why do we assume it was always the New Right that was at the centre of constructing neoliberalism? If that was found not to be the case, how might the story we are told about the origins of neoliberalism need to be rewritten? And, controversially, why do we accept that the labour movement was simply the victim of neoliberal change, rather than involved more intimately in its manufacture? These questions are central to understanding the present condition of the labour movement and its prospects for the future. This book looks to the particular case of Australia, to demonstrate the interconnections between organised labour and neoliberalism that are largely missing from accounts of economic transformation since the end of the long boom.

1 The ALP & ACTU Accord

Jamie Peck, Neil Brenner and Nik Theodore have urged scholars to consider the diverse ways that neoliberalism has been constructed, through path-dependent and context-specific development. They argue that neoliberalism takes variegated forms across different regulatory environments, and that the development of neoliberalism takes place 'among its others' (Peck, Theodore, and Brenner 2009, 104). For these authors, the 'notion of neoliberalism somehow standing separate from other social formations and political projects seriously misconstrues both the character of neoliberalism and the nature of its advance' (ibid 2009, 103). This book examines one such spatially distinct outcome: the simultaneous implementation of the Accord social contract and advance of neoliberalism in Australia.

Between 1983 and 1996, a social contract was instituted between the political and industrial wings of the Australian labour movement. The *Statement of Accord by the Australian Labor Party and the Australian Council of Trade Unions Regarding Economic Policy* ('the Accord') profoundly shaped the political economy while extending the country's longstanding corporatist arrangements. The agreement was framed as consensual economic decision-making in the national interest, and was signed after a decade of failed attempts, by successive governments, to resolve the economic crisis of the 1970s. The unions viewed the social contract as a way to maintain the living standards of their members, given the strategy of industrial militancy of the 1970s and early 1980s was at the point of exhaustion. In return for labour agreeing to moderate wage claims to the level of inflation, the social contract promised to restrain prices, introduce economic and taxation reform, and extend the social wage.

Although the Accord was a wide-ranging document with an expansionary emphasis, it was quickly narrowed to focus on wage control. The period of the Accord also involved the advance of 'vanguard' neoliberalism. The vanguard period—from the mid-1970s until the late 1980s—was a key moment in the construction of neoliberalism in various advanced capitalist countries, and the period is characterised by an initial and intense period of implementation in order to reorient national economics. Key vanguard locations included Chile, Argentina, the US, the UK, Australia and New Zealand (NZ). I detail how the Accord deepened Australian corporatism at the same time as vanguard neoliberalism was constructed.

The economic malaise in the period before the Accord was deep and intractable in Australia, with five recessions in the decade between 1973 and 1983. What many refer to as the Golden Age of the advanced capitalist nations—the long post-war boom—came to an abrupt end in the early 1970s with a widespread crisis of profitability. During those years, consecutive governments unsuccessfully tackled the situation. The cornerstone of the Australian welfare system—the centrally indexed full-time wage and its associated conditions—came under increasing pressure from concurrently rising inflation and unemployment. Sections of the labour movement sought to preserve wages and conditions through workplace-based struggle, and industrial militancy reached its highest point in the nation's history. A resources-led boom at the end of the 1970s gave brief respite to the recessionary tendencies, before the Australian economy contracted again in 1981.

In the early 1980s, the union strategy of confrontation with business and government to protect living standards was fatigued. The assault on the labour movement by the conservative Fraser Government (1975–1983)[1] had also flagged. Neither side had won a decisive victory. The 'exhaustion' of industrial struggle, plus the search for an alternative, brought a new political project to centre stage as part of an effort to resolve the crisis. The Accord, as a consensual approach to economic and industrial relations policy, underpinned the landslide election victory of the Bob Hawke ALP government in March 1983—using the campaign slogan 'Bringing Australia Together'.

The election of the ALP government was a watershed moment in Australian politics. In contrast to most of the post-war period, the Labor Party held office nationally and in four of the six states. The party re-emerged as the major political force after many years of conservative dominance, and in most cases the party won with resounding majorities. The conservative Liberal and National Parties were in disarray around the country. Prime Minister Hawke would win four elections as leader in 1983, 1984, 1987 and 1990, while his successor Paul Keating would lead the ALP to victory in 1993—an unprecedented five consecutive terms as federal incumbents. This ALP Government is now considered 'one of the most successful [post World War II] governments of the western world' (Harcourt 2013).

Soon after the election in 1983, the ALP implemented the already-signed Accord agreement as government policy. During the 13 years of Labor rule, the agreement functioned as the primary statement of domestic economic policy (Ahlquist 2011, 133). In return for the trade unions restraining wage demands to the level of inflation (and making 'no further claims' via industrial action), prices and non-wage incomes were to be moderated, the social wage was to be expanded and tax reform was to be implemented. The Accord reintroduced central wage fixation and sought to promote growth through economic management and central planning. The Accord stated that reducing inflation by moderating wage claims was fundamental to achieving expansion. For this reason benefits for workers would be enhanced and delivered through an increased social product and social wage.

The Accord period is commonly presented as the high point of relations between the ALP and ACTU, and as being beneficial to the working class in a period marked by the policies of the New Right in overseas countries. Australia was purported to be the progressive alternative to the approach taken by Thatcher's Conservative Party and Reagan's Republican Party (Markey 2013). For many in the ALP and the trade unions today, these remain halcyon years—electoral successes only dreamed of in a contemporary era of low ALP primary

1 A list of Australian governments from 1972 onwards is provided in Appendix A.

votes, declining party and union membership, and the consolidation of a political challenger to the left of Labor in the form of the Australian Greens.

The Accord was reconstituted through national wage cases and renegotiated terms between the parties over 13 years and eight 'editions' (Mark I–VIII). The original statement (ALP & ACTU 1986) set out wide-ranging economic and social policy. However, it is generally acknowledged that the process quickly narrowed to focus almost exclusively on wages. Real wage levels, to be maintained under the Accord, declined markedly. Early in the period, the ALP adopted a policy—'the trilogy' commitment—not to increase taxation, government expenditure or the size of the budget deficit as a percentage of gross domestic product. This significantly curtailed the planned social wage spending. Many core elements of the original statement were not implemented and, on frequent occasions, policy contrary to the text was adopted. Australia's tariff system was dismantled and free tertiary education was abolished, in contravention of the agreement. Taxation—which was to be restructured under the Accord to ensure business paid a 'fair share'—moved in the opposite direction.

2 The Social Contract's Gala Dinner

The 30th anniversary of the Accord, and other key events managed by the social contract, occurred during the writing of this book. The anniversaries involved various celebrations, as well as a resumption of analysis about the social contract's role in political economic transformation. For the most part, the events and discussions provided an untroubled account of a period of dramatic change.

In 2012 there was an Accord reunion of sorts, at the annual gala dinner of the ACTU. Many of the crucial players involved in the development of the agreement were there. Paul Keating, Prime Minister (1991–1996) and Federal Treasurer (1983–1991), and Bill Kelty, Secretary of the ACTU (1983–2000), delivered the keynote speeches. Keating was asked to commemorate Kelty's leadership in the labour movement, and in particular his commanding role in the Accord. Bob Hawke, Prime Minister (1983–1991) and ACTU President (1969–1980), led a rendition of the traditional union anthem, 'Solidarity Forever', and all speakers sang the praises of the social contract. Speakers urged a renewed partnership. A new agreement between the Labor Party and the trade unions was necessary, they argued, in an effort to deal with uncertain economic times (Lucas 2012).

Public events continued into 2013 as the formal 30th anniversary of the signing of the Accord took place. At the main academic conference organised around the event, a number of the architects of the social contract extolled its virtues. Former politicians and union leaders Hawke, Kelty, Ralph Willis (Federal Treasurer 1993–1996) and Simon Crean (ACTU President 1985–1990) took credit for restructuring the Australian economy to meet the challenges of globalisation. One of the speakers dubbed the opening panel, which also included business representative Bert Evans, Chief Executive of the Metal Trades Industry Association (MTIA) (1981–1996), the 'Accord Quintet'. They celebrated their roles in the dramatic restructuring of the Australian economy, which, alongside the suppression of wages and industrial action through the social contract, involved financial 'deregulation' (re-regulation), floating the Australian dollar, and mass privatisations. Yet, in the same moment as this event, state and federal Labor parties were recording some of their lowest primary votes in a century and the union movement's coverage of workers was languishing. The panel failed to assess candidly the impact of the Accord on the Labor Party and labour movement, a task that must include an assessment of the decline of the Labor Party and trade union density. The anniversary event had an air of the surreal, like a party in a cemetery.

Later in the conference and after the departure of these men of the 1980s, more difficult questions about the Accord's legacy within the Labor Party and wider labour movement were raised. Ged Kearney, then President of the ACTU, gave the Accord only guarded support. Kearney (2013) called the agreement the 'highpoint of the political and industrial wings of the labour movement linked informally and formally in the national interest to deliver economic stability and historic reforms'. But, Kearney (ibid 2013) also noted that the Accord can be 'a heavy cross to bear'. She argued that an assessment of any achievements of the Accord should also recognise defects and unintended consequences. Kearney asserted that the period after the Accord had included the spread of precarious work, escalating executive salaries, exploitative and illegal business practices, as well as a lack of concern over inequality on the part of business elites. Kearney placed the responsibility for these deficiencies at the feet of capital. However, she also stated that the Accord's reintroduction of centralised wage fixation had held back unions from doing their core work of bargaining with employers. Kearney explained that the shift in policy around wage bargaining had long-term consequences and the labour movement was still paying the price. The agreement, in her view, had resulted in some unions 'forgetting' how to organise.

Although Kearney did not provide the same gloss as the opening panel, she equally did not reflect candidly on the content of the Accord. Open debate about the legacy of the Accord in the context of Labor's neoliberal agenda remains rare in the union movement. I would argue that there is also a lack of critical assessment of the Accord in the scholarly literature. This book highlights the troubled legacy of the Accord, and examines questions that arise from understanding the social contract's legacy as part of a period of dramatic and problematic neoliberal change. The Accord voluntarily suppressed real wage levels and industrial action, and it is pertinent to examine how this suppression might have broken capacity for workers' self-activity and organisation. The centrality of the labour movement in designing the Accord raises crucial questions about the role of the labour movement in constructing neoliberalism. Subsequently, because the labour movement helped design and implement the Accord, a key issue is to what extent did the labour movement itself play an active role in creating the context for and policy of its own subsequent disorganisation.

3 Neoliberalism's Corporatist Origins

Most accounts of the Accord suggest that the social contract and neoliberalism were contradictory and counterposed sets of ideas, policies and processes (Peetz 2013; Spies-Butcher 2012). In contrast to those accounts, I argue that the Accord and neoliberalism were not alternative, exogenous or antagonistic to each other. Rather, the social contract and neoliberalism were interrelated elements of a hegemonic state-centred project to restore accumulation after the 1970s economic crisis. The relationship between the Accord and vanguard neoliberal transformation in Australia as one of concord, not opposition, which I describe as *simultaneously deepening corporatism and advancing neoliberalism*—where those processes are aspects of a unified moment of class rule. This framework provides a unique insight into how vanguard neoliberalism developed among its corporatist 'other'. Corporatism and neoliberalism were two sides of a unitary project of capitalist class rule through politics and the state, and when examined as such we can gain a richer understanding of both.

The development of neoliberalism in Australia through the Accord forces a reconsideration of the dominant narrative about neoliberalism's global advance. Reconsidering the dominant narrative does not necessarily mean displacing existing accounts of the development of neoliberalism in other locations in their entirety. Rather, by closely examining concrete exceptions to the prevailing story we can enrich our understanding of the global development of neoliberalism. The Australian experience points to how alternative geographic accounts to the dominant narrative can usefully 'write in' the ways that social democratic parties and organised labour were active agents in the construction of vanguard neoliberalism. Such a process may provide a more satisfactory explanation of the multi-faceted and diverse forms of neoliberalism in its early years, thereby offering a more useful perspective for understanding its underlying commonalities and trajectory over time. It also opens up a consideration of the relationship between corporatism and neoliberalism in other locations and moments, such as in the New York City Council fiscal crisis and the more recent process of neoliberalisation in Finland (as discussed in Chapter 9).

In the case of Australia, the implementation of vanguard neoliberalism occurred through a 'positive' corporatist project centred on working class sacrifice in the national interest. In turn, the use of corporatism within vanguard neoliberalism led to a particular method of labour disorganisation—one marked by the labour movement itself implementing successful wage suppression and self-policing of industrial activity. Trade union officials did not act only as 'representatives' of the workers, but as agents of control over them—enveloped by a political society they had been drawn more closely into.

It is too simple to argue that the Accord assisted the introduction of neoliberal policies through its various effects, although it did have that result in many ways. Rather, and more distinctively, the agreement engendered consent for the neoliberal project to take place by integrating the unions and the working class into the efforts of political society to construct a new form of social rule. In this book, I pursue a more compelling theorisation of the Australian Accord—one which recognises the social contract as the process by which vanguard neoliberalism was constructed, and as a central component in the transformation of civil society in the process. Corporatism was the *form* and *method* that vanguard neoliberalism took in Australia, and corporatism and neoliberalism were internally related.

The disorganisation of working class power has generally been seen as one of the central objectives or outcomes of neoliberalism. In this book, I demonstrate how the social contract was integral to the disorganisation of labour that took place in Australia. Consensual agreement on the part of the trade unions took the form of submission to, and active implementation of, the suppression of wages, industrial activity and organisation of rank-and-file labour. I detail how this process of disruption took place through the Accord's components—and that this occurred despite the social contract being signed at a time of peak power and organisation for an historically strong trade union movement, and the agreement resulting in unions gaining unprecedented direct political influence in the state. Central to the analysis is the paradox between the Accord only being possible because of the size and strength of the Australian union movement, and that same agreement ultimately contributing to the movement's internal disorganisation.

What follows interrogates the role of organised labour and its representative structures in the construction of vanguard neoliberalism in Australia. In the process of constructing and implementing the social contract, the unions helped execute key aspects of neoliberal transformation. These changes included real wage decline, structural adjustment through industry policy, the suppression of industrial action, and the re-regulation of the industrial relations system in a manner that weakened organised labour's position. The Accord, and thus neoliberalism, was not a process enacted only from above, as it involved the consent and active involvement of the trade union movement. This is the story of how labour made neoliberalism.

4 A Hegemonic Political Project

This book analyses the class-based nature of the Accord and its role in establishing neoliberal hegemony in Australia in the wake of the political and economic turbulence of the 1970s. This book understands neoliberalism as a *state-centred hegemonic political project remaking capitalist production and social reproduction since the end of the long boom.* Neoliberalism is not simply a process of state-led economic transformation necessitated by economic crisis, nor is it merely an ideology or a set of ideas. Neoliberalism involves the development and implementation of a political project that utilises modified neoclassical economics to bring coherence to a suite of characteristic policies and economic changes—even if neoliberalism in theory varied from neoliberalism in practice.

As will be discussed in Chapter 4, neoliberalism does not involve strict fidelity to a certain economic doctrine. Neoliberalism is a project utilising different means in different locations, and is carried out by the state and political society in the interests of the dominant social group. The key aim of neoliberalism was the restoration of capitalist profitability and stable capital accumulation, which had been disrupted by economic crisis and, to lesser or greater extent globally, by worker resistance. Its consequences have included the diminution of organised labour's power, the disorganisation of labour movements, and a significant upward shift of national income from the working class to the capitalist class (Harvey 2005). Emphasising neoliberalism as a political practice, rather than simply assessing it on the basis of conformity to a particular ideological model or series of policies, enhances our understanding of 'actually existing' neoliberalism (Cahill 2014).

Neil Davidson has argued that any catalogue of neoliberal reforms cannot be exhaustive given the geographic specificity of the political project. However, he includes in his list of those that 'proved more enduring':

> [P]rivatisation of state-owned industries and utilities, flexible labour markets, outsourcing of non-core functions, deregulation of financial markets and the removal of exchange controls, abolition of protective tariffs and subsidies on essential goods, commodification of services once provided free at the point of use, the shift from direct and progressive to indirect and regressive taxation, and a monetary policy dedicated to the maintenance of low levels of inflation (2013, 190).

Neoliberalism is shaped by a macroeconomic approach that sees inflation as a greater risk to economic development than unemployment and promotes the benefits of markets over state action (Bieler 2007, 112). In general terms, most scholars agree 'that neoliberalism can be broadly defined as the extension and installation of competitive markets into all areas of the economy, politics and society' (Birch 2015, 571). In Australia in the Accord era, the state implemented an 'inflation first' strategy and a suite of economic and social reforms similar to those usually viewed as part of the advance of neoliberalism globally. These reforms included: floating the Australian dollar and abolishing exchange controls; deregulating the financial and banking sectors; dismantling the tariff system and promoting 'free trade'; widespread industry deregulation; privatisation of government-owned entities; corporatisation of government departments and contracting out of services; marketisation of the retirement payments system; the adoption of competition policy frameworks; imposition of a level of austerity on the working class; and, over time, the introduction of a 'deregulated' labour market in the form of enterprise bargaining.

Neoliberalism as a concept in the anglophone world has been dominated by the transformations that took place in the UK and the US. By interrogating the variety of ways in which neoliberal policies were introduced in other locations, new light can be shed on what is common among diverse processes. The neoliberal project has not always been connected to the election of New Right political currents, or those that might be historically rooted in particular economic traditions. Social democratic parties have also implemented vanguard neoliberalism in response to changes in capitalist accumulation, such as in Australia and NZ (1984–1990).

The implementation of vanguard neoliberalism by social democratic parties in Australia and NZ is distinct from the phenomenon of social democratic adoption of an already established neoliberalism, as in the case of British Labour's 'Third Way' turn (1994–2010). Unlike in the dominant narrative, neoliberalism in Australia took hold through a consensual social contract with the trade union movement. Consequently, this book reconceptualises the *political* nature of neoliberalism and reflects on the durability and antinomies of it as a mode of political practice.

5 Corporatist '*involucro*'

Most analysis of the Accord—and corporatism in general—tends to presume rather than demonstrate an underlying harmony in contemporary capitalist societies. This book problematises the notion of a shared national interest between classes. The analysis argues that such social harmony is not possible because of the fundamental features of modern capitalist society, which were explained by Marx in his pioneering critique of political economy. In summary, the alienation (or 'abstraction') of living labour in the process of social production produces:

- A directly antagonistic relationship ('exploitation') between capitalist and worker.
- A bourgeois civil society in which all individuals live in constant competition, alienated from each other by the logic of the social system.
- An 'abstract' political state which itself stands 'over against' the particular interests of civil society, but which is dependent on the continuation of capitalist social relations for its survival.

Thus, the state is *always already* partisan—and, despite having its own interests, these interests cannot break free of the need to defend and promote the stability and health of capitalist society on a national and international scale. The modern nation state is a *capitalist* state—not because it is inhabited by capitalists, under their control or directly tied to them, but because it is the state of a capitalist (national) civil society.

As will be discussed in Chapter 3, corporatism requires working class assent to the idea that there exists a national interest (Panitch 1981, 1976). Moreover, corporatism has a basic dilemma at its core—it translates working class loyalty to a social democratic party into loyalty to the state, and sees 'coercion in the name of harmony' rear 'its ugly head' (Panitch 1976, 247).

In a parallel conception utilised by this book, Gramsci's concept of the integral state posits that civil society is enwrapped ('*involucro*') by political society. The notion of the integral state can usefully support and extend Panitch's analysis by understanding '"political society" as a "container" of civil society, surrounding or enmeshing and fundamentally reshaping it' (Thomas 2009b, 189). In this way, the concept of the integral state emphasises how corporatism is a mechanism to address (temporarily) the separation and antagonism within the state–civil society relationship.

This book develops a framework that considers the complementary nature of the integral state and Panitch's analysis, in order to examine the relationship between the Accord and vanguard neoliberalism. Such a framework assists in re-examining the legacy of the Accord, concluding that the Accord was a collaborative project between the state and civil society in order to implement a specific and partisan political-economic transformation. As such, the Accord cannot be considered as an alternative economic plan in the interests of all, or for the advance of socialism as some trade unions believed.

6 A Note on Method

This book identifies a dominant narrative about the origins of neoliberalism in scholarly literature. I argue that the nature and processes of neoliberalism can be enriched, if the developments of neoliberalism in locations that sit at odds with the prevailing account are taken seriously. In this regard, the analysis employs Gramsci's approach (2011, 128–129; Q1 §43) seeking to locate 'the real identity underneath the apparent differentiation and contradiction and finding the substantial diversity underneath the apparent identity'. Further, following Gramsci, the research for this book commenced from a concrete examination of the national, in order to understand its originality and uniqueness, but never divorcing that from the international. As Gramsci (1971, 240; Q14 §68) argued in relation to the international capitalist state-form:

> The problem which seems to me to need further elaboration is the following: how, according to the philosophy of praxis (as it manifests itself politically)—whether as formulated by its founder or particularly as restated by its most recent great theoretician—the international situation should be considered in its national aspect. In reality, the internal relations of any nation are the result of a combination which is 'original' and (in a certain sense) unique: these relations must be understood and conceived in their originality and uniqueness if one wishes to dominate them and direct them. To be sure, the line of development is towards internationalism, but the point of departure is 'national'—and it is from this point of departure that one must begin. Yet the perspective is international and cannot be otherwise. Consequently, it is necessary to study accurately the combination of national forces that the international class will have to lead and develop, in accordance with the international perspective and directives.

Taking the national as the point of departure, Gramsci immediately re-emphasised the international—stressing their interrelationship and the 'dialectical tension between these perspectives' (Thomas 2009, 215). While neoliberalism is an international phenomenon, the study of specific national variants helps us understand the historically and contextually specific ways it is implemented. At the same time, an examination of the national context sheds further light on what is essential and extraneous in neoliberalism as a process in general. It is from this perspective that the study proceeds, in examining the development of neoliberalism in Australia and assessing it in light of, and a critique of, the prevailing narrative as to neoliberalism's advance globally.

Gramsci's theoretical conceptions are used throughout this book, in particular those of the integral state and hegemony. His formulations were developed in a close study of various locations and historical moments—not least of all the *Risorgimento* in Italy. As such, the context of Gramsci's analysis raises the question of how his work might usefully aid social inquiry about other moments and spatial locations. As Adam Morton explained in *Unravelling Gramsci* (2007), it is crucial to be attentive to how Gramsci's ideas developed within a specific historical context before discerning any contemporary relevance. Quoting and contesting Randall Germain and Michael Kenny, Morton (2007, 16) noted that there is a 'need to historicise Gramsci and display "greater sensitivity to the general problems of meaning and understanding in the history of ideas" as well as pay "far greater attention to the problems of meaning and interpretation"'. With Gramsci, perhaps more so than some other theorists, this task is complex because of the open-ended form of the *Notebooks*, their circular and progressive structure and incomplete form. Buttigieg (2011, x) notes that 'only by doing violence to the text of the *Prison Notebooks* could one conceal their fragmentariness and reconstruct them into a conventional, more or less unified format'. Similarly, the history of alteration and adaptation of Gramsci's conceptions in the secondary literature, often without making such shifts clear, further complicates this task. In using Gramsci's work in this book, the analysis has sought to be attentive to the historical specificity of his terminology, and to work in an acknowledgement that the form of the *Notebooks* means this is not always plain.

In response to this fragmentary nature, Thomas (2009, 117–118) urges that the more productive approach is not to 'search for origins or telos' but rather simply 'to admit the obvious: history happened the way it did'. He suggests we should examine the *Prison Notebooks* in the manner Gramsci (1971, 384; Q16 §2) suggested we read others—in a search 'for the Leitmotiv, for the rhythm of the thought as it develops' and that this 'should be more important than ... single casual affirmations and isolated aphorisms'. As Boothman (2007, 116) argued of Gramsci's methodology in relation to translation, the adoption of terms from one context to another is not always a question of uncomplicated integration, but often of reinterpretation within the new location. He suggested that (for Gramsci and us) translation need not necessarily be a problem, as language can be flexible—where the process of translation demonstrates:

> … how discourses may be rendered 'open', renewed and updated by means of a critique and modification of the concepts used in other discourses, not always or often, by their simple unmodified incorporation into one's own.
>
> BOOTHMAN 2007, 136–137

This book takes this approach in considering the relevance and limitations of the conception of the integral state.

The research for this book focused on: analysing how the key elements of the Accord were developed and implemented; how the Accord was related to wider neoliberal reforms; the changing nature of the relationship between the ALP and the trade unions; as well as the evolution of the labour movement. Archival research in trade union collections examined items from the 1960s until the 2000s, deposited by the ACTU, Victorian Trade Hall Council (VTHC), Australian Manufacturing Workers' Union (AMWU), Amalgamated Manufacturing Workers' Union (AMWU), Amalgamated Metals Foundry and Shipwrights' Union (AMFSU), Amalgamated Metal Workers' and Shipwrights' Union (AMWSU), the Electrical Trades Union (ETU), the Builders Labourers' Federation (BLF) and the Williamstown Naval Dockyards Combined Unions' Shop Committee, among others. As explored in Chapter 8, many authors have identified the key role of the AMWU in constituting and implementing the Accord (Bramble and Kuhn 2011, 102; Stilwell 1986, 96). Without the backing of the AMWU, as the largest and most powerful union in the Australian labour movement, the social contract would not have been possible. For this reason, archival work focused particularly on that union and its predecessors.[2] The project also examined materials such as political party policy statements, political ephemera, contemporaneous news articles, government economic data, media analysis and audio recordings. The analysis also included biographies, autobiographies and interviews with participants in the Accord processes completed by other researchers.

---

2 The acronym 'AMWU' is used in this book to refer to the metals union through its regular name changes, with the details of the key name changes included in Appendix B.

7 Structure of the Book

The book begins by considering the state–civil society relationship, which is key to examining both neoliberalism and corporatism. Chapter 2 traces a line of theorisation from Karl Marx's critique of Hegel, to Gramsci's conception of the integral state. It sets out how Marx's clarity on the antagonistic logics of the social (civil society) and political (state and political society) spheres—together with Gramsci's dynamic model of how political society and the state organise to manage civil society—usefully frame a consideration of the incorporation of organised labour into the neoliberal project.

The context of corporatism in Australia is examined in Chapter 3, through a focus on Leo Panitch's conceptual framework. Although analysis of the Accord has emphasised it as a consensual project in the national interest, corporatism is best understood as a political structure to manage civil society (in particular trade unions) and increase exploitation of labour in the interests of capital (i.e. the extraction of surplus value). The Accord is contextualised in the history of corporatist arrangements in Australia. Gramsci's conception of the integral state is shown to usefully support and extend understandings of the use and content of corporatist arrangements—measures that increase the exploitation of labour by drawing them into a macroeconomic project in the national interest. The chapter proposes that the conception of the integral state, discussed in Chapter 2, can usefully support and supplement the important insights developed by Panitch.

Neoliberalism is a state-centred hegemonic political project remaking capitalist production and social reproduction since the end of the long boom. Chapter 4 sets out a paradox in the contemporary critical literature analysing its development. On the one hand critics of neoliberalism argue for an emphasis on the diverse and geographically specific way in which neoliberalism advanced globally. Yet, on the other hand, a very particular set of originating features is usually posited as common across multiple national histories. The chapter delineates this narrative—constructed based on neoliberalism's advance in the US and UK—as having four elements. This narrative is widely present in the radical and Marxist literature, and I evidence this through an examination of the widely cited and key accounts of David Harvey and Naomi Klein, as well as the work of radical geographers Peck, Brenner, Theodore and Adam Tickell. In order to bring increased clarity to what was common and divergent across spatial locations in the global advance of neoliberalism, the dominant narrative must be destabilised.

Chapter 5 sets out a periodisation of neoliberalism in Australia, contextualising the development of the Accord within this. Developments in Australia are framed within a periodisation of neoliberalism internationally. The chapter argues that periodising neoliberalism allows analytical separation within the historical phase, in order to highlight shifts in content and coherence over time. This is central to demonstrating, empirically, that neoliberalism has been constructed in different locations through a lengthy process of structural adjustment—including efforts before and after vanguard phases—with the involvement of parties across the political spectrum. The chapter examines the neoliberal project's continuity with, and rupture from, the previous historical period—in a way that accounts for its contingent emergence 'from among its others'. The periodisation divides the neoliberal era in Australia into four stages: a proto-neoliberal stage; a vanguard neoliberal stage; a piecemeal neoliberalisation stage; and a crisis stage. The periodisation outlines shifts in the hegemony and coherence of neoliberalism, shedding light on the weaknesses of the dominant narrative outlined in the previous chapter.

The stated intention of the Accord was to buffer citizens from the deep economic crisis that began in the 1970s. Chapter 6 outlines the historical development and content of the agreement, and empirically focuses on the core element of wages policy through the initial and subsequent revisions (Accord Mark I–VIII). The Accord quickly narrowed from a broad framework—covering price moderation, wages policy, social wage improvements (including universal health care), taxation and increased government expenditure—to one that facilitated control over organised labour through the widespread and successful suppression of wages and industrial action. The chapter demonstrates how consensual wages policy was central the advance of neoliberalism, through the trade union leadership offering up organised labour—and its ability to increase its own exploitation—as a macroeconomic solution to the protracted crisis. Moreover, it was the wages policy approach that was key in the disorganisation of labour.

Chapter 7 establishes how the social contract was shaped—and reshaped—to be 'fit for purpose' within the wider neoliberal transformations of the era. Contrary to most scholarly accounts, which posit the Accord and vanguard neoliberalism as exogenously related or competing processes, the chapter argues that they were internally related aspects of bourgeois political rule—described as *simultaneously deepening corporatism and advancing neoliberalism*. The chapter also critically assesses the progressive credentials of the social wage gains, while examining how they were related to neoliberalism. The Accord is argued to represent a high point of successful integration of key civil society subaltern groups by the state, as well as the assimilation of the organised labour movement into the reorganisation of class rule after the economic and political turmoil of the 1970s.

Chapter 8 details the evidence for the most controversial claim of the book, which is that organised labour was central to the construction of neoliberalism in Australia. This refocuses the examination of vanguard neoliberalism undertaken in the book, in order to demonstrate, at a higher level of detail, the role of the labour movement in its construction. It explains how the development of Australian neoliberalism diverged from the dominant narrative of neoliberalism's advance globally. The chapter casts the labour movement as not simply an object of neoliberal change, but an active constructor, and details the impact of the union movement shifting from workplace-based union organising to the centralised Accord. The chapter details the suppression of industrial struggle, and in particular the role of the ACTU and labour movement in policing unions that sought to go outside the Accord's 'no further claims' framework. The chapter analyses the implementation of enterprise bargaining as a process of re-regulating the industrial relations system, and as an outcome actively sought by the labour movement—not one chiefly facilitated by business and the New Right.[3] Despite finding that Australia's trajectory diverged from the dominant narrative, this chapter argues that key outcomes were analogous to the seminal accounts that informed that narrative—most particularly the multi-layered disorganisation of labour and state-led restructuring of the economy to restore conditions for stable capital accumulation.

In the wake of the destabilisation of the dominant narrative through the examination of vanguard neoliberalism in Australia, Chapter 9 inquires into the impact of this for understanding the advance of neoliberalism internationally. This is explored through indicative evidence from NZ, the UK, the US and Finland. Interrogating the relationship between corporatism and neoliberalism, and the role of labour in key neoliberal antecedent moments, reemphasises how the dominant narrative of neoliberalism narrows our understanding of neoliberalism's global advance. The chapter argues that the agency of labour can usefully be 'written in' to the wider origin story of neoliberalism, and a more compelling account of the origins of neoliberalism can be obtained when the dominant narrative is destabilised.

3 In the context of Australia, 'New Right' is used to refer to a political movement of the late 1970s and early 1980s onwards. It refers, on the one hand, to the organisational form of the movement, which cohered both inside and outside the two main political parties of the right—the Liberal Party of Australia and the National Party of Australia. On the other hand, it refers to the political orientation of the movement, which can be described as neoliberal. Various business organisations are associated with the New Right (such as the Business Council of Australia), as are a number of conservative think tanks (such as the Institute of Public Affairs and the H R Nicholls Society). Chapter 8 discusses efforts of the New Right in undermining trade unions in the vanguard neoliberal period.

CHAPTER 2

Theorising the State–Civil Society Relationship

> There is, unfortunately, no form of state that can do away with existing class-antagonisms; for the form of state is the expression and result of class-antagonisms and not their cause.
>
> PAUL LEVI 2012, *The Retreat from Leninism*

1 Introduction

Political economists, historians and philosophers have all sought to explain the particular character of the contemporary capitalist state, yet its nature remains opaque. David Held (1983, 1) maintained that while 'this may seem peculiar for something so pervasive in public and private life [it is] precisely this pervasiveness which makes it difficult to understand'. Michel Foucault (2004, 77) asserted—in a more extreme view—that the state's nature was unknowable and that analysis should proceed 'without a theory … as one can and must forgo an indigestible meal'. Yet, for all the difficulties inherent in developing a framework to understand the state, it remains a key task for Marxist scholarship.

Advancing a wide-ranging theory of the state is beyond the ambit of this book, and this chapter focuses on the state–civil society relationship in order to investigate the association between the Accord and the neoliberal project in Australia. The analysis emphasises the separation and dialectical unity of the state and civil society, in setting out an approach applicable to the modern representative states of advanced capitalism. Such a theory of the state–civil society relationship frames not only how empirical evidence has been analysed and understood, but also how the research for this book was conceptualised and pursued.

The chapter begins by examining Marx's critique of Hegel on the state, law and politics. It then considers Marx's argument regarding the separation and antagonism between the state and civil society, developed in his writings of the mid-1840s. The chapter then explores Gramsci's conception of the integral state, through which he argued there is an interconnection and dialectical unity of the state and civil society—integrating the latter under the leadership of the former. The analysis considers the tension between the positions of Marx and Gramsci, concluding that the distance between the accounts is bridged when the integral state is understood as being always necessarily unstable.

 | DOI:10.1163/9789004383463_003

This is because a state based on an atomistic and internally divided civil society cannot ever fully overcome the logic of the fundamental social relations that produce those contradictions.

1.1 *Some Preliminary Comments*

Although this chapter cannot set out a wide-ranging theory of the state, it is important to note and clarify a number of issues. Firstly, there is no settled general theory of the state within Marxist political economy. Although the 1960s and 1970s saw a revival of discussion amongst western Marxists as to the nature of the state, no clear resolution was achieved. Further, despite the changes wrought by neoliberalism directly impacting on the question of the state *vis-a-vis* civil society and market, this has not provoked a major rethinking among Marxists in more recent decades. Contemporary analysis is often confined to the concrete changes regarding the functions of the state under neoliberalism and, usually, sets aside explicit analysis of the general nature of the capitalist state. Of course there are some exceptions to this (Jessop 1990; 1982; Panitch 1999), and at the height of the Global Justice Movement at the turn of the century state theory was more widely debated inside and outside the academy (Holloway and Callinicos 2005; Holloway 2002; 2000). Other more recent works of Marxist political economy, such as Panitch and Sam Gindin's *The Making of Global Capitalism* (2012), have outlined a view of the state primarily to make previously worked-out theory explicit rather than to focus on extending it.

Secondly, a key concern of Marxist theorising of the state has been to understand precisely why and how capitalist states come to serve the interests of capitalism. On one level this is a simple question—why would a state within capitalism *not* serve the longer-term interests of the economic structures that gave rise to it? Yet, given that class conflict is inherent to capitalism, and also that various civil society groups place pressure on the state to act (or not act) in certain ways, the structural mechanisms that ensure the state serves the longer-term interests of capitalism have been widely discussed. As will become clear, this book doesn't accept the presumption that there can be 'interests of capitalism' *in general*—let alone that the capitalist state does, or even can, serve them. The capitalist class is internally divided by competition between atomised individuals. Although members of the capitalist class seek to act together at times, to pursue what might be their shared interests on particular matters, there can be no overall general interest of the bourgeoisie in the stronger sense meant by many Marxist theorists—except perhaps at the point when the overthrow of capitalist social relations is immediately threatened.

Thirdly, over the last two decades there has been 'ubiquitous concern with the concept of civil society', and this has 'rekindled an interest in Gramsci's reflections on the subject' (Morton 2007, ix). The line of reasoning set out below argues that a productive contribution to understanding the contemporary state–civil society relationship can be developed by tracing a theoretical line through the work of Marx and Gramsci. Again, this is not proposed to articulate a wide-ranging theory of civil society, but instead provide a useful lens to consider the relationship of labour to the state in the Accord period in Australia.

Fourthly, and crucially, this chapter proposes that Marx developed a mostly coherent theory of the state in his early writings, in the course of a critique of the conceptions of Hegel and certain of Hegel's followers. Some scholarship asserts that Marx either abandoned, broke with or superseded his early conceptions of the state in his more 'mature' writings (Balakrishnan 2015, 2014). The analysis in this book draws on Colletti (1975) and his argument that Marx's later theorisation involved a deepening and enhancement of his initial critique of politics and the state via the critique of political economy—that is, the critique of the (alienated and exploitative) capitalist social relations that produce bourgeois civil society. Further, such an approach continues to provide a useful framework for thinking about the state–civil society relationship, especially when supplemented with Gramsci's conception of the integral state—which was also developed, in part, via a critical engagement with Hegel.

This chapter argues that Gramsci provided an essential elaboration of the fundamental relationship between civil society and state in the era of mass representative politics. Gramsci's conception of the integral state can draw out the complex contradictions and interconnections between capitalist social relations, civil society, political society and the state apparatus. The chapter proposes that the frameworks articulated by Marx and Gramsci should be considered to be complementary. In developing a framework of the state–civil society relationship, the chapter emphasises an integrated analysis of production, exchange and the state (capitalist totality), without either: (a) reducing these to the same level of abstraction; (b) reducing their specificity to mechanical causation; (c) denoting a free agency to the state; or (d) failing to integrate a theory of the state with the international competitive system of states and global competitive capital accumulation (and thus capitalist social relations). This is important in understanding the relationship between the Accord and neoliberalism because: (a) state managers and politicians were not simply personifications of the capital relation in driving through the reforms of that era; (b) neither were those actors reflexively responding to changes at the 'economic' level; (c) nor were those actors free from the challenges and constraints set by the economic conditions of the day; and (d) those actors made those changes in response to national economic conditions (such as deindustrialisation) in a situation of global crisis, economic restructuring and political change.

2 Marx's Critique of Hegel

At the heart of Marx's social critique was what those who followed him often called 'historical materialism', which argued not only that any given society had to be understood in terms of the determinate relationships between living human beings (his theory's materialism), but that the temporally-specific arrangement of social relations of production shaped the entire society in which they dominated (its historicism). In the third volume of *Capital*, Marx (1991, 927–928) wrote:

> The specific economic form, in which unpaid surplus-labour is pumped out of direct producers determines the relationship of domination and servitude, as this grows directly out of production itself and reacts back upon it in turn as a determinant. On this is based the entire configuration of the economic community arising from the actual relations of production, and hence also its specific political form. It is in each case the direct relationship of the owners of the conditions of production to the immediate producers—*a relationship whose particular form naturally corresponds always to a certain level of development of the type and manner of labour, and hence to its social productive power*—in which we find the innermost secret, the hidden basis of the entire social edifice, and hence also the political form of the relationship of sovereignty and dependence, in short, the specific form of the state in each case. This does not prevent the same economic basis—the same in its major conditions—from displaying endless variations of innumerable different empirical circumstances, natural conditions, racial relations, historical influences acting outside, etc., and these can only be understood by analysing these empirically given conditions.

This statement, among others in Marx's 'mature' writings, makes explicit that he saw the form of the state in any given mode of production as specific to that mode of production. This is because, in any such social formation, one form of exploitative social relations of production dominates over others (Banaji 2010). Thus, those dominant social relations 'assign rank and influence to the others' and the form of production 'is a general illumination which bathes all the other colours and modifies their particularity' (Marx 1973, 107). But such statements are unclear on how to theorise what relationship the state and politics have to capitalist social relations at the base of society. This has led many Marxists to contend that Marx himself never completed a theory of the capitalist state, in particular because he never completed his planned volume of *Capital* on the topic—in which he would presumably have expounded his view at a more concrete level of analysis than the highly abstract critique of political economy in the first three volumes (Hay 1999; Jessop 1990; 1982).

Bob Jessop (1982, 1) stated that there are 'discontinuities and disjunctions' in the work of Marx on the state, and that this 'incompleteness and indeterminacy account for the wide range of so-called Marxist theories of the state'. Jessop (ibid pp. 2–31) argued that aspects of the writings of Marx and Engels can be found to support competing claims that the state is an 'instrument of class rule', a 'factor of cohesion' and 'an institutional ensemble'. This, Jessop claimed, means that despite Marxists long claiming special knowledge of the state's strategic significance, debate has often been 'esoteric' and disconnected from those writing in other traditions. Thus, despite Marx's frequent journalistic and polemical writings on contemporary politics and actually existing states, it has been argued he never produced a coherent theory of the modern state, based in his most important lifework: the critique of political economy.

I would maintain, however, that in some of his earliest theoretical writings (in the years 1842–1847 in particular) Marx did lay down an important and relatively comprehensive theory of the state and politics. Moreover, this 'early' theorisation provides an incisive and useful approach to understanding the relationship between the state and civil society—one that can assist in analysing the implementation of neoliberal reform via the Accord. The origin of Marx's views are located in his critique of Hegel's philosophy of the state, and below the chapter sets out the most relevant components of Marx's writings and integrates these with his subsequent critique of capitalist social relations. This line of exploration then allows comparison with Gramsci's conception of the integral state.

Marx's starting point in the early 1840s was a critical engagement with Hegel, the pre-eminent theorist of the state, law and politics to that time. Contrary to the view among some Marxists that Marx's 'youthful' writings are predominantly 'philosophical' in content and follow Hegel by being 'idealist' in method (Althusser 2005; cf Teeple 1984), Marx himself lauded Hegel's contribution to a materialist understanding of the state (1975c). Marx agreed with Hegel (1967) when the latter insisted that because modern (bourgeois) civil society is atomistic and composed of competing particular, private, individual interests, there is a necessary separation between civil society and the universal or common social interest implied in the form of the state. Hegel argued that modern society allowed individual freedom unthinkable in previous social formations, but also recognised that the constant competition between private individuals in civil society (Hobbes's (1997) '*bellum omnium contra omnes*' or 'war of all against all') produced unceasing social instability, which required some kind of organism to hold society together: the modern state.

While Marx saw Hegel as the most advanced theorist of the modern state, he took Hegel to task for claiming that the state could truly express the universal social interest. For Hegel, the legislature mediated between a civil society of particular interests and the modern representative state embodying universal interests. But for Marx (1975b, 158) the legislature was incapable of bridging the divide between individual and universal interests, and instead brought out that contradiction—because 'it is the antinomy of political state and civil society, the contradiction of the abstract political state with itself'. In other words, Marx identified that the antagonism between civil society and the state was unable to be resolved, precisely because in a society composed of competing particular interests, the state itself would be just another particular interest—even if in a formal or abstract way it claimed to stand for the general or collective interest of the society that it governed over.

Marx and Engels made the more general point that in every class society, the state (no matter what its specific relationship to the rest of society) was the political form of class rule. Marx and Engels (1976, 98) defined the historically contingent development of a specifically bourgeois civil society thus:

> Civil society embraces the whole material intercourse of individuals within a definite stage of the development of productive forces. It embraces the whole commercial and industrial life of a given stage and, insofar, transcends the State and the nation, though, on the other hand again, it must assert itself in its external relations as nationality and internally must organise itself as state. The word 'civil society' [*bürgerliche Gesellschaft*] emerged in the eighteenth century, when property relations had already extricated themselves from the ancient and medieval community. Civil society as such only develops with the bourgeoisie; the social organisation evolving directly out of production and intercourse, which in all ages forms the basis of the state and of the rest of the idealistic superstructure, has, however, always been designated by the same name.

Furthermore, the nature of the capitalist class in bourgeois society was that it was itself internally divided by competition. Therefore, bourgeois society required a state that was formally separate from its individual members and standing 'over against' them (Marx and Engels 1976, 83–84). Marx and Engels (ibid 1976, 99) stated that:

> Since the state is the form in which the individuals of a ruling class assert their common interests, and in which the whole civil society of an epoch is epitomised, it follows that all common institutions are set up with the help of the state and are given a political form. Hence the illusion that law is based on the will, and indeed on the will divorced from its real basis—on free will.

It follows that the historic uniqueness of bourgeois society was that the capitalist class ruled *politically* via a state that was formally separate from the private existence of its individual members, each one of whom already ruled *socially* in their respective firm or business. As a result, capitalist class political rule appeared as its own opposite. Thus, the state appeared to stand over all of society, including the capitalist class, in the general interest.

Marx argued that Hegel's error was that he missed seeing the fundamental basis of the state as an estranged expression of civil society, but that this relationship exists in inverted form in reality—in other words, the state appears to be prior to civil society, and politics appears to dominate and drive social relations. Hegel, Marx stated (1975c, 64), was 'not to be blamed for depicting the nature of the modern state as it is, but rather for presenting what *is* as the *essence* of the state'. Put another way, Marx concluded that it was not that Hegel's description inverted what was really happening, but that social reality existed in an inverted and mystified form, because of the dominance of capitalist social relations, and that Hegel did not see this.

Marx located the sharp separation between the state and civil society, and between political and social relations, as emerging historically with the rise of capitalist modernity. Marx (1975b, 90) stated that the 'abstraction of the *state as such* ... was not created until modern times. The abstraction of the *political state* is a modern product'. Modern civil society could, therefore, only organise itself as a state on the basis of this separation. Furthermore, the abstraction of politics from civil society in the form of a state involved the depoliticisation of civil society (Marx 1975d). Colletti (1975, 34) has summarised Marx's view thus:

> ... the analysis hinges upon the simultaneity of these two fundamental divisions: the estrangement of individuals from each other, or privacy within society, and the more general estrangement of public from private, or of the state from society.

This antagonism meant that for Marx the notion of 'political representation' is a misnomer. As soon as individuals deputed from civil society enter the state, they stop being deputies and instead become part of the abstract state. In so doing, the role of political representatives changes to one of furthering the interests of the state—and the political society around it—over the interests of those sections of civil society from which they emerged (Marx 1975b).

This aspect of Marx's argument can throw light on the limits of political representation of workers' social interests within corporatist arrangements or via labourist parties. It also illuminates how historical debates over the extent of 'relative autonomy of the capitalist state', by Poulantzas (2001) and others (Panitch and Gindin 2012), are potentially misplaced. This is because the state is both fully separate from bourgeois civil society—and, moreover, operates on the basis of a political logic that is antagonistic to social logic—yet is also entirely dependent on the perpetuation of the specifically bourgeois civil society from which the state is abstracted.

Nevertheless, while Marx rejected Hegel's notion that the state could truly represent the general interest, he did argue there was no other social force that could act across an entire society to *attempt* to manage the interests of the capitalist class. This was why Marx and Engels (1976) called the state 'an illusory community': not because it wasn't real, but because it was not a true community of the individuals who formed its social basis. In considering and citing Marx's point in *The German Ideology*, Colletti argued (1973, 88):

> The collective interest ... 'takes an independent form as the State, divorced from the real interests of the individual and community', insofar as 'just because individuals seek only their particular interest which for them does not coincide with their communal interest—in fact, the general is the illusory form of communal life—the latter will be imposed on them as an interest "alien" to them and "independent" of them, as in its turn a particular, peculiar "general" interest'. Hence 'the social power' transformed into the power of the state 'appears to these individuals ... not as their own united power, but as an alien force existing outside them, of the origin and goal of which they are ignorant'.

Thus, for Marx, there were severe limits on what the state could do to further the management of shared interests for two reasons. The first was that in a society of irreconcilable particular interests, at best the state could enforce some kind of hypothetical 'average' of those different interests (Marx 1975b). The second was that the modern state's basis in bourgeois society meant that it could never challenge the fundamental social relations that produced such a society—relations based on bourgeois private property—lest it risk eradicating the basis for its own existence (Marx 1975a). Thus, the state could at best manage or administer the social evils produced by capitalist social relations differently, but never directly challenge the sources of those social harms.

3 From Critique of Politics to Critique of Political Economy

Marx's (1975e, 425) theoretical critique of the state and politics led him to the next stage in the development of his social analysis:

> My inquiry led me to the conclusion that neither legal relations nor political forms could be comprehended whether by themselves or on the basis of a so-called general development of the human mind, but that on the contrary they originate in the material conditions of life, the totality of which Hegel, following the example of English and French thinkers of the eighteenth century, embraces within the term 'civil society'; that the anatomy of this civil society, however, has to be sought in political economy.

From the early studies in the *Paris Manuscripts* of 1844 to the conclusions of the three volumes of *Capital*, Marx located the basis for the specific nature of civil society in capitalist social relations—that is, in the process of abstraction of value in the exploitation of labour power. Yet, as Colletti (1973, 232–233) has noted, Marx employed a corresponding approach in both his critique of the state and his critique of political economy. In the former, Marx attacked the speculative aspects of Hegel's philosophy of the state, by contrasting the abstract form of the state with its concrete basis in civil society. Marx thereby revealed how Hegel has uncritically accepted mystified forms precisely because he engaged in the 'crassest materialism' and had not gotten to the essence of the matter (see also Marx 1975b, 174). In the latter, Marx attacked the political economists for accepting the mystified, fetishised forms of appearance of capitalist social relations at face value, rather than grasping their basis in concrete relationships between real individuals (see also Marx 1976, 163–177). In each case reality itself is upside down and must be turned right side up through practical activity.

Crucially, Marx understood capitalist social relations, including exchange relations, as extending beyond the geographic territory of any one nation. As Marx (1973, 407–408) stated:

> [Just] as capital has the tendency on one side to create ever more surplus labour, so it has the complementary tendency to create more points of exchange. … the tendency to create the world market is directly given in the concept of capital itself. Every limit appears as a barrier to be overcome.

Thus, there can be no theory of the state without recognising the presence of a global system of states. And such a 'system of states' is both presupposed by and constitutive of the world capitalist market. As Barker (1978) put it, the implication for a Marxist understanding of the state is that it must always already be understood as one of 'many states'.

Marx and Engels (1998, 37) famously stated that the 'executive of the modern state is but a committee for managing the common affairs of the whole bourgeoisie'. Barker (1978) takes them to task on this point for missing the divisions between nation states. *Contra* Barker, Marx and Engels point must be considered in the context of where it appeared, within a polemical document intended to orient communists on the independent working-class tasks in the German bourgeois revolution of 1848. Thus, it arguably makes more sense to read this famous phrase as referring to a whole *national* bourgeoisie and not the entire *global* bourgeoisie. If we interpret Marx and Engels's description in this manner, it is suggestive of how the state must manage both capitalists' *intra*-national relations among each other and with other social groups, as well as their *inter*-national affairs (Marx and Engels 1976, 57). States have to respond not only to changes in domestic circumstances but also to international factors—dynamics that affect not just accumulation (such as the international slide into economic crisis in the 1970s), but political circumstances also (such as destabilising wars like that in Vietnam, the undermining of the racialised Australian settlement with the rise of post-colonial regional nationalisms, and the competitive pressure of state-led restructuring among Australia's closest economic partners and rivals).

4 From Marx to Gramsci

The century from Marx's death to the election of the Hawke government was marked by a tremendous growth in the social weight and apparent importance of the state and political society to the functioning of modern capitalist societies. So much so that, for workers' movements in advanced Western countries, talk of a separation or antagonism between state and civil society would seem divorced from the experience of mass trade unions, electorally successful social democratic parties, and large-scale state intervention in capitalist economic life. In that sense, representation of the social interests of civil society actors in politics and the state could seem not only to have been nearly completely won, but also to have overcome the antinomies that Marx described. Such a view might rest on what *seemed* incontrovertible empirical evidence during the long post-war boom: unions with power to demand higher wages; a social democratic 'consensus' or Western model of development that could deliver full employment; a rapidly-growing welfare state; and 'Keynesian' policies that *appeared* to have all but eliminated capitalism's tendency to crisis.[1] However, these pieces of 'evidence' would be challenged and eventually buried in practice, by the return of capitalist crisis from the early 1970s and the state-led responses to it. Central to this was the collapse of the so-called Keynesian social-democratic consensus, which faltered under the contradictions within the accumulation process during that phase of capitalism.

While Marx could only have seen small clues of such tumultuous changes, Gramsci analysed the early decades of mass representative politics in his attempt to theorise the revolutionary potential of 'the West' (and its failure to be realised) in the wake of World War I. This necessitated an understanding of the concrete changes in the state–civil society relationship occasioned by these historic shifts. Like Marx, Gramsci's starting point was to engage with Hegel's conceptions and to build on them, using the toolbox provided by those of Marx's writings that were available at that time. Because many of Marx's key theoretical expositions regarding the state and politics were unpublished when Gramsci set about composing his *Prison Notebooks* (2011a), he often couldn't rely on Marx's positions from those texts. Thus, while Gramsci sought to develop his theory as closely as possible to Marx's approach, some tensions will also become apparent in the course of mapping out Gramsci's conception of the integral state.

4.1 *Lo stato integrale*

A key contention of this book is that the neoliberal political project was made possible in Australia through the active participation of the union movement in the Accord process. The theoretical framework for understanding how this took place is Gramsci's conception of the integral state:

---

1 Of course, not everyone was included in the era of mass politics or through the Keynesian consensus, with race and gender—in particular—excluding many from equal participation in economic and social life.

> ... as a network of social relations for the production of consent, for the integration of the subaltern classes into the expansive project of historical development of the leading social group.
>
> THOMAS 2009, 143

Gramsci's *Prison Notebooks*, in which the conception of the integral state was first elaborated, were composed in the wake of the mass working class struggles that followed World War I. The conception of the integral state was a distinct innovation, not drawn from Gramsci's predecessors, and built on the foundation of insights by Hegel and Marx. Gramsci was also attempting to redefine Marxism in the wake of the Great War: not so much 'against' Marx, but hostile to particular brands of 'Marxism'. Such writings were in critique of 'interpretive traditions within and outside Marxism: both Second International and Stalinist instrumentalisations' (ibid 2009b, 97).

His writings have inspired a broad range of academic projects, from disciplines in philosophy to education. The open-ended form of the *Notebooks*—both their circular and progressive structure and incomplete form—mean there is no 'true' Gramsci. Yet, despite the varied interpretations of his work on offer, it is difficult to ignore a unifying concern in Gramsci's theorising: to develop a sophisticated, historically-informed appreciation of how capitalist social relations in civil society relate to how the state operates. Gramsci analysed the complex and interrelated mechanisms of consent and coercive rule under capitalism. Sections of the *Notebooks* examine the winning of consent ('hegemony') and the coercive aspect of rule ('domination'), and how these distinctions allow the capitalist state to rule in a way that defends the dominant social relations. Gramsci was not only concerned with how accumulation occurs and how the integral state might try to ensure that this continues, he was also concerned with how the character of production and accumulation—and the civil society which arises from this—lead to contradictions that allow openings for hegemonic struggles by subaltern groups against capitalist class rule.

The analysis in the first half of this chapter emphasised Marx's elucidation of the sharp separation of and antagonism between civil society and the state (and the political society that exists around the latter). The analysis of Marx also emphasised the depoliticisation of civil society produced by this separation. The discussion now turns to Gramsci's conception of the integral state as an expanded understanding of how the state and political society come to lead or direct civil society politically. Rather than seeing the state as genuinely universalising in its project, Gramsci argued, like Marx, that the integral state is a process of capitalist class domination and hegemony. This aspect of Gramsci's argument is frequently overlooked in the secondary literature (Morton 2007,

89). The integral state was a conception that Gramsci developed specifically as part of a critique of the liberal conception of the 'separation of powers' (ibid 2007).

For Gramsci, the integral state concept described the particular relationship between the state (political society and the state apparatus) on the one hand, and civil society (atomised social interests and the relations between them) on the other. He conceived the integral state not as an 'identity' between the two (i.e. the same as each other), nor as a 'fusion' (i.e. distinct but in union)—but rather as a *dialectical unity* (Thomas 2009b, 69). He deployed a specific understanding of this dialectical unity as a process of envelopment or enwrapping (*involucro*) of civil society by political society. Peter Thomas explained (2009b, 189):

> [T]he definition of political society as an '*involucro*' in which a civil society can be developed would not seem to correspond in any sense to the concept of the state apparatus; for, whereas the latter is normally conceived as a coercive instrument applied externally in order to regulate civil society's inherent tendency towards anarchy, Gramsci here presents the image of 'political society' as a 'container' of civil society, surrounding or enmeshing and fundamentally reshaping it.

In summary, there is a more complex interplay of economic, political and institutional forms to create an 'integral unity of capitalist state power' (ibid 2009b, 94–95) and Gramsci is attempting to think through the question of the state specifically in advanced capitalist countries ('the West') (Fiori 1973, 242–243).

Within the integral state conception, processes of consent (hegemony) in civil society are just as important as openly coercive state rule (domination). For Gramsci, conceiving of the state as something that simply sits above civil society, involved in regulation and coercion alone—even through democratic means—overlooks that it is in practice a:

> ... complex of practical and theoretical activities with which the ruling class not only justifies and maintains its dominance, but manages to win the active consent of those over whom it rules.
>
> GRAMSCI 1971, 244; Q15 §10

Thus:

> ... the general notion of the [s]tate includes elements which need to be referred back to the notion of civil society ... in the sense that one might

> say that the State = political society + civil society, in other words hegemony armoured with coercion.
>
> GRAMSCI 1971, 263; Q6 §88

Far from civil society and political society only being in contradistinction, civil society is (in Gramsci's conception) in dialectical unity with the state. Civil society and political society are better conceptualised not as geographical locations, but as different sites of social practice: civil society is the location of hegemonic practice and political society is the site of direct domination. Further, the state apparatus plays:

> ... an important role in concretising this unifying supplement to civil society's constitutive divided particularity—but the 'political' as such necessarily exceeds the institutions that seek to organise and regulate it, just as, from another direction, civil society necessarily exceeds the political society that attempts to impose meaning upon it. If the political represents the 'consciousness' of the supposedly 'non-political' or civil society, the state apparatus functions as the moment of 'self-consciousness' of the political itself.
>
> THOMAS 2009b, 189

In this way, the state apparatus is a supplement to the naturally fragmented entity of civil society. It is 'naturally fragmented' because it is based on capital accumulation and atomised market actors.

5 Gramsci *contra* Marx? The Limits of Integration

It is here that a tension may be detected between Marx's argument about the essential state–civil society antinomy and Gramsci's notions of enwrapment (*involucro*) or dialectical unity. But the distance between the two accounts is bridged when the integral state is considered as always necessarily unstable, because a state based on an atomistic and internally divided civil society cannot ever fully overcome the logic of the fundamental social relations that produce those contradictions. At no point does Gramsci accept the inverted existence of society as its essence; he repeatedly returns to Marx's arguments from the 1859 *Preface* that capitalist relations of production remain the basis for all other developments, including those within broader civil society and political society (Thomas 2009b, 98). Gramsci's insight is that the chaos of civil society (as it is produced and reproduced by the anarchic process of capital accumulation) can break through the political container in which it finds itself enwrapped and which seeks to neutralise its radical potential to disrupt, and even end, capitalist rule.

For Gramsci, any initiative from below to win hegemony on the terrain of civil society cannot help but enter the terrain of 'the political', because it pushes against the enwrapment of civil society by political society and is comprehended in political terms (Thomas 2009b, 194). Thus, as soon as a social movement starts to contest bourgeois rule on the terrain of civil society, it will come into contact with political society and the state. It is important to note that, in this book, when discussing the rule of the ruling class in capitalist society—i.e. the capitalist class or bourgeoisie—a distinction is drawn between its *social* rule in civil society (rooted in its dominance in social relations of production, which in Gramsci's writings are sometimes described as 'economic' relations) and its *political* rule, through the institutions of the modern state. The question is, therefore, to what extent can political society enwrap and ultimately incorporate non-ruling social groups in its projects?

The *Prison Notebooks* developed detailed historical accounts of how opposed processes of contestation and integration have played out in a variety of societies, but especially in Italy. Gramsci was particularly interested in various civil society organisations—whether explicitly 'political' or not—which played their parts in these processes. He chiefly examined overlapping epochs of rising and consolidating mass politics, stretching from late 1800s to when he was imprisoned. This gave him an historical substrate from which to draw conclusions that went beyond what Marx could theorise in his lifetime. Marx lived in an age where the infiltration of civil society by political society was relatively limited, and where (as an important example) direct representative institutions based on the working class were virtually non-existent. Thus, in Marx's time, the antagonism between the state and civil society was less obscured by the complex (and organic) institutional connections that developed between them with mass politics. For Marx and Engels, the need to understand how organisations such as trade unions and workers' parties could become incorporated into bourgeois rule was not as clear as it later became, especially with the role of the social democratic parties in defeating revolutionary movements after World War I. In this, Gramsci was consciously following in the footsteps of Lenin, who was forced to rethink Marxist political perspectives and renovate received Marxist theory in the wake of the capitulation of most of the Second International parties to their national war efforts (Harding 2009).

Gramsci spent many pages of the *Notebooks* dissecting the specific internal histories and logics of different parties (such as Catholic Action), organisations and institutions, in an endeavour to understand the micro and macro level processes that underpinned activities of contestation and integration—from sudden about turns to subtle 'molecular changes' in which their orientation would reverse in almost imperceptible increments (Gramsci 2011b, 257; Q8 §36). The rest of this book will utilise Gramsci's conception of the integral state and associated interrelated concepts such as hegemony, in order to critically analyse the component of class rule implemented by the state and political society in the administration of Australian capitalist society during the vanguard phase of neoliberal restructuring. It will, in particular, focus on the integration of the labour movement and trade union leadership into this process.

Political responses to the crises and contradictions afflicting Australian society in the 1970s and early 1980s can thus be perceived as able to come 'from above' and 'from below'. However, latter responses—such as those embodied by labourism and its corporatist aspects—were based on attempts to integrate subaltern groups into political society (or state) imperatives in a way that could directly undermine subaltern social groups' interests. This book will propose that given the fundamental instability of capitalist social relations and the limits to integration of social contradictions by the political sphere, the outcome of the Accord process was never destined to occur regardless of the actions of the various actors involved. Rather, the outcome was always a contingent one. Further, the resulting victory for the actors involved in reconstituting bourgeois political rule through the institutions of the state in this period, via the Accord, laid the basis for future difficulties in maintaining that rule—which both Gramsci and Marx can help us theorise.

6 Conclusion

The above analysis has reflected on a conception of the state and its relationship to civil society through an examination of the work of Marx and Gramsci. Marx's early writings were used as a basis to characterise the state–civil society relationship in a way that explains how his later critique of political economy could be integrated with that characterisation. This analysis emphasised Marx's conception of the state as both abstracted (separate) from, and antagonistic to, the civil society from which it emerges. Further, it noted Marx's theorisation that civil society's nature—its atomism and internal competition—arises from the abstraction of value within capitalist social relations of production. The argument found that Gramsci elaborated and extended Marx's basic critique, in order to analyse later developments in the relationship between the social and political spheres. In particular, Gramsci analysed how the growth of mass politics led to the further enwrapment of civil society by political society in the form of an integral state, and how civil society thereby became further incorporated into processes of bourgeois political rule. This conception of separation and dialectical unity of the state and civil society provides additional tools to understand why the Accord became the high point of integration efforts in the neoliberal era. Nevertheless, like Marx, Gramsci never saw this integration as capable of being completed, precisely because of the unstable and chaotic social foundations—those of civil society—on which it is built. It is crucial to understand this in analysing how corporatism as a state-led class strategy attempts to manage the state–civil society relationship, but in doing so engenders tensions within the process. This is the focus of the next chapter.

CHAPTER 3

Corporatism in Australia

> They had miles of proof that when Labor men got into power they had forgotten the class that put them there. For twenty years they had been urged to obtain Labor majorities. They had gotten those majorities, but where was their heaven? … Where were the golden streets? They could see plenty of slums, of misery, of prostitution and poverty. They had been following a vain dream and mirage.
>
> Adelaide unionists, 1910, quoted in JIM MOSS (1985) *Sound of Trumpets*

1 Introduction

In order to understand why the Accord was introduced, and its relationship to neoliberalism, it is necessary to examine the nature of corporatism. This chapter briefly explores the use and content of social democratic corporatist arrangements, most particularly through Panitch's paradigmatic Marxist account, before examining the historical structures of state-centred arbitration in Australia. Rather than understanding the Accord as the 'arrival' of corporatism in Australia (Dabscheck 2000), it argues the social contact deepened and intensified already existing arrangements—a process of *corporatism within corporatism*.

While scholarly literature on the Accord has emphasised it as a consensual project in the national interest, this chapter argues that social contracts are best understood as a political arrangement to manage the exploitation of labour in the interests of capital. Panitch's account of corporatism, rooted in a materialist analysis of its class character, provides a valuable method for understanding the formation and use of the Accord. The investigation demonstrates how Gramsci's conception of the integral state can support and extend Panitch's analysis. The chapter considers corporatism at both the general level (through an examination of Panitch's work), and in its concrete expression in the Accord (an examination commenced here at a higher level of abstraction and continued throughout the book in more concrete terms).

 | DOI:10.1163/9789004383463_004

2 Understanding Corporatism

A pivotal 1974 article concluded that we were 'right smack in the middle of the century of corporatism' (Schmitter 1974, 126) and, by the 1980s, academic attention to the concept was 'almost obsessive' (Molina and Rhodes 2002, 305). Yet, within only a few decades, preoccupation with corporatism had fallen away. Some argued this mirrored the decline of corporatism as a strategic program, 'defeated on the ground by the actual evolution of employment relations', as a result of Keynesian welfare ideology being supplanted by neoliberalism (Grahl and Teague 1997, 418). Others argued the fall from favour was not simply a result of being usurped by neoliberalism, but the failure to find new ways of exploring contemporary reality (Molina and Rhodes 2002, 325). Although it has been argued that in the 1980s 'corporatism entered a terminal crisis as corporatist arrangements were unable to contain distributional conflict in a context of economic crisis and recession' (Upchurch, Taylor, and Mathers 2016, 10), in practice corporatist arrangements continued in some countries in the neoliberal era even if in a revised form (Urban 2012; Molina and Rhodes 2002). However, scholars have noted that social pacts have been conspicuous by their absence since the 2008 global economic crisis, suggesting that the exclusion of unions from economic decision-making is due to the declining social legitimacy of organised labour (Culpepper and Regan 2014).

In certain locations, the roll-out of vanguard neoliberalism was concurrent with the use of corporatist arrangements (Adkins et al. 2017; Krinsky 2011). One of the limitations of the literature on both corporatism and neoliberalism has been its limited exploration and analysis of these moments. Although some authors have noted how neoliberalism emerged from 'among its others', encompassing a mix of 'non-neoliberal' features, such work has been of a general and suggestive character (Peck, Theodore, and Brenner 2010; Jessop 2002). The Australian Accord was a distinct spatial example of neoliberalism emerging alongside—and through—corporatism, and this relationship is examined throughout this book.

While there is variation between corporatist agreements, they have been understood as distinct from pluralism, which is centred on group multiplicity and a passive or dispassionate state (Panitch 1981, 25). Corporatism has been variously understood as interest representation; institutionalised patterns of policy formation; interventionist state economic policy directed predominantly at business; a structure for managing conflict in advanced capitalism; and a tool of social control (Wilson 1983, 106–107). For many scholars, corporatism is understood at a basic level to refer to 'a political power structure and practice of consensus formation based on the functional representation of professional groups' (Czada 2011).

Gerhard Lehmbruch's (1977) influential work argued corporatism is a mode of policymaking. On this account corporatism is:

> … an institutional pattern of policy formation in which large interest organisations cooperate with each other and with public authorities not only in the articulation and even intermediation of interests, but also in the authoritative allocation of values and the implementation of policies.
> MOLINA and RHODES 2002, 307

Lehmbruch has been criticised for assuming corporatism is a 'consensual collaboration between capital and labour' (Singleton 1990b, 167). Philippe C Schmitter's (1979, 9) prominent approach defined corporatism as a 'system of interest and/or attitude representation' where institutional arrangements link the 'associationally organised interest of civil society with the decisional structures of the state'. His understanding of corporatism, however, did not interrogate the location of corporatism in the wider capitalist system. Schmitter's approach provided 'little theoretical invitation to challenge pluralism's assumption of state neutrality between the groups or to address the differential power position of the groups themselves in the society' (Panitch 1980, 167). Indeed, it remained 'a "group-theoretical" rather than a "class-theoretical" approach' (ibid 1980, 169).

3 Panitch's Approach

Panitch's (1986, 1981, 1980, 1977, 1976) analysis of corporatism is a Marxist account of the use of corporatist frameworks by liberal democratic governments, and in particular considers their deployment in periods of economic crisis. Panitch (1981, 24, 1977, 66) argued that the corporatist paradigm is:

> … a political structure within advanced capitalism which integrates organised socioeconomic producer groups through a system of representation and cooperative mutual interaction at the leadership level and of mobilisation and social control at the mass level.

This structure is:

> …based on a form of systematic political exchange between the state and trade union leaderships based on a trade off between wage moderation

> and state economic and labour market policies that attempts to resolve distributional conflicts and the employment-inflation dilemma'.
>
> UPCHURCH, TAYLOR, and MATHERS 2016, 10

In the Accord, corporatist mutual rights and obligations were manifest for the trade union movement as the right of representation in decision-making and an assumption that the relationship of labour to the state 'would deliver special access to power and its benefits' (Hampson 1996, 57), and the obligation to prioritise the 'national interest' and impose this on the labour movement (Kelly 2009, 2; Cahill 2008). In this way, corporatism is 'an actual political structure, not merely an ideology' (Panitch 1981, 24). Panitch noted, however, that in comparing the scholarly literature, a minimal descriptive definition of corporatism is difficult to construct and might have limited substantive value. Panitch (1980, 183–184) argued that this is because the 'debate over definitions is really a debate between different theoretical frameworks, in which normative and ideological preferences play their part'.

In reflecting on the experience in Europe after World War II—and in particular on corporatism in the UK—Panitch (1977, 74) stated that in almost all liberal democratic nations 'in which corporatist structures become at all important, an incomes policy designed to abate the wage pressure of trade unions was the frontispiece of corporatist development'. Panitch's account emphasised corporatism's class nature, its role in social control, and the subjective agency of political society in bringing about such arrangements. Thus, corporatism and, in particular, the incomes policy component:

> … involves the explicit acceptance by the organised working class of the claim that there is a community of interests within existing society, [and] that the harmony between classes posited by a national integrative political party does in fact exist.
>
> PANITCH 1976, 3

As a result:

> … when social democracy translates working class loyalty to its party into loyalty to the nation, the basic dilemma of corporatism—coercion in the name of harmony—comes to rear its ugly head'.
>
> PANITCH 1976, 247

In regard to British corporatist frameworks, Panitch (1976, 26) argued the success in wage suppression was because trade union officials did not only act as 'representatives' of the labour movement, but also as agents of control over them. This was chiefly because the state could not directly apply a policy of generalised wage suppression, given it would have resulted in mass industrial unrest.

The previous chapter highlighted a line of Marxist state theory that both recognised the real separation of the state and civil society in modern times, and also delineated the efforts of political society to enwrap and integrate civil society actors. Panitch's (1981) account helps to fill in the concrete details of how such a process can occur through the establishment of corporatist political structures. Importantly, while Panitch focused on corporatist arrangements whereby explicitly class-based interests are accorded privileged representation within the operations of the state, he also acknowledged that these operate alongside and in connection with more standard democratic representative structures—those based on citizenship and individual voting rights. Corporatism and parliamentary democracy can be usefully thought of as two processes by which the integral state can operate in certain circumstances.

Panitch provided two further insights that are important to the analysis in this book. First, Panitch (1981, 34–40) argued that there were two waves of corporatism in the post-World War II period. He argued that classic post-war corporatist efforts were designed to deliver wage moderation in the context of economic boom and full employment, but that a second wave of such arrangements occurred in circumstances of rising unemployment from the mid-1970s. High levels of labour militancy immediately preceded these latter corporatist efforts, in a period of economic crisis. This experience of industrial militancy meant workers had the confidence to press for large wages claims, despite the economic malaise. In agreements from the mid-1970s, state and political society actors felt constrained in using the threat or reality of legislative coercion against organised labour. Instead, the state shifted to allowing greater rank-and-file participation in industry committees and investment planning bodies, in order to achieve wage suppression and limit industrial action. While coming later, and in even more difficult economic conditions, the Australian Accord is more akin to second wave efforts—like the British Wilson Labour Government and Trade Union Congress's social contract (1974–1979)—than various European arrangements of the 1940s to 1960s.

The second relevant insight of Panitch (1981, 37) is that this greater depth of union participation in state structures led some labour leaders and left-wing political activists to the (somewhat naïve) belief that this ushered in 'the possibility of class struggle occurring in the corporatist "heart" of the state apparatus'. The reality, Panitch argued, was that such participation amounted to the opposite of class struggle: class collaboration. As discussed below, some Australian unions believed that participation in the social contract would involve the labour movement pressing for socialist concerns in the heart of the state.

Even though Panitch did not draw on the same state-theoretical lineage as I do in this book, his conclusions from analysing the practice of corporatism post World War II allow his insights to be integrated with such a viewpoint. This is especially the case in Panitch's demonstration of corporatism as a flexible tool for attempting to integrate civil society forces that threaten to destabilise state rule, which can sit alongside or in connection with other processes (such as parliamentary democracy). What Panitch has not done sufficiently, however, is elaborate what it is about the nature of the state–civil society relationship, more abstractly and generally, that means corporatist structures are particularly well suited to integrating elements of civil society.

While Panitch was clear that corporatism is a state-centred and state-managed class project of integration, Gramsci's conception of the integral state highlights corporatism as a formalisation of the process of enwrapment. The integral state concept shows how social contracts are successful not simply because they are class projects of a capitalist state, but because they are efforts to integrate (or reintegrate) civil society groups—in particular trade unions and the broader labour movement—when they threaten to destabilise state rule or accumulation. Gramsci was clear on how political society enwraps and overdetermines the social. The importance of this is in highlighting how corporatism is a mechanism of the integral state seeking to address (temporarily) the separation and antagonism between civil society and the state. Thus, the conception of the integral state can usefully support and extend Panitch's analysis.

4 Corporatism and the Accord

The Accord has variously been referred to as a modified 'antipodean' application 'of corporatism' (Dabscheck 1989, 1); 'corporatism without business' (Matthews 1994, 209); and 'bargained corporatism' (Singleton 2000, 85–86). Debate in the scholarly literature has, in part, been concerned with whether the Accord can be considered 'fully' corporatist given capital was not an official party to the agreement. I take the view that the Accord comfortably fits within the notion of corporatism as understood by Panitch. The British social contract, like the Accord, was also a bilateral agreement in which the labour movement accepted 'voluntary wage restraint [to] assist the Labour Government to solve Britain's economic problems' and in return the government undertook 'to restore full employment, move towards economic equality and pursue a program of legal and social reforms desired by the union movement' (Odom 1992, 21). Further, and as elaborated later in this book, others have argued that the Accord was somewhat more tripartite than it first appeared, because of the industry-focused structures and organisations that flowed from the agreement (Stilwell 1986, 34). Panitch (1981, 40) argued that:

> The resuscitated corporatism of the 1970s was very much dependent on the bargains struck between social-democratic parties and trade unions; involving the promise that the compromises made by the working class in corporatist structures would be compensated for via the parliamentary process, whether through the 'social wage', industrial relations legislation or direct impositions on capital.

If this way, although commencing in the early 1980s, the Accord fits neatly into the conception of corporatism.

Panitch argued that there are recurring problems in the international scholarly literature analysing corporatism, and these flow from the pervasive assumption that class harmony can be secured through corporatist agreements. As will be described below, the problems Panitch identified also arise in the literature analysing the Accord. First, Panitch argued that scholars tend to presume that 'liberal capitalist societies, while subject to tension and strain, are no longer subject to [class] contradiction with the coming of the welfare state and state economic planning' during the long boom (ibid 1977, 66). In other words, there is a presumption rather than demonstration of 'an underlying harmony in modern capitalist societies and that ... the concept of national or public interest is an unproblematic one' (ibid 1977, 66–67). From this flows the lack of a precise theory of the state (on this point see also Wilson 1983, 111; and Jessop 1979, 190). Second, there is an assumption by scholars of equivalence on the part of those involved in corporatist arrangements, in particular a correspondence between trade unions and business organisations. The literature presumes that because the corporatist process was voluntary, it was equal. And third, the literature tends to not acknowledge the high degree of instability that marks corporatist structures.

These problems are replicated in the scholarly literature on the Accord. First, an assumption of social harmony is prevalent, and the social contract is generally viewed as one that can achieve outcomes in the interest of *all* Australians through effecting compromises (Castles, Gerritsen, and Vowles 1996, 216–223). Most analysis fails to develop an explicit theory of the state and, on the occasions where it is explored, the consideration is underdeveloped (Bramble and Kuhn 2011; Stilwell 1986, 36) or conflated with a consideration of the nature of social democracy or labourism[1] (Singleton 2000; Beilharz 1994). This has led scholars to deploy a thin conceptualisation of corporatism.

Second, the scholarly literature tends to assume parties had equivalent power, because there was mutual agreement to the Accord (Dabscheck 2000; Singleton 1990b). Given that the social contract committed the parties to certain actions and compromises on some level, authors tend to assume that all parties would (or could) equally be made to implement components of the agreement and that the consequences of any compromises were equal (or at least involved mutual sacrifice for the national interest). While the literature acknowledges that the Accord varied over time and that key components were not implemented, it generally fails to consider whether the nature of corporatism itself produced this outcome. Instead, the literature typically posits that wider political-economic circumstances left the Accord parties with little or no choice (Pierson 2002; Singleton 1990b). Further, the literature tends to presume rather than demonstrate that, on the whole, the unions and the working class fared better under the social contract than they would have without it (Spies-Butcher 2012; Ahlquist 2011; Castles, Gerritsen, and Vowles 1996). A presumption assessed later in the book.

Third, the literature underestimates the instability of corporatism, by looking at it narrowly and based simply on whether the Accord 'survived' (Buchanan, Oliver, and Briggs 2014, 296). Panitch has argued that corporatist agreements are challenging to establish, that once established they are difficult to protect from internal tensions, but that they can prove durable—'spanning the rise and fall of particular governments' (Panitch 1981, 40). In regard to internal tensions, corporatist frameworks are difficult to manage, not only because of the nature of the component groups, but also because the function of the agreements is founded on the suppression of labour movement interests—interests that cannot be made party to a corporatist agreement.

While the lengthy period of operation of the Accord and the failure of the rank and file to revolt against the union leadership would appear, at first

1 There is debate in the literature over whether the Accord is corporatist or labourist (Dabscheck 2000; Singleton 2000). However, there is no reason to see these as mutually exclusive (Pusey 1991). If the 'essence of labourism is the achievement of union objectives through the exercise of political power' (Singleton 2000, 87) via the intervention of the trade union movement bureaucracy into the political sphere, and corporatism is understood as a form of managing class conflict, then a commitment to labourism is one way the trade unions come to be incorporated into the corporatist framework. This book describes labourism empirically in this way, in reference to the actual social relationships between people in civil and political society, rather than in reference to some sort of consistent or ongoing ideology in the ALP or unions.

glance, to contradict Panitch's argument of instability, a deeper consideration reveals this is not the case. When the trajectory of the Accord is considered holistically, including its final phase in the neoliberal re-regulation of industrial relations in the form of enterprise bargaining, we can appreciate a more passive decay of the social contract. The Accord was also undermined through the 'exit voice' model of dissent, as union members left trade unions in significant numbers (Dabscheck 2000). Over the Accord period, there was an historic collapse in trade union membership. Dabscheck (2000, 103) argued that this rapid decline in union density should be read as an exit-voice model of dissent to the Accord framework, where dissent manifested not in rank-and-file revolt forcing unions to break with the social contract (as in the 'Winter of Discontent' in Britain), but in members leaving trade unions altogether. This is discussed further in Chapter 9.

Dabscheck has undertaken the only detailed application of Panitch's framework of corporatism to understand the Accord. Dabscheck (2000, 94) summarised what he terms Panitch's 'life-cycle theory of corporatism' as involving the following steps: (1) the rationale or need for corporatism; (2) conditions for the establishment of corporatism; (3) incorporation of union leaders; (4) the *real* role of union leadership in corporatism; (5) reactions by the rank and file; (6) instability of corporatism; and (7) neoliberal responses. He concluded that Panitch's analysis is appreciably accurate in regard to the Accord's implementation in Australia, in that it largely fitted 'like a glove'. Dabscheck (2000, 103) explained that the 'ALP used its special relationship with the ACTU to secure the union movement's pursuit of a pro employer/business/capital agenda'. However, Dabscheck's analysis stopped short of integrating Panitch's more general argument that corporatism must be seen as a process of state-structured class rule. Dabscheck also posited that neoliberalism was a response to the instability of the Accord, which diverges from the argument in this book that corporatism and neoliberalism developed simultaneously in Australia. And as will be discussed in Chapters 6–8, the terms of the Accord embodied key aspects of the neoliberal reform process.

Ian Hampson (1997) argued that two notions of corporatism specifically motivated elements of the labour movement to participate in the social contract. First, the unions believed that 'democratic' corporatism and its ideology of 'consensus' would usefully subordinate domestic antagonisms to the requirements of successful industrial adjustment. The model form of corporatism was argued to be Sweden through the 1960s and into the 1970s, and that this inspired involvement in the Accord within the Australian trade union movement (ibid 1997, 541). Second, the ALP and labour movement generally argued that the Accord was the basis for implementing 'democratic socialism' (ALAC 1981, 9). Many proponents of the Accord argued its consensus approach was an opportunity for the unions to 'enter into new debates and stake out new areas of legitimacy for the movement in Australian politics' (Burford 1983, 8). For a minority radical element within the trade unions, the notion of corporatism as a pathway to socialism was a significant attraction (AMWSU 1978; Carmichael 1983). Such an argument was grounded in the view that the state can be transformed, radically, through the involvement of trade unions in corporatist arrangements (given they can push for their concerns in the heart of the state).

Yet, as Panitch (1981, 41) pointed out, such views are 'particularly barren'—this is because they involve 'an insufficient appreciation of the role corporatist structures necessarily play, as arenas of top-level bargaining, in forestalling or constraining working-class mobilisation'. While the founders of the Accord argued it was an alternate project to the Thatcher and Reagan models (Hawke 1987, 8) and the *only* alternative model to that of a rising local New Right (ACTU 1987; AMWU 1987), the Hawke-Keating era in practice implemented many policies similar to those of the New Right governments in the UK and US—albeit through a different mechanism. As Michael Pusey (1991, 7) argued in his key analysis of vanguard neoliberalism in Australia,[2] the ALP government and its policy agenda was ultimately dominated by a 'semi-Thatcherite "Right" faction whose ministers control[led] Prime Minister and Cabinet and Treasury and other key departments'.

5 The Context of Arbitration

The Accord has been repeatedly portrayed as the 'arrival' of corporatism in Australia, with the parties to the social contract and analysts positing it as a revolution in, or reconstruction of, Australian politics (Peetz 2013; Dabscheck

2 Pusey's book was called *Economic Rationalism in Canberra*. Initially neoliberalism was called 'economic rationalism' in Australia, terms treated as synonymous by many authors (Frankel 1997) and in this book. The 'term originated under the Whitlam government [1972–1975], where it had the positive connotation of policy formulation on the basis of reasoned analysis, as opposed to tradition, emotion, and self-interest, but, with the exception of support for free trade, did not imply a presumption in favour of particular policy positions. Over time, however, most "economic rationalists" came to assume that reasoned analysis would always lead to support for free-market policies. Hence, the analytical process could be dispensed with, and replaced by advocacy of a predetermined set of policies, those of market reform' (Quiggin 2001, 83). This was the case in the Accord period. Weller and O'Neil argue the terms are not synonymous, in that 'economic rationalism was autocratic but committed to interventionist government in the service of the community's (rather than capital's) interests'. Such an approach is problematic in that it understands neoliberalism as related to ideas, in particular *laissez-faire* government, and levels of fidelity to that doctrine (see Cahill 2013 for a critque of ideas-centred explanations of neoliberalism).

2000; Kelly 1992; Singleton 1990a). However, the suggestion that the Hawke government had novel corporatist intentions is a sign of the 'social amnesia' that often accompanies great crises (Beilharz and Watts 1983, 27–28). Such a position disconnects the corporatism of the Accord from a century of arbitration, and elides the implementation of the social contract with Hawke's consensus personality (ibid 1983, 28). Since the early years of the 20th century at least, Australian trade unions were heavily tied into the state at two key levels—their connection to an electorally successful labourist political party and their participation in a formal and highly legally regulated arbitration system. Therefore, more or less formal corporatist arrangements can be found at various points since federation of the Australian colonies in 1901. The Accord was not corporatism visiting Australia but a deepening of already-existing corporatist arrangements: a process of *corporatism within corporatism.*

Trade unions have been prominent in Australian politics through their close relationship to the ALP, a party that was constructed in the late 1800s out of a combination of various political currents and by unions themselves. Many trade unions remain formally affiliated to the ALP, have voting rights within its structures, and provide significant funds to the party. The ALP has also been 'integrally identified' with what is termed the Australian Settlement: 'the social and economic programme of the (then) new Australian Commonwealth—White Australia,[3] arbitration and conciliation, tariff protection and the primitive beginnings of a welfare state' (Kelly 1992). The party incorporated the labour movement into political society and running the state through this framework.

The ALP has been in power and key to managing almost every significant economic crisis since federation—the Scullin Government in the Great Depression (1929–1932); the Whitlam (1972–1975) and Hawke Governments (1983–1996) during the crisis that ended the long boom; and the Rudd and Gillard Government during the Global Financial Crisis (GFC) (2007–2013) (Johnson 1989). Thus:

> ... the ALP must be seen as a national party of crisis management, a party that seeks to integrate the representatives of the major organised power blocs into a corporatist political structure while it expands the ranks of the marginal and claims to represent all people.
>
> BEILHARZ and WATTS 1983, 29

3 White Australia is the name given to the official state policy frameworks that intentionally favoured immigration from English speaking countries and certain other European ('white') nations. White Australia policy had various forms, and only officially ended in the 1960s (see Kelly 1992).

Soon after Federation a unique form of highly structured and state-centric industrial bargaining, involving both labour and capital, was constructed in Australia. Its legacy profoundly shaped Australian politics and (later) the Accord process. In 1904 the Commonwealth government created a Court of Conciliation and Arbitration. Since then, Australia has had some form of centralised compulsory arbitration.[4] The court determined any matters unable to be resolved between unions and employers; set a minimum living wage; registered unions and defined their coverage; and developed industrial awards for occupations (legally enforced wages and conditions).

The idea of compromise in the national interest played an historical role in arbitration. Justice H B Higgins (1915, 14), the first Chief Judge of the Court, stated that:

> ... the process of conciliation with arbitration in the background is substituted for the rude and barbarous processes of strike and lockout. Reason is to displace force; the might of the State is to enforce peace between industrial combatants as well as between other combatants; and all in the interests of the public.

While Higgins may have hoped for industrial peace via arbitration, the result was not as simple as that. Centralised arbitration ensured industrial action continued, built into the centralised system, but it managed militancy and led trade unions to be (at least partly) shaped by its structures. Right-wing critics of arbitration have argued that the process of centralised wage setting increased industrial disputation beyond what it would have been in a decentralised system. They argue that although the rate of industrial disputation declined over the Accord period, it had historically and consistently been above the OECD average as a result of the system of arbitration (Moore 1998).

4 This structure is unique globally, although a similar system operated for a period in New Zealand (Barry and Walsh 2007; W A (Bill) Howard 1977, 262). In 1956 the Arbitration Court was split into the Conciliation & Arbitration Commission and the Commonwealth Industrial Court. The former made industrial awards and the latter enforced them. The direct descendants of these arbitration bodies in the Accord era were the Australian Industrial Relations Commission (IRC) and the judges of the Federal Court who heard industrial law cases—although the Fair Work Commission has now replaced the former. Up until the introduction of enterprise bargaining in the final years of the Accord, these were changes of form rather than substance. Throughout this book I use the term 'arbitration' or 'Commission' to cover these bodies, unless otherwise specified. I note that Australia also has two side-by-side systems, for constitutional reasons—a federal system for cross border employment and a state-based system for employment wholly within a state. State courts in general have mirrored federal ones, although at times one could be significantly more punitive for workers than the other.

Analysis of arbitration in Australia has focused on whether or not it produced 'dependent union movements' (Markey 2002; Gahan 1996). The most influential account of this position, by W A Howard (1977), argued that arbitration caused Australian unions to develop so as to address the requirements of arbitration, as opposed to those of their own members. Thus, Howard (1977, 255) argued, Australian trade unions have been incapable of 'carving out for themselves an industrial role that is independent of the arbitral system'. The enmeshment of unions with the state is particularly obvious when considered in light of compulsory membership in various sectors in the pre-Accord era (i.e. 'closed shops'), and very high membership density in others. This resulted in some unions developing as servicing bodies, rather than organising the local membership and encouraging active participation. Closed shops were a legacy of compulsory arbitration and historically non-union labour was not more attractive to employers in a number of key industries, as firms were required to meet the labour award conditions for both union and non-union members (ibid 1977, 262). This led to some of the largest unions remaining 'thinly' organised and industrially weak (Barry and Walsh 2007, 58). The dependency thesis argues that the evolution of the unions and arbitration were closely intertwined, and that each has been dependent on the other.

Some Marxist accounts have argued the legacy of arbitration is that union organising has often been a model of addiction, and that trade unions developed an unwillingness to engage in industrial action to win wage increases, instead preferring conciliation and centralised indexation. This is, in part, evidenced by the large number of strikes in Australia of one day or less duration, their purpose being 'to bring a dispute to the attention of the Arbitration Court/Commission' (Bramble 2001, 5–6). Further, in a study of the role of union officials in the South Australian Branch of the Vehicle Builders Employees' Federation (VBEF) between 1967 and 1980, Tom Bramble (1992, 137) argued that the 'practices of Australian unions are significantly circumscribed by the arbitration system'. Bramble (1992, 137) noted that the leadership of the VBEF believed 'in the superiority of arbitration over industrial action in the pursuit of union goals' and that this created 'an atmosphere of legalism in relations with management and a top-down approach to internal union affairs'.

There have been periods, however, where various unions have had a more mobilisational approach, focused on rank-and-file organising (Bramble 2001). Other research has questioned the simplicity of the dependency thesis by demonstrating diversity across union strategy in various time periods (Gahan 1996). It is, however, clear that compulsory arbitration moulded the general shape of Australian trade unions. As Rae Cooper and Bradon Ellem (2008, 536) have argued, while the dependency thesis might not be as simple as posited by some, the 'argument has the merit of alerting us ... to the importance of the relationship between national unions and the state'.

The assumption in much of the scholarly literature is that compulsory arbitration and the election of ALP governments reduced the necessity for union organising. Unions were seen as 'simply "receiving" membership rather than engaging in purposive action to build themselves' and this meant that they were not the 'active agents in deciding their own destiny' (Cooper and Patmore 2002). However, the line of tension with respect to the legacy of arbitration is not that unions failed to be active agents in their own destiny or that arbitration built union density for them. Rather, it is that trade union strategic orientation was developed through accepting the terms set by arbitral structures and processes.

While this process provided opportunities for union growth and high density in certain circumstances, it did so by limiting the development of the unions' independent social power beyond those narrower terms. When confronted with the Accord and the development of neoliberalism, this weakness in labour movement strategy contributed to an inability to enact a break with the social contract—precisely because of the unions' historical corporatist logic, the labour movement's development within a context of arbitration, and its particular relationship with the ALP. The history of arbitration and the relationship of the unions to the Labor Party contributed to an inability to seriously challenge the specifically neoliberal politics and structural reform embodied in the Accord process and the actuality of the Hawke and Keating ALP governments. This was, in part, because of the labour movement's long-term corralling within corporatist structures.

Arbitration in Australia must be considered both as a form of long-term corporatism and as a class conflict management method in place for more than a century. Panitch's argument that corporatism has historically been deployed to manage labour and wage growth in periods of full employment can assist in placing the Accord in the longer-term corporatist framework of arbitration, given that: 'the problem of labour supply, scarcity, and skill or education has been a central theme throughout Australia's economic history' (Ville and Withers 2014, loc 1744). This can assist in understanding both corporatism and the Accord as class strategies. The importance of the Accord is not simply that it is 'more' corporatism, but that it was an especially formal arrangement that incorporated the trade union leadership into the highest levels of national economic policy and governance during a protracted crisis. In that sense, the Accord could be considered the high-water mark of not only Australian corporatism but of labourism as an institutionalised political project.

Regarding the impact of corporatist political structures on trade unions, Panitch (1981, 32) concluded that the:

> ... primary *organisational* effect is to articulate the collective mass organisation with centralised state apparatus, by encouraging the *centralisation* of the union movement so that union policy is increasingly made not at the level of locals or individual unions but *via* the permanent apparatus of confederal centrals.

The Accord intensified this centralisation and articulation, but as part of a longer history in Australia. The Accord is therefore usefully understood as both a continuation of Australian corporatism, and a 'break' with the arbitration-based corporatism of the past (in that it involved a more formal and highly structured regime). The concept of *corporatism within corporatism* throws light on the continuity of the ALP's management of trade unions in relation to capital accumulation.

The importance of focusing on the corporatist nature of the Accord and the concept of *corporatism within corporatism* lies, firstly, in the need to recognise and delineate the classically corporatist technical arrangements between the unions, the ALP and the Australian state embodied in the agreement. But, secondly, it is essential as the basis of a framework that can explain the following:

- Why was the Accord arrangement apposite to the specific conjuncture in which it arose?
- Why was the Accord successfully implemented so soon after a period of confrontational union militancy?
- Why did the Accord not end in an open rank-and-file revolt?
- How has the Accord's success, in serving the interests of the state, also ensured that the social basis for another social contract was dramatically undermined and perhaps eliminated?

These questions have been noted here, but are explored in greater detail in following chapters.

6 Conclusion

This chapter began with a critical appraisal of corporatism, and Panitch's work was highlighted because it rejects the idea that the corporatist state can overcome social antagonisms in civil society in some imagined national interest, and also because it highlighted how state action creates outcomes that favour capital over labour. A Marxist approach to corporatism was articulated, given its superior ability to understand the internal relationship between corporatism and neoliberalism. Further, Gramsci's insights around the integral state were argued to support and theoretically extend Panitch's account of corporatism, in order to better delineate how—under capitalism—the political enwraps and overdetermines social developments.

In considering how corporatism has been understood within the scholarly literature on the Accord, I concluded that such analysis has been problematic and insufficiently attentive to the nature of the capitalist state and the class content of corporatist arrangements. The scholarly literature on the Accord assumes, incorrectly, that there is an underlying social harmony and a national (cross-class) interest in modern capitalism. The Accord was also situated in the longer historical context of arbitration, articulating the social contract as a process of *corporatism within corporatism*. The wider historical background of state–labour relations is important, not because arbitration and the Accord were identical, but because they were both state efforts to manage the labour movement organisationally, by drawing it into a centralised apparatus and tying it to political society. The book now turns to considering the nature of neoliberalism, before examining (over the remaining chapters) how neoliberalism developed in Australia from amongst its corporatist 'other'.

CHAPTER 4

Destabilising the Dominant Narrative

> The political home of neoliberalism in Australia is, of course, the Liberal Party itself.
>
> KEVIN RUDD, 2009, *The Monthly*

1 Introduction

This chapter outlines how we might understand this thing we call neoliberalism, and proceeds in two parts. The first part of the chapter addresses the specificity of the historical development of neoliberalism by engaging with some of its most influential radical critics, in particular Harvey, Klein and the geographers Peck, Theodore, Tickell and Brenner. The dominant narrative accepted by most critical and radical scholars, as to neoliberalism's historical origins, is delineated and subjected to criticism. As was noted in the Introduction, this dominant narrative posits that:

- The origins of neoliberalism are to be found in the 'vanguard' projects of the late 1970s to mid-1980s in Chile, the US and UK.
- These geographically specific experiences represent original types, from which neoliberalism was later exported elsewhere.
- Neoliberalism was a project of the political (New) Right and that social democratic parties were not significant to its vanguard phase, instead implementing it later in a moderated form.
- Neoliberalism is a state-led coercive project and that it is imposed on labour.

I destabilise this prevailing account by outlining how, in Australia, a social democratic party working through a consensual social contract with the labour movement constructed neoliberalism. This claim is supported by more detailed and concrete evidence in the remaining chapters.

The second part of the chapter argues it is particularly useful to understand neoliberalism as a state-centred hegemonic political project remaking capitalist production and social reproduction since the end of the long boom. I argue for an approach that rejects tendencies toward economically, politically or ideologically determinist explanations. Neoliberalism is understood as

 | DOI:10.1163/9789004383463_005

a political project that cannot be defined only by a simple and consistent set of ideas, policies and/or economic outcomes across different spatial and temporal instances. Nevertheless, it does constitute a relatively coherent and understandable response to the specific features of the protracted economic crisis of the 1970s and 1980s in both national and global economies. The centrality of political practice, specifically how under capitalism political society enwraps civil society, is emphasised. Thus, the economic and ideological aspects of neoliberalism come together in the cohering of a contingent political project that draws from and impacts on capitalist social relations.

Importantly, the neoliberal project is at its heart a class project, systematically defending and extending the social power of the ruling social group in capitalist society—the capitalist class or bourgeoisie. While the first section of the chapter critiques Harvey's 'dominant narrative' view of the origins of neoliberalism, the second section scrutinises his understanding of neoliberalism as a class project—contrasting this with the work of Michael Howard and John King (2008) and Neil Davidson (2010). The chapter concludes by considering how the conceptualisation of neoliberalism outlined in this chapter can inform a more detailed political-economic account of the Accord as the central element of the vanguard neoliberal period.

1.1 *Conceptual Diversity*

It is important to note that the term neoliberalism is diversely deployed within the social sciences. The term's meaning is often imprecisely defined and is the subject of contestation (Flew 2014). In the hands of various authors it can refer to: (1) a doctrine, set of ideas and/or ideology; (2) a set of economic policies, an entire economic regime and/or a distinct phase of capitalism; (3) a political project, form of political rule and/or type of state; (4) a category of denunciation or criticism; (5) a governing rationality; and (6) a complex mix of some or all of these elements.

Deployment of the term has often obscured its meaning more than illuminated a coherent story (O'Connor 2010, 691). At times authors refer to a 'neoliberal era', signposting the term as the period after the end of the long boom (Cooper 2008), while others claim it is a theoretical rejection of Keynesianism (Lavelle 2010, 56) or related to the policy-led transformation of institutions (Prasad 2006). A growing number of writers emphasise that 'actually existing neoliberalism' is a departure from the neoclassical and neoliberal theoreticians who are its supposed inspiration (Cahill 2010a; N. Brenner and Theodore 2002b). More recently, debates have raged since the 2008 economic crisis as to whether neoliberalism persists or has faltered (Duménil and Lévy 2011; Crouch 2011; Saad-Filho 2010).

Most recently, scholars have questioned the usefulness of the term neoliberalism and highlighted the tendency for new work simply to add another more precise definition of the concept (in the mind of its author) in an effort 'to refine, complicate and extend old concepts, or to proliferate new ones' (Venugopal 2015, 171). Some have urged caution (Konings 2014), while others have suggested the conception be set aside because of its incoherence, imprecision and the disagreements around it (Dunn 2015; Venugopal 2015). While authors may have found solace in emphasising neoliberalism's hybridity and variegation, this has not necessarily enhanced understandings of the nature of the neoliberal project.

So before proceeding, and in the midst of this controversy, it is important to be clear on why it is useful to use the term at all. Peck (in an interview with Brogan 2013, 183) has suggested there is 'no point in holding onto the concept of neoliberalism for its own sake [and] it has to be doing some work'. The 'work' Peck (ibid 2013, 183) has said the term does 'is to force you to think through connections across different geographical sites and historical time periods'—to consider 'connections between neoliberal projects in one place and another, their family resemblances and structural features'. The connections—be they the response to the global profitability crisis that emerged in the 1970s or the efforts of elites to restrict union power—must be considered concretely in any location, but also understood as part of changes beyond that location. It is for this reason that this book is particularly concerned with the prevailing narrative of the development of neoliberalism, and how this has shaped and limited a consideration of neoliberalism's global development and content—including an analysis of the Accord and political economic change in Australia—in the scholarly literature.

There is still work to be done—including by Marxist scholars—to deliver increased clarity on the processes of neoliberalism and the nature of economic reform in the wake of the end of the long boom. In short, 'it is fair to say that we do not know all there is to know about this thing we call "neoliberalism" and, moreover, that its usefulness as an analytical category is still contested' (Birch 2015, 581).

2 The Dominant Narrative

While recent scholarly work argues neoliberalism takes diverse forms (N. Brenner, Peck, and Theodore 2010), most critical accounts have tended to cleave closely to what this book terms the 'dominant narrative' of neoliberalism's historical development. This dominant narrative has four key features that concern the analysis in this volume. First, most accounts locate inaugural events and paradigmatic cases of neoliberalism in the NYC fiscal crisis of 1975–1981; during the mid-1970s in Chile during the dictatorship of Augusto Pinochet; and in the New Right governments of Thatcher in the UK (1979–1990) and Reagan in the US (1981–1989). Second, such a story sees the widespread development of neoliberalism as being based on its later export from these original (ideal type) locations to elsewhere, rather than understanding it as a global process from the start. Third, the narrative holds that social democratic parties were not significant in the introduction of neoliberalism in its 'vanguard' period (of the late 1970s to mid-1980s), implementing it only in moderated forms and in the wake of projects of the New Right. That is, social democrats and labour movements follow the neoliberal path opened by the Right (Peck, Theodore, and Brenner 2010). Fourth, the story contends that coercive state action has been the key method by which reforms were implemented, including direct state repression by dictatorships; defeat of trade union resistance by the state through set-piece confrontations; imposition of structural adjustment in the Global South; and the use of 'shock' or crisis to impose neoliberal change (Mirowski and Plehwe 2009; Klein 2007; Harvey 2005). Of particular interest to this book is that the dominant narrative casts the labour movement as almost exclusively an object and victim of change.

These aspects of the dominant narrative are found in much of the scholarly literature (see Weller and O'Neill 2014; Peters 2011; Davidson 2010; Klein 2007; Harvey 2005; Peck and Tickell 2002; and Teeple 2000 as examples). This chapter interrogates the manifestation of this dominant narrative in three significant and influential accounts—those of David Harvey, Naomi Klein and the jointly written work of Neil Brenner, Jamie Peck, Adam Tickell and Nik Theodore. The work of these authors is central to critical appraisals of the neoliberal era. Notably, even in the work of geographers Brenner, Peck, Tickell and Theodore—who emphasise the 'variegation' of neoliberalism across time and space—the dominant narrative persists. However, the following discussion will consider how analysis might move beyond the prevailing origin story of neoliberalism through their notion of neoliberalism developing 'among its others' (Peck, Theodore, and Brenner 2010, 104).

2.1 *Harvey:* A Brief History of Neoliberalism

Harvey's seminal book *A Brief History of Neoliberalism* (2005) has provided a detailed exposition of the development of neoliberalism, building on a conceptual framework he earlier developed in *The New Imperialism* (2003). Harvey (2005, 13) has cultivated an historical narrative within a framework that emphasises the uneven geographical development and 'the complex ways in which political forces, historical traditions and existing institutional arrangements all shaped why and how the process of neoliberalisation actually occurred'. He argued that neoliberalism is a project to restore class power, made possible by capital and national states, in the wake of the economic crisis and social conflict of the 1960s and early 1970s.

Harvey has posited the origins of neoliberalism as principally the story of its development in Chile, through to the NYC Council fiscal crisis, and then to the US more widely under Reagan and the UK under Thatcher.[1] These four locations form the cornerstone of his analysis. He has argued that, inspired and influenced by the intellectual efforts of University of Chicago-trained economists and the Mont Pèlerin Society, Reagan and Thatcher led governments that implemented neoliberalism in two of the world's largest economies. Reagan and Thatcher 'seized on the clues they had (from Chile and NYC) and placed themselves at the head of a class movement that was determined to restore its power' across the globe (ibid 2005, 63). These actors:

> ... plucked from the shadows of relative obscurity a particular doctrine that went under the name of 'neoliberalism' and transformed it into the central guiding principle of economic thought and management (ibid 2005, 2).

Harvey has argued (2005, 8) that the 'first experiment with neoliberal state formation' in Chile, in the wake of the Pinochet coup on 11 September 1973, was achieved through the US's central role in overthrowing the Salvador Allende government and the influence of 'the Chicago boys' when they were 'summoned to help reconstruct the Chilean economy'. Harvey (2005, 88) has also argued that, although a map of neoliberalisation is difficult to construct because of only partial progress in most countries, clearly 'the UK and the US led the way'.

Harvey has emphasised a distinction between the introduction of neoliberalism by dictatorships, in Chile and Argentina, and its 'democratic' introduction by Thatcher and Reagan. Harvey (2005, 40–41) has argued the introduction of neoliberalism in the latter locations was achieved through the construction of consent. He drew on Gramsci's notion of 'common sense' to argue assent was developed through various ideological and cultural mechanisms assembled on the material basis of the experience of daily life under capitalism in the 1970s. Central to his analysis of how consent was constructed, however, are acts of

1 Although Harvey discusses China at length, this is not common across the dominant narrative.

state coercion. For example, Harvey has viewed the disciplining of labour by Thatcher and Reagan—through economic policy and industrial disputes—as fundamental to their ability to introduce reforms. Inflation and a rising wave of unemployment in Europe and the US 'created the conditions for a new discipline of labour' imposed by the state (Duménil and Lévy 2005, 11). Those governments used set-piece confrontations as a coercive tool to defeat unions. Reagan defeated the PATCO union when he fired striking air traffic controllers and jailed their union leaders in 1981, despite promising in 1980 to work cooperatively with the union (who supported his election) over industrial and safety matters (Harvey 2005, 25, 59; Armstrong, Glyn, and Harrison 1984, 418–423). In March 1984, Thatcher triggered a confrontation with the National Union of Mineworkers (NUM) by announcing a wave of redundancies and pit closures (Harvey 2005, 59). The NUM strike lasted for a year and, despite widespread public support for the miners, was won by the conservative government (Davidson 2010, 36–37; Harvey 2005, 59). Thus, according to Harvey, coercive methods had to be used to push through neoliberalism in both democracies and dictatorships.

Harvey (2005, 3) has argued that following the introduction of neoliberalism in these particular places almost all states have 'embraced, sometimes voluntarily and in other instances in response to coercive pressures, some version of neoliberal theory and adjusted at least some policies and practices accordingly'. While Harvey has referred to neoliberal reforms by social democratic parties in later periods, he did not consider locations where the introduction of neoliberalism in the vanguard period was accomplished by such political formations—most particularly the social democratic and labourist governments in Australia (from 1983) and NZ (from 1984). Similarly, for Harvey (2005, 63) social democratic governments were 'followers' of vanguard neoliberalism:

> [The] genius [of Reagan and Thatcher] was to create a legacy and a tradition that tangled subsequent politicians in a web of constraints from which they could not easily escape. Those who followed, like Clinton and Blair, could do little more than continue the good work of neoliberalisation, whether they liked it or not.

Harvey's restricted choice of paradigmatic locations produces an incomplete and one-sided account of neoliberalism's origins and trajectory, whereby: it is led by the forces of the New Right; where state coercion of organised labour is needed not just by authoritarian but also by democratic governments implementing it; and, where labour movements and left-wing parties are at best followers and at worst passive victims of vanguard neoliberal change. This is not simply an issue of Harvey failing to mention the country of study involved in this book. Harvey's oversight of Australia is problematic because of the scholarly recognition of how the implementation of neoliberalism in Australia influenced the British Third Way (Johnson and Tonkiss 2002; Pierson and Castles 2002).

2.2 *Klein:* The Shock Doctrine

Klein's account of neoliberalism in *The Shock Doctrine* (2007) has been frequently discussed in the scholarly literature. With over seven thousand citations in Google scholar it is distinguished as one of the most citied texts on neoliberalism, and has been widely influential on social movement activists campaigning against neoliberal policies. Other authors have also developed Klein's ideas through their analysis of corporations and state power in the contemporary era (Loewenstein 2015). Klein has argued that nation states have used 'disasters' of various kinds to transform aspects of society and implement neoliberal policies. Klein's approach has been to conceptualise transitions to neoliberalism as 'eventful temporality: the coups, crisis and shocks that usher in neoliberal policies' (Krinsky 2011, 387). She has cited Friedman's argument that 'only a crisis—actual or perceived—produces real change [and that when] a crisis occurs, the actions that are taken depend on the ideas that are lying around' (Friedman 1962, xiv; Klein 2007, 140). Klein has viewed 'neoliberalism as the manifestation of the inner logic of corporate capitalism and "shock" as the means by which it can be realised' (Davidson 2010, 16). For Klein, the timing of such shock therapy is related to a political 'counter-revolution' against the Keynesian economic policies and social 'compromise' effected during the long boom (Klein and Smith 2008, 583).

Klein (2007, 75–87) has argued that the origins of neoliberal 'shock therapy' are to be found in the 'laissez-faire laboratory' of the Pinochet coup in Chile, followed by the Argentinian military dictatorship of 1976–1983 (ibid 2007, 98–115). Like Harvey, she has proposed that the implementation of neoliberalism by Thatcher was a process of its transition to a democratic footing. Klein (2007, 140) has argued that, in the UK, neoliberalism's advance was made possible by the manufactured shock of the Falklands War being able to:

> … unite the country, [during] a set of extraordinary circumstances that justified [Thatcher's] use of emergency measures and repression—a crisis that made her look tough and decisive rather than cruel and regressive.

In *The Shock Doctrine*, Klein examined the rise of 'disaster capitalism' through various other 'shocks', including the disintegration of the Soviet Union, natural disasters like Hurricane Katrina, and the invasion of and wars in Iraq and

Afghanistan. Prominent in Klein's account is her observation that neoliberalism does not enjoy common assent and it has come about through forcing economic change on populations in moments where social resistance is unlikely to develop. For Klein, neoliberalism is—to a significant extent—built on secret and hidden processes, when the population is distracted by the impact of shock events.

There are a number of problems with Klein's approach, some of which result from her acceptance of the dominant narrative and others that arise from her thesis of 'shock'. Klein has placed ideas at the centre of her analysis and provided little to substantiate why certain ideas become influential in certain locations (Cahill 2013, 72). In understanding neoliberalism as the ideological defeat of Keynesianism (Klein and Smith 2008, 584), she has largely limited her analysis to those locations where New Right governments enacted the political-economic transformation in the 1970s and 1980s. Like Harvey, she has failed to acknowledge where and how social democratic parties introduced neoliberalism in the vanguard neoliberal era. Klein has also failed to explain examples of crisis and shock where neoliberalism was not implemented (Davidson 2009, 168). In the case of the former, she cannot account for why neoliberal restructuring took place in some locations without shocks (such as Australia and NZ). In the case of the latter, she cannot account for the greatly different economic policies that were implemented following different US-backed coups (eg. Indonesia's coup in 1965 being followed by vastly different policies to those of Chile's coup in 1973).

Most pointedly, if Klein's thesis of shock were correct, then the Fraser Government in Australia should have been able to introduce neoliberal policies in the midst of a protracted economic crisis and in the wake of the political upheaval of the 1975 administrative 'Dismissal' of the Whitlam government. As described in the next chapter, those circumstances of crisis and 'shock' underlay why Fraser and the New Right could *not* cohere a neoliberal project. While Klein has usefully highlighted how politics can shift quickly in situations of crisis—with neoliberal reforms able to be introduced more quickly than at other points in some cases—this is more generally true of the history of capitalism. Klein has failed to provide specificity to her understanding of the neoliberal era. Further, as John Krinsky (2011, 387) usefully notes, the focus on 'turning points may obscure strong continuities with the past'.

2.3 *Peck, Theodore, Tickell and Brenner: 'Neoliberalisation'*

That neoliberalism developed on different time scales, in different locations, and in varied sequences, has been emphasised in the work of Peck, Theodore,

Tickell and Brenner.[2] While the work of these theorists is not entirely compatible with a class-based account of neoliberalism as advanced in this book, the strength of their analysis is that they have comprehended neoliberalism as a process rather than an outcome, and its development as variegated (Birch 2015). These authors have argued that, given the multifaceted ways in which neoliberalism has concretely developed, there 'is no paradigmatic ground zero' (Peck, Theodore, and Brenner 2010, 104). They have used the term 'neoliberalisation' to emphasise it as a process of ongoing renovation. Peck, Brenner and Theodore (2010, 104) have argued it is not a process with a fixed endpoint—a utopian vision that capitalism struggles towards—but rather that it:

> ... should be conceived as [a] hegemonic restructuring ethos, as a dominant pattern of (incomplete and contradictory) regulatory transformation, and not as a fully coherent system or typological state form. As such, it necessarily operates among its others, in environments of multiplex, heterogeneous, and contradictory governance.

Yet even in arguing this, these authors have posited an origin and transmission thesis for neoliberalism that reflects the aforementioned dominant narrative such that:

> ... neoliberal doctrines were deployed to justify, inter alia, the deregulation of state control over industry, assaults on organised labor, the reduction of corporate taxes, the downsizing and/or privatisation of public services and assets, the dismantling of welfare programs, the enhancement of international capital mobility, and the intensification of interlocality competition.
>
> Pinochet's Chile represented the first example of neoliberal 'shock treatment', while Thatcherism and Reaganism were among its defining, vanguard projects. More moderate and muted forms of a neoliberal politics have also been mobilised in traditionally social-democratic or Christian democratic states such as Canada, New Zealand, Germany, the Netherlands, France, and Italy. Furthermore, following the debt crisis of the early 1980s, neoliberal programs of restructuring were extended selectively across the global South through the efforts of US-influenced

2 Peck, Theodore, Tickell and Brenner have published analysis together, in various combinations. For the purposes of the discussion in this section, the commonalities in their analysis are treated as a common body of work.

> multilateral agencies to subject peripheral and semi-peripheral states to the discipline of capital markets.
>
> PECK, THEODORE, and BRENNER 2009, 50

In this passage, Peck, Theodore and Brenner have presented an origin story that begins with Pinochet, Thatcher and Reagan. These seminal projects are then followed by, on the one hand, neoliberalism in social democratic states where it appears in a 'moderate or muted' form and, on the other, by the transmission of neoliberalism to the Global South. Further, neoliberal doctrine is seen as being deployed to justify the project's assault on organised labour, where trade unions are the object and victims of that project.

Peck and Tickell (2002) and Brenner and Theodore (2002a) have also deployed the terms 'roll-back' and 'roll-out' neoliberalism in relation to the dominant narrative. Both of these are processes and periods of neoliberalism, in which the former relates to 'the Thatcherite and Reaganite era of privatisation and deregulation, and the latter is represented by Third Way doctrines of state building and marketisation of public services' (Birch 2015, 579; see also Tickell and Peck 2003). While the strength of this approach is how it tentatively periodises neoliberalism and its contingent development across the globe (a method also undertaken in the next chapter of this book), it is too constrained by the dominant narrative to map the case of Australia—and as will be argued in Chapter 9, to account for other between these words. Should read to other locations as well.

While emphasising the 'more than contingent differences' between 'the actually existing reform programs found' internationally, the authors have implicitly accepted the UK and the US as original models that other countries are measured against (Peck, Theodore, and Brenner 2010, 104). This is clear, for example, in their claim that the introduction of neoliberalism in New Zealand by a social democratic government was a restrained version of the 'full' model in other locations (ibid 2009, 50). It is difficult to maintain the view that the vanguard neoliberal experience in NZ was a 'moderate' or 'muted' version of those that were developing simultaneously in the UK and US, given 1980s reforms in NZ: re-regulated the country's finance sector; undertook significant structural adjustment of its largely protected economy; extensively restructured the state and welfare sector; suppressed the labour movement; ensured a significant shift in the distribution of wealth and income away from the working class; and caused a split the country's Labour Party by provoking bitter internal party dissent to these processes (Kelsey 2014, 1995; Roper 2005). Indeed, it was noted from early on that the 'New Zealand Experiment' implemented a 'Reagan-style program of market reforms' and became 'a privileged prototype for neo-liberal reform, endorsed by international agencies (IMF), business associations (European Management Forum) and think tanks (International Institute for Economics)' (Clancy 1996, 1). Jessop even remarked that neoliberalism in NZ was perhaps the 'least impure form' over the early shifts to neoliberalism in uncoordinated market economies (Jessop 2002, 457).

2.4 *Destabilising the Dominant Narrative*

The above limitation aside, Peck, Theodore, Tickell and Brenner have also moved the conceptualisation of neoliberalism forward in their warning against erecting a theoretical wall between neoliberalism and its 'others'. They have emphasised that neoliberalism does not stand 'separate from other social formations and political projects', and that seeing it as such 'seriously misconstrues both the character of neoliberalism and the nature of its advance' (Peck, Theodore, and Brenner 2010, 103). As such, neoliberalism (as highlighted earlier in this chapter) 'necessarily operates among its others, in environments of multiplex, heterogeneous, and contradictory governance' (ibid 2010, 105). And:

> More than this, neoliberalism invariably exists in an essentially parasitical relationship with those extant social formations with which it has an antagonistic relationship, such as state socialism, social democracy, or neoconservative authoritarianism.
>
> ibid 2010, 105

It is by understanding neoliberalism as advancing among and through it others—and in the case of Australia through corporatism and the Accord—that a richer narrative as to neoliberalism's origins can be located. This is explored concretely in coming chapters by examining the relationship between the Accord and the neoliberal project in Australia.

Employing a somewhat different framework to that of Peck, Theodore, Tickell and Brenner, but arriving at a similar conclusion, is John Krinsky's (2011) account of the NYC budget crisis of the mid-1970s. In examining a process of austerity and restructuring, Krinsky has highlighted how long-established corporatist structures of trade union cooperation with the NYC Council were deepened at the same time as the neoliberal project was driven through (discussed further in Chapter 8). In Australia, neoliberalism was also entwined with the deepening of longstanding corporatist arrangements through a formalised social contract in the form of the Accord.

Meanwhile, Connell and Dados (2014) have taken to task the predominance of Northern narratives of neoliberalism in the social sciences, in which both intellectual drivers and political economic changes are seen as emanating from US and European examples. They have argued that the story of neoliberalism in mainstream theory is of a phenomenon arising in the global North (in the US and UK in particular) and later exported to the global South. For them, such interpretations place the global North at the centre of the development of neoliberalism and eschew the experience of the global South. Connell and Dados's argument is that neoliberalism in the global South should be understood as a development strategy, supplanting those pursued prior to the 1970s. Connell and Dados (2014, 132) have not argued that the Northern narrative needs to be replaced by a Southern one, even if a single 'Southern narrative' were possible, but that there can be an 'enriched understanding of neoliberalism … when the social experience and intellectual production of the global South are prioritised'.

In a further destabilisation of the dominant narrative is tackled in Chapter 9, in considering how others analysing the US and UK have pointed to the fact that, in the period prior to the election of Reagan and Thatcher, trade unions played an active role (working in tandem with business, the state or both) in efforts to hold down wages or industrial action in the midst of the 1970s crisis. Such alternative analyses allow for the examination of a new set of issues that are excluded from the dominant narrative. Analysis of the consensual role of labour in the production of neoliberalism in Australia requires this kind of approach. This is not to argue that the advance of neoliberalism in the UK and US is less important or less 'typical' than elsewhere. In fact, it is in many ways the opposite, because of the economic size and the relative geopolitical weight of those two countries. Both countries could and did play a decisive role in the development of neoliberalism within their respective regions and globally, particularly the US. That is different, however, from seeing developments in those locations as prototypical or primarily causative of developments elsewhere. Rather, there is a tension between commonalities and divergences in different neoliberal projects. As Gramsci wrote in his *Prison Notebooks*, and as mentioned in the Introduction:

> … finding the real identity underneath the apparent differentiation and contradiction and finding the substantial diversity underneath the apparent identity is the most essential quality of the critic of ideas and of the historian of social development (2011, 128–129; Q1 §43).

In examining tensions between the concrete experiences of vanguard neoliberalism and the dominant narrative, greater clarity can be gained as to the content of neoliberal social development. The foregoing critique of the dominant narrative offers more than just the possibility of expanding the range of national locations and historically specific paths within and along which neoliberalism has developed. Destabilising the dominant narrative also opens the possibility of grasping neoliberalism as a political project centred on class relations and class power—not one necessarily attached to the ideas and actions of the New Right. It is to mapping out a class-centred definition of neoliberalism that this chapter now turns.

3 A Class Approach to Neoliberalism

This next section critically reviews class theoretical approaches to neoliberalism, arriving at a definition that is consistent with the framework of state–civil society relations established in Chapter 2. The starting point is a further engagement with Harvey's *A Brief History of Neoliberalism*, in order to highlight his pivotal application of Marxist categories. While Harvey's overall contention that neoliberalism represents a form of class rule is compelling, one of his key theorisations requires closer examination—his definition of neoliberalism as 'the restoration of class power'. While the argument developed in this section—that neoliberalism is best grasped as a hegemonic political project—would seem to be compatible with Harvey's thesis of the 'restoration of class power', I set out the divergence in our approaches. Davidson's work is similar to Harvey's, in that they both conceive of neoliberalism as a political project and as being about class power (although they differ on how they understand this). The strength of Davidson's analysis over Harvey's is his periodisation of neoliberalism, which emphasises shifts in form and content in relation to global and national politics.

This book has sympathy for, but rejects, the explanation of neoliberalism offered by Howard and King (2008, 2004). Howard and King have viewed neoliberalism as a new phase of capitalism, where the development of the productive forces (i.e. technological development) causes processes of market creation and expansion to outpace processes of market elimination. Their position has a great strength over many other explanations of neoliberalism in that it attempts a materialist account of one important feature: that, from the late 1970s onwards, there was a generalised increase in the prominence of markets in areas of economy, politics and ideology. Yet there is a difficulty in their theorisation, which is based on Cohen's (1978) reinterpretation of aspects of Marx's theory of history, in that they have understood various social and political actors as largely passively following behind technological change—even if they have allowed for certain feedback mechanisms from social relations and so-called 'superstructures'.

Howard and King's account, therefore, has tended to reduce a wide variety of forms of political development—in the period when neoliberalism became hegemonic—to the idea that the return of markets to prominence (over a prolonged period) was eventually and inevitably followed by a delayed adaptation of social relations, legal and political forms, and ideas. While perhaps having power as a 'broad sweep' theory of the underlying reasons for neoliberal change, it has remarkably little to say about the actions of real people engaged in social and political contests.

Nevertheless, Howard and King (2008, 8) have usefully challenged simplistic left-wing accounts of the rise of neoliberalism in that:

> … we do regard the existing explanations of neoliberalism cast in terms of economic and political factors as flawed. Most particularly, what has become the orthodoxy of the Left is deficient. The emphasis here is placed upon the decline in profitability that engulfed advanced capitalism in the late 1960s. This, it is claimed, activated property owners to pressure and support state policies seeking to break the power of the organised working class, and restore the profitability of capital through neoliberal reforms. Again we can accept the facts upon which this account is based, but the interpretation fits Britain and New Zealand far better than Western and Central Europe or the United States. And it fails to explain why the working class was defeated so easily, and remained defeated in the ensuing decades. Nor is it explained why the instruments of defeat were neoliberal policies rather than a resort to extra-economic disciplinary measures. Finally, the abandonment of Social Democratic principles in favour of neoliberalism by the political parties of the Left throughout advanced capitalism hardly fits with this class struggle perspective.

It is the contention of this book that a more developed understanding of the relationship between civil society (and the 'economic' relations at its foundation) and the state, of the sort outlined in Chapter 2, can account for the gaps in the 'orthodox' Left perspective. Moreover, this can be achieved without needing to reject a central Marxian concern with how capitalist social relations produce class struggles, and how these play out in the social and political spheres.

3.1 *Harvey: 'The Restoration of Class Power'*

While Harvey's work has been productively criticised by other authors who see class as central to understanding neoliberalism (Cahill 2014; Ashman and Callinicos 2006), his analysis remains the most cited and widely read of any Marxist account. Harvey (2005, 16) has argued that neoliberalism is 'a project to achieve the restoration of class power' in the wake of the economic crisis of the 1970s. Harvey (2005, 19) has asserted that we can:

> ... interpret neoliberalisation either as a utopian project to realise a theoretical design for the reorganisation of international capitalism or as a political project to re-establish the conditions for capital accumulation and to restore the power of economic elites.

For Harvey, the second understanding is correct. Although emphasis on the mechanisms through which this has occurred vary, a similar argument that neoliberalism was an attempt to 're-establish the conditions for capital accumulation' has been made by many other Marxists (Selwyn and Miyamura 2014; Panitch and Gindin 2012; Duménil and Lévy 2011; Saad-Filho 2010; R. Brenner 2006).

For Harvey, the development of neoliberalism was purposive and intentional even if experimentation occurred to determine preferred paths. Harvey (2005, 2) has argued that neoliberalism is a distinct and new phenomenon, involving an 'emphatic turn ... in political-economic practices and thinking'. This analysis has placed political-economic change at the centre of understanding the contemporary era, in particular problems of capital accumulation. Yet Harvey's definition has partly foregrounded neoliberalism as synonymous with, and deriving supremacy from, its ideology even as he is deploying 'a class-based analytical lens' (Cahill 2013, 72). This is problematic because it can lead to aligning neoliberalism with its ideological facade, both in terms of its relationship with neoclassical economic theory and in how the state should function.

Furthermore, by stating that ruling class power needed to be 'restored', Harvey has implied that the capitalist class suffered diminution of its power during the long boom. Such a claim requires careful consideration given the long boom was the most stable and successful period of capital accumulation in history. Harvey has presented two key arguments for his 'restoration of class power' thesis: first, economically, that there was a drastic shift in the share of income and wealth away from labour in the neoliberal period; and second, politically, that neoliberalism was a reaction to the rising social movements of the 1960s and 1970s.

The key piece of evidence Harvey (2005, 17) has mobilised in support of his first argument is the shift in share of national income for the top 0.1 percent of the population in the United States, the graphical representation of which in *A Brief History of Neoliberalism* bears the title 'The Restoration of Class Power'. He also deployed the work of Duménil and Lévy on income shifts, quoting approvingly their argument 'that neoliberalism was from the very beginning an endeavour to restore class power to the richest strata in the population' (Harvey 2007, 28). Thus, neoliberalism is seen as the articulation of particular class interests, in response to economic and social changes, which drove the transformation from the post-World War II era to the superficially market-based neoliberal framework that emerged in the 1970s (Duménil and Lévy 2012).

The second part of Harvey's argument was premised on the growing strength of labour and social movements and their threat to capitalism, both in the US and more globally (Harvey 2005, 14–15). Harvey has argued that there was a significant threat to the ruling class in the form of economic crisis and organised labour's efforts to maintain wages and conditions. The crisis threatened the viability of certain sectors of capital, as well as the fiscal integrity of government budgets through declining taxes, and therefore the ruling class sought the restoration of accumulation and power in restructuring production and attacking workers' wages and conditions. Harvey's contention was that the:

> … conjoining of labour and urban social movements throughout much of the advanced capitalist world augured a socialist alternative to the social compromise between capital and labour that had grounded accumulation so successfully in the postwar period.
>
> HARVEY 2007, 27

However, Harvey's class power formulation is problematic in that it suggests that the capitalist class was less powerful in the period of the long boom and that capitalism was placed under increased constraint by civil society (this position is also argued in Klein and Smith 2008; and Duménil and Lévy 2011). How the most stable and successful period of capitalist accumulation in history was also one where the ruling (capitalist) class was ultimately losing or lacking power is never fully spelled out. Furthermore, the long boom was accompanied by what was universally experienced as profound social stability in most rich Western countries, with low levels of industrial action, rapid growth of corporate power and frequent popular pronouncements of the death of class and 'the end of ideology'. Labour's share of GDP in countries like the United States and Australia was high throughout the long boom (when social stability was high and struggle low); not just when large-scale social struggle emerged in the late 1960s and early 1970s. Even then, while there was a relatively high level of strikes and protests in most of the rich West during this final phase of the boom, not even at its highest point (in the general strike that shook France in 1968) did subaltern elements of civil society come close to overthrowing the capitalist system in any one country.

Thus, Harvey's 'restoration of class power' adds confusion to any attempt at locating the rise of neoliberalism in an analysis of class relations. It deduces from the class *effects* of neoliberal restructuring a specific class *motivation* that cannot be sustained on the basis of empirical facts about the long boom. So, Harvey creates an exaggerated picture of the power and economic position of labour *vis-à-vis* capital in the pre-neoliberal period. Harvey's analysis also lacks the specificity required to explain why governments took the neoliberal road in a variety of locations with greatly divergent balances of class power—something that is more usefully developed in Davidson's work.

3.2 *Davidson: 'An Entirely New Political Regime'*

Davidson's analysis of neoliberalism—chiefly set out in *Neoliberal Scotland* (2010), 'The Neoliberal Era in Britain' (2013), 'The New Middle Class and the Changing Social Base of Neoliberalism' (2015) and Crisis Neoliberalism and Regimes of Permanent Exception (2017)—has provided a useful conceptualisation in terms of Marxian class theory. He has traced neoliberalism's ideological and socio-economic antecedents and, like other Marxist scholars, has argued that neoliberalism developed out of the economic crisis of the 1970s, with its breakdown in stable accumulation and profitability. Davidson has posited that the term 'neoliberalism' can be defined in three ways: first, as a body of theoretical or ideological work, developed and prosecuted by neoliberal theorists and their supporters (especially after World War II); second, as a political-economic strategy evolved by the ruling class in response to the crisis of profitability of the 1970s and involving the necessity to impose greater controls on working class; and third, as an era initiated by the end of the long boom (Davidson 2015, 4–5).

Davidson doesn't dwell on the autonomous power of ideas to lead neoliberal transformation, thereby putting distance between himself and thinkers who posit an ideas-centric understanding of neoliberalism (see Cahill 2013 for a detailed analysis of this tendency in the scholarly literature). Davidson (2013, 173), however, has raised the question of 'whether neoliberalism is a useful way of characterising the entire historical period from 1973 to 2008 and possibly beyond'. To answer his own question, Davidson has proposed a periodisation of the 'neoliberal era', in order to clarify its course and internal shifts. This is an innovative contribution, and is a method that this book draws on and applies to the Australian example in the next chapter.

Davidson's periodisation emphasises aspects of continuity between the post-war boom and the neoliberal period, while rejecting the argument that neoliberalism represents a more fundamental change to capitalist social relations (eg. as a result of globalisation). Davidson (2013, 181) has argued that neoliberalism is conceptually valuable because it acknowledges significant structural changes to capitalism since the early 1970s, and also draws out the 'failure of Keynesianism' and the political and policy arrangements with which it was associated. The power of constructing a periodisation is that it goes beyond acknowledging the historical continuity and change represented by the rise of neoliberalism. Such an approach also allows further continuity and change to be tracked, rather than treating neoliberalism as fixed and immutable once introduced.

Davidson periodised neoliberalism into three key phases: the first is what he terms 'vanguard neoliberalism'; the second he terms 'social neoliberalism'; and the third is the post-2008 period of 'crisis neoliberalism'. Vanguard neoliberalism is described as 'a regime of reorientation'. Davidson (2013, 183) argued that neoliberalism, in each location it has been introduced, has usually required a vanguard phase that includes 'an entirely new political regime' and 'one which did not reluctantly acquiesce in policies they would rather have avoided [and was] fully committed to their implementation'. Meanwhile, Davidson (2010, 46) argued that social neoliberalism represents 'a regime of consolidation' that is 'characterised by social or liberal democratic rhetoric, during which governments were able to incorporate the rhetoric of social solidarity while maintaining and even extending the essential components of neoliberalism'. Davidson argued that the term 'Third Way', usually defined as a path between social democracy or Labourism and neoliberalism, is misleading. He argued that the phase of social neoliberalism is more accurately understood—as described by Alex Law and Gerry Mooney (2007)—as an adaption of the former to the latter, and not as a synthesis (Davidson 2013, 195). Finally, crisis neoliberalism is understood as 'a regime of permanent exception' (Davidson 2017).

Davidson emphasised the political aspects of the neoliberal shift in his description of the 'entirely new political regime' represented by the vanguard phase. Neoliberalism's emergence was 'a conscious ruling class strategy, rather than an esoteric ideological doctrine' (Davidson 2013, 181). Therefore, hegemony had to be remade 'in response to the end of the post-war boom, but in changed conditions created by that boom' (ibid 2013, 181). While Davidson's emphasis on the political is useful, the separation between the capitalist class and the state remains inadequately theorised. Emphasising neoliberalism as a conscious 'ruling class' strategy passes over the bourgeoisie's existence as atomised, competing, private individuals and their separation from the state. This fails to distinguish clearly how state and civil society operate on different logics—political and social. This can lead to an economic reductionism in analysis of the behaviour of political actors, because they tend to be seen to act in line with an imputed general class interest of capital. In order to sustain this view in light of mainstream Western political parties pursuing economically damaging 'austerity' policies along apparently neoliberal lines, Davidson (2015) has argued that neoliberalism has become increasingly irrational with respect to the general interests of the capitalist class.

Despite its overall innovation and flexibility, Davidson's argument has also absorbed aspects of the dominant narrative. In particular, Davidson (2013, 183) has argued that neoliberalism was a coercive project of 'the established parties of the right' in its vanguard phase. Similarly, he has tended to portray the role of social democrats as following in the wake of the right's vanguard efforts, rather than being capable of carrying such reforms through themselves. Davidson (2013, 183) has, for example, stated that it was 'only in the exceptional case of New Zealand after 1984 [that] an incumbent social democratic party transform[ed] itself into the agent of neoliberalism before it became the dominant form of contemporary capitalist organisation'. The implication in his analysis is that Australia, under the Hawke-Keating governments, did not undertake the country's vanguard neoliberal turn. As will become clear in the following chapters, it is not tenable to view the Hawke-Keating era as anything but a vanguard period of neoliberal reform under the auspice of a social democratic government.

3.3 *A Hegemonic Political Project*

While both Harvey and Davidson's works are attuned to the political nature of neoliberalism, and both see it as a question of class power, they differ in how this is conceptualised. For Harvey, neoliberalism is a process that sees a strengthened ruling class displace and weaken the working class. He has posited the long boom as an era of working class ascendancy that forced a Keynesian compromise, which then had to be overturned by a process of 'restoration'. Davidson, by way of contrast, has understood the neoliberal period as one where there is a change in how class interests are being deployed through the state to stabilise capitalist accumulation. The strength of Davidson's work over Harvey's is that it provides a clearer understanding of the mediations between the interests of capital and the actions of the state, also it is less prone to eliding the two. In addition, while never satisfactorily clarified, tensions between capital and the state are recognised in Davidson's effort to periodise neoliberalism, in order to account for divergences between countries and within countries over time.

This book argues that the key to understanding neoliberalism is not in identifying its internal consistency or fidelity to an ideal type, but in recognising it as a transformative political project with the ability to provide enough *political* coherence to deliver capitalist restructuring and social change—including the defeat of those social and political forces standing in the way of its aims. It is not that ideas and ideology are unimportant; rather, they are how individuals and groups come to understand, justify and argue for their material interests and practices. In this way, ideology is central to the development of any political project.

However, ideology cannot be considered to have an existence autonomous from social practice. Therefore, while many of the agents who drove neoliberal restructuring may have come to understand what they were doing in terms of some form of what might usefully be described as neoliberal ideology, this book focuses on the coherence of the *practice* of neoliberalism rather than subordinating it to those sets of ideas. The accounts of Harvey and Davidson look at the key historical developments in the implementation of neoliberalism internationally, in order to highlight its coherence and nature as a *practical* class project. While neoliberalism does tend to share key features in all locations (the disorganisation of labour; financial sector reforms and re-regulation; marketisation of public goods; etc.), those ideological and policy factors had to be underpinned by a political project that was able to achieve hegemony in practice.

In that sense, neoliberalism is best understood as a material practice of political society and the state—one that represents a clear break from the political arrangements of the preceding period. Neoliberalism's three integrated aspects can only be separated analytically as the ideological, the economic, and the political. The ideological roots of neoliberalism are found in classical and, in particular, neoclassical economic theory and its neoliberal revisions. These bodies of theory have been fundamental to its development, even if neoliberalism in practice diverges (sometimes dramatically) from those canons of work. Neoliberalism is therefore not synonymous with how it is presented ideologically in order to justify the political project (for example: as a retreat of the state, in order to cut the welfare state; as the expansion of individual liberty and freedom, in order to increase corporate and ruling class power and decrease labour and subaltern rights; as a development project to enhance the wellbeing of all, when its effect is the opposite; or as an economic project to provide stability to capitalism after the 'failure' of Keynesianism, which in reality often produces more instability).

Neoliberalism is a project intended to restore stable capital accumulation after the global economic crisis of the 1970s, and it is here that its economic origins can be located. It has been a contingent response to fundamental problems of profitability in the global economy, and this is discussed further in the following chapter. This context has explanatory usefulness both in terms of why neoliberalism was introduced *when* it was, and in terms of *what* sort of economic and policy reforms were implemented—particularly why the suppression of wages was crucial to the introduction of neoliberalism in Australia. Neoliberalism is, therefore, a state-centred hegemonic political project of economic transformation.

The realisation of a neoliberal political project cannot be understood outside of the political-economic conjuncture of the 1970s—including the economic crisis and relative social strength (and resulting confidence) of organised labour in the later decades of the long boom—but must also be understood in terms of the interests of the state (and the political actors around it) in addressing those developments. Such features shaped the neoliberal political project, but also shaped further changes as they unfolded. Neoliberalism-as-ideology does not become neoliberalism-as-phase-of-capitalism until this ideology is made manifest in a political project, implemented by political society through the state. It was when politics—i.e. the activities in the political sphere centred on the state—was deployed to change national societies as a whole that neoliberalism had the potential to become a hegemonic political project, one that could effect a significant shift in the balance of social forces.

4 Conclusion

This chapter has contended that it is necessary to destabilise the dominant narrative of the origins of neoliberalism in order to account adequately for the diverse trajectories of neoliberal restructuring internationally. Existing radical and Marxist versions of the dominant narrative often posit that it was a coercive project of the New Right, only subsequently or reluctantly pursued by social democrats and imposed on unwilling labour movements. This narrative fails to integrate fully (or in some cases at all) the case of Australia in the Accord era.

Once the dominant narrative is destabilised, it becomes possible to develop a richer theorisation of the nature and trajectory of neoliberalism. This chapter has done so from a materialist or Marxian perspective, by drawing on the insights of Harvey and Davidson in particular. Firstly, both authors have emphasised the class nature of the neoliberal project, as a response to the economic and political crisis at the end of the long post-war boom. Secondly, Davidson has offered a deepened understanding, because of his attention to periodising neoliberalism, thus enriching its theorisation by countering a tendency in many accounts to imply that, once neoliberalism is introduced, it is effectively static or immutable. Additionally, a multiphasic trajectory of neoliberalism provides the basis for understanding how neoliberal ideology and neoliberal economic policies alone are not enough to ensure that a neoliberal-restructuring regime wins out. Rather, ideology and economic policy need to be brought together in a contingent political project, which draws significant civil society actors under the direction of politics and the state. Thirdly, and finally, while they do not always clarify this aspect of neoliberalism's nature, Harvey and Davidson have both focused on the state as implementing a project of class rule.

Concretising the insights drawn from Marx and Gramsci in Chapter 2, the analysis in this chapter defined neoliberalism as capitalist class rule in the form of a *state-centred hegemonic political project remaking capitalist production and social reproduction since the end of the long boom*. The next chapter will deploy this concept in outlining the historical trajectory of neoliberalism in Australia.

CHAPTER 5

Periodising Neoliberalism

> Australia stands poised on the threshold of the 1980s more divided within itself, more uncertain of the future, more prone to internal conflict, than at any other period in its history.
>
> BOB HAWKE, 1979, *The Resolution of Conflict*

1 Introduction

Neoliberalism has been constructed in different locations through a lengthy process of structural adjustment—including efforts before and after vanguard phases—with the involvement of parties across the political spectrum. In this chapter I propose a periodisation of the neoliberal era in Australia, contextualising the development of the Accord within this. My intention in undertaking this method of analysis is to demonstrate the neoliberal project's continuity with, and rupture from, the previous historical period—in a way that accounts for its contingent emergence 'from among its others' (Peck, Theodore, and Brenner 2009).

The periodisation divides the neoliberal era in Australia into four stages: a proto-neoliberal stage; a vanguard neoliberal stage; a piecemeal neoliberalisation stage; and a crisis stage. Underpinning the periodisation are four key contextual issues: 1) the antecedents of neoliberalism in Australia; 2) the unsuccessful attempts by the Whitlam and Fraser Governments to suppress wages and control industrial militancy; 3) the circumstances that allowed the vanguard stage to be cohered; and 4) the reasons for the end of the vanguard neoliberal period.

The analysis emphasises the impact and form of the 1970s economic crisis on political and civil society, while considering political efforts in response to it. The discussion also examines the relationship between the dominant narrative of neoliberalism's origins internationally and the vanguard neoliberal period in Australia. By considering shifts in the hegemony and coherence of neoliberalism in Australia over time, and by comparing this to the dominant narrative of neoliberalism outlined in the previous chapter, the periodisation provides a more comprehensive account of the origins of the neoliberal project and the role of Accord as its central facet.

 | DOI:10.1163/9789004383463_006

2 Periodising Neoliberalism in Australia

The value of constructing a periodisation of neoliberalism is that it allows analytical separation of different historical phases of change, in order to highlight shifts in content and coherence over time. The purpose of periodising capitalism is:

> … to interpret an otherwise undifferentiated 'flow' of historical time by classifying events and/or processes in terms of their internal affinities and external differences in order to identify successive periods of relative invariance and transitions between them
>
> JESSOP 2001, 283.

To not periodise neoliberalism, itself a phase of capitalist development, would be to risk 'the analytical delivery of an "undifferentiated mush" in tracing different conditions of class struggle across space and time' (Bieler, Bruff, and Morton 2010, 31). If, as has been argued, neoliberalism is a state-centred hegemonic political project, periodisation can assist in teasing out the relevance of contingent local factors within a broader global political-economic conjuncture, as well as focusing more closely on the changing strength of neoliberal hegemony. In Australia, the contingent local factors included, most importantly, the method of removal of the Whitlam ALP Government in 1975 and the impact of that event on the following conservative Fraser Government—constraining its ability to undertake a national reform project to address the economic crisis.

Despite the clear analytical benefits of periodisation, scholars have not attempted to periodise neoliberalism in Australia. Even when seeking to delineate various political interventions in response to the end of the long boom (in order to ask 'was this government neoliberal?') scholars have usually emphasised linear chronology over the more complex interplay of contingent factors, or connected neoliberalism simply to changes in government and their respective imputed ideological frameworks. For example, geographers Weller and O'Neill (2014) set out a definition of neoliberalism that looks for 'recognisably neoliberal' policies in a chronology of government changes from the 1970s onwards. Such an approach seeks to locate a 'typical' neoliberalism based on the dominant narrative previously outlined and, when failing to find a match to this ideal type, declares successive Australian governments decidedly non-neoliberal. This approach fails to understand how neoliberalism emerges and operates 'among its others', and instead sees the existence of any Keynesian policies or a corporatist framework as 'proof' against the existence of neoliberalism. Cottle and Collins (2010) have argued that the ruling class strategy of neoliberalism cannot be squared with the social democratic ALP being in power for 13 years, in an agreement with the labour movement. They suggested that the ALP's adoption of neoliberal policies can only be explained as a necessarily pragmatic approach in response to external political economic factors in the midst of a crisis. The authors argued it would be 'nihilistic' to claim that a marriage of heaven (social democracy) and hell (neoliberalism) occurred in this period, as this would be to admit defeat for the project of social democracy—especially a form of that project that directly involved the trade unions in the running of the state during the Accord. Cottle and Collins' approach establishes the character of governments from the imputed ideological frameworks of political parties, rather than through a materialist analysis of the practices of political society.

Drawing on the approach of Davidson, outlined in Chapter 4, I present a periodisation of Australian neoliberalism as a spatially distinct outcome (within a national formation) of the global neoliberal project. By focusing on neoliberalism as a hegemonic political project, the periodisation provides increased demarcation within a period of capitalism often simply referred to as 'the neoliberal era', and greater delineation of how the neoliberal political project was constructed. The periodisation offers a framework for comparing Australian neoliberalism with the dominant narrative of neoliberalism's global advance. The historical account set out in this chapter also acts as a guide to orient the analysis in Chapters 6–8.

An emphasis on the trajectory of neoliberalism creates an opportunity to ask when the project was most effective and when it waned—a method that also emphasises neoliberalism's protracted course of development within and 'among its others'. The concept of 'among its others' (Peck, Theodore, and Brenner 2009, 104) is used throughout this book to denote that the key mechanism to advance neoliberalism in Australia was a corporatist social contract. It was by drawing the trade unions more directly into the project of running the state, thereby enwrapping their civil society organisation politically, that vanguard neoliberal structural adjustment was able to occur in civil society—primarily in terms of real wage reduction and the suppression of industrial militancy. The process in Australia simultaneously reinvigorated corporatism *and* advanced neoliberalism, albeit temporarily in regards to the former.

There were four key stages of neoliberalism in Australia:

1. A proto-neoliberal stage from 1973–1983.
2. A vanguard neoliberal stage from 1983–1993.

3. A piecemeal neoliberalisation stage from 1993–2008.
4. A neoliberal crisis stage from 2008 onwards.

The 'vanguard' phase of neoliberalism represents a set of political manoeuvres that bring together state and civil society actors to address key problems faced by a national capitalism. In Australia, that was constituted by efforts to drive through a sharp and rapid shift from the previous crisis-ridden political arrangement—in terms of both policy and ideological justification. This shift was centred on the Accord.

This chapter focuses most heavily on the proto-neoliberal stage—the Whitlam and Fraser years—in order to provide the background to the shift into the vanguard stage in 1983. The vanguard period is discussed briefly here, then extensively in the following three chapters. The current chapter also outlines what factors shaped the exhaustion of the vanguard phase in 1993. Finally, given the focus of the book on the Accord era, attention is only briefly given to the period after the 1996 electoral defeat of the Keating Government in order to complete the periodisation.

3 Proto-neoliberal Stage: 1973–1983

Before the arrival of vanguard neoliberal reform in Australia, there was a period marked by the failure of the Whitlam and Fraser governments to push through decisive and effective responses to the economic crisis that ended the long post-war boom. The book refers to this period as the proto-neoliberal stage, because it involves some early pragmatic attempts at policy shifts that would later be closely associated with neoliberalism. The proto-neoliberal stage is characterised by an inability to break completely from the old Keynesian project in order to implement a new hegemonic regime. The following analysis of this stage first describes the economic context of the end of the boom and then the (ultimately) unsuccessful efforts of successive governments to address this.

3.1 *The Economic Crisis*

Australia, like many advanced Western economies, experienced an extended economic crisis in the 1970s and 1980s—a crisis that was an obvious contrast to the preceding long boom. As the post war boom came to an end, economic growth contracted sharply in the early 1970s and there were six periods of recession between then and when the ALP was elected in 1983 (see Table 5.1). The global economic situation was characterised by the intractability of

TABLE 5.1 Recessions in Australia, 1960–2015

Commenced	Ended
1 Apr. 1961	30 Sep. 1961
1 Oct. 1971	31 Mar. 1972
1 Jan. 1974	30 Jun. 1974
1 Jul. 1975	31 Dec. 1975
1 Jul. 1977	31 Dec. 1977
1 Oct. 1981	31 Mar. 1982
1 July. 1982	30 Jun. 1983
1 Jan. 1991	30 Jun. 1991

Note: Recessions are defined as two or more consecutive quarters of zero or negative GDP growth.
Source: OECD 2015

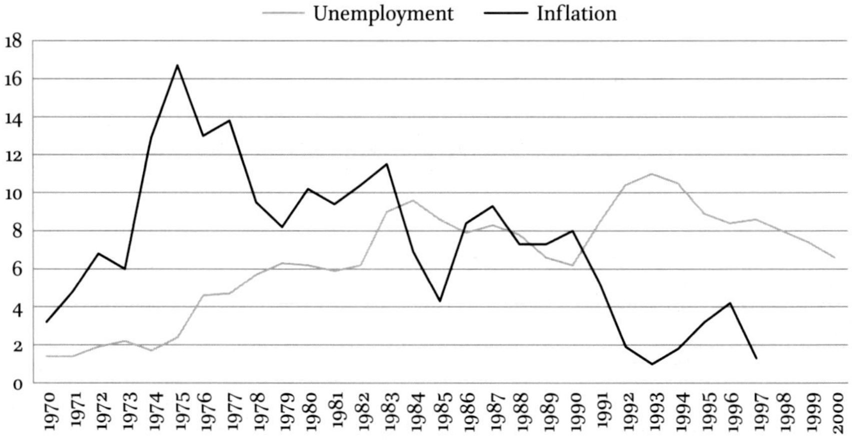

FIGURE 5.1 Unemployment and inflation in Australia (%), 1970–2000
SOURCE: BUTLIN, DIXON, AND LLOYD 2014

inflation and rising unemployment. Such features also ruled domestically—inflation grew sharply in the early 1970s and remained high until after the 1991 recession, while unemployment grew (mostly) steadily through the 1970s and 1980s (see Figure 5.1). Rising inflation and unemployment were coupled with declining government revenue and an increasing social welfare expenditure burden. This was the context in which political parties and trade unions debated how to restore strong and stable capital accumulation as a basis on which to pursue their policy agendas. It would form the background for the development of the Accord.

Accounts of the 1970s economic crisis emphasise diverse drivers. Many have agreed it was centrally characterised by stagflation, which discredited Keynesianism and prompted a search for other policy solutions (Catley 2005, 99; Singleton 1990b, 162; Stilwell 1986, 6–8). As such, in some accounts of this period, policy makers are seen as less able to use trade-offs between inflation and unemployment as part of a macroeconomic policy strategy. Other analysts have emphasised the oil shocks and their impact on inflation; the imbalance of trade relations; the devaluation of the US dollar; and collapse of the Bretton Woods system (Beggs 2015; Bryan 1991; Armstrong, Glyn, and Harrison 1984, 311). Each component variously features and fades in competing assessments. Rick Kuhn and Tom O'Lincoln (1989, 45–46) argued that although all these events and changes were 'factors in the timing of the short-term recessions during the longer run crisis', analysis that focuses on these features alone does not explain satisfactorily why the international and Australian economies became so susceptible to 'policy failings' and 'external shocks'.

The generally accepted explanation for the weakness of the advanced economies in this period is that there was a general decline in profitability. It is most commonly accepted that the decline in profitability was caused by higher real wages constraining profits (Armstrong, Glyn, and Harrison 1984; Body and Crotty 1976; Glyn and Sutcliffe 1972). Although the crisis in Australia was in large part driven by its interrelationship with the global economy, and although international instability fuelled domestic inflation (Beggs 2015, 149), versions of 'wage-push' or 'profit-squeeze' theory have been widely accepted as an explanation for the protracted malaise within Australia's borders (Beggs 2015, 177; Hancock 2014, 10; Megalogenis 2012, 38; Kelly 1992, 50–51). Such accounts argued at a basic level, that full employment pushes up wages and this in turn 'squeezes' profits. An alternative account, argued by some Marxists, is that the underlying problems of the economy were best explained by a tendency for the rate of profit to fall over time in a capitalist economy (Roberts 2012; Duménil and Lévy 2011; Brenner 2006; Mohun 2003; Weisskopf 1979). This explanation posits that a downward secular trend in the rate of profit from either the 1950s or 1960s onwards 'can be regarded as a key feature of the economic crisis of the 1970s and 1980s' (Kuhn and O'Lincoln 1989, 48; see also Roberts 2012). Such arguments portray this secular trend in the rate of profit as underpinning the:

> ... sensitivity of the world economy to shocks and policy mistakes resulting in ... cyclical recessions ... interpolated by 'recovery' periods of high unemployment and unstable growth (Kuhn and O'Lincoln 1989, 48).

Despite disagreement on causation, both profit-squeeze and rate of profit explanations concur in arguing that the crisis expressed itself as a decline in business profitability.

Broader political-economic changes shaped how the crisis following the long boom unfolded, and how the situation was tackled by nation states and capital. Davidson (2013, 178) noted that alongside the historically unequalled global growth of the 1950s and 1960s, several other changes took place:

- The first was an 'unprecedented three-fold expansion of international trade, growing twice as fast as actual output across the period, with the biggest increase taking place in the decade immediately prior to the crash of 1973'.
- The second was 'an increase in the extent of cross-border production, utilising world forces of production ... to achieve economies of scale that were only possible within a multinational market'.
- The third was the internationalisation of finance.

These changes resulted in a deeper interpenetration of national capitalisms and established the parameters for the political-economic response and the development of neoliberalism.

The economic context and the accumulation crisis resulted in a collapse of the Keynesian consensus that characterised, at a general level, the post WWII boom in Australia. As Paul Dibley-Maher (2012, 64) argued, the long boom in Australia saw unemployment and inflation largely in check, and 'the economy requiring litter attention other than the accepted Keynesian orthodoxy built around fiscal policy to [maintain] aggregate demand'. The emphasis in Australia (and in many other locations) once the boom had collapsed, was on 'neoliberal' adaptation through reduced protectionism, increased marketisation and financial sector re-regulation (Bryan 1991, 295).

Australia faced additional and more particular challenges. Capitalism in the former British colony was historically centred on agriculture and mineral extraction, with a small and heavily protected manufacturing base (Kaptein 1993, 81–82). In the 1960s and 1970s, Australian commodities faced increased competition on the world market, partly due to the winding down of the Commonwealth trade preference systems. State managers and governments had long held concerns about the lack of international competitiveness of many Australian commodities, believing that reduced protectionism was an important way to deal with this (Kelly 2009). Given Australia's medium size, surges in mining extraction resulted in the Australian economy tapping into niche markets, which impacted positively on the economy in terms of GDP growth, employment and investment. But, when these booms receded—such as in the midst of the global crisis in the 1970s and in the collapse of a brief mining led recovery in the early 1980s—serious economic problems were revealed. Key figures within the corporate sector and government argued for a sharp change, away from protectionism, if Australia was to remain a significant force internationally (J.K. Campbell 1979). Further, the Australian economy had also experienced 'industrial stagnation as early as the mid-1970s' with the process of neoliberal adaptation accentuating 'this historical phrase of structural retrenchment' (Lucarelli 2003, 77). This process took place in the context of a global restructuring of manufacturing production, which had profound impact on the scope for worker's struggle.

Regardless of the correctness and/or relative weight of the above-mentioned explanatory factors, in elite business, political and media circles it became increasingly accepted that not only were rising real wages the cause of the predicament in Australia, but that their suppression was the essential solution. This explains the overriding policy focus on suppressing wage claims and industrial militancy as a solution to the crisis, as will become clear in the remainder of this chapter and the next.

3.2 *The Whitlam Government*

The first years of the proto-neoliberal stage were during the Whitlam ALP government, and this section discusses two key events: the 1973 referendum on prices and incomes; and, efforts to cohere a social contract in the period.

In 1972—after 23 years of centre-right rule—the Whitlam Government was elected on a program of economic development and social reform. This took place in a period of increased social and labour movement activity. Workers' confidence had been boosted by steadily increasing affluence during the long boom, alongside close to full employment, and a new generation of union militants had emerged. Between 1967 and 1969, the number of strike days doubled (O'Lincoln 1993, 14). Laurie Aarons, Secretary of the Communist Party of Australia (CPA),[1] stated in 1969 that the 'time has come for a determined, militant

1 The CPA began as a socialist organisation inspired by the Russian Revolution, existing from 1920 to 1991. Although the CPA remained small, and had little electoral success, it was the largest political formation to the left of the ALP and was influential in trade unions and social movements. Beilharz argued that the CPA was traditionally closer to the mainstream than similar parties overseas. He also notes that by the 1960s it was criticising the Soviet invasion of Czechoslovakia, while being increasingly Eurocommunist in orientation (1994, 98).

confrontation with the employer-arbitration-Government class structure' (cited in O'Lincoln 1993, 15). The CPA won a number of key union elections in the period that followed, and Australia's most intense period of industrial militancy commenced.

Whitlam arrived in office promising modernisation and progressive reform. Over the next three years a large range of policies were introduced, including: the Medibank public health scheme; increased funding for education; free tertiary education; publicly-funded childcare and women's services; extensive regional development programs; increased social security; plus, various labour market initiatives (Kuhn 1986). While these reforms were in part a response to political and social struggles of the era, many also aligned with the interests of business. Social policy initiatives such as 'Medibank and changes in funding for school and higher education met the need of increasingly capital-intensive production for a more literate, more skilled and healthier working class' (Bramble and Kuhn 2010, 314). The mass expansion of higher education was necessary to underpin the growth of skilled work. Similarly, long-term structural problems in the economy (as mentioned above) drove industry and labour market initiatives to retrain the workforce and redevelop capital (ibid 2010, 314).

In 1973, six months after his election and before the long boom officially ended in Australia, Whitlam announced a 25 percent reduction in tariffs. While the tariff reduction was introduced to force structural change (by modernising or bankrupting unprofitable sections of industry in primary production, manufacturing, textiles and footwear), it was publicly justified as a strategy to address rising inflation (Leigh 2002, 491–493; Johnson 1989, 57). It is important to note, however, that the 25 percent reduction occurred alongside a further reduction of tariffs on manufactured goods, but also increases in other areas. The net result was actually no change in average effective protection for manufacturing—with a 27 percent to 25 percent shift in average effective rates of assistance, due to the changed size of parts of the sector (Garnaut 2002).

Politically, however, the decision to reduce tariffs was momentous. Historically tariffs and industry protection were deeply embedded in the policy of the ALP and the ACTU, particularly among the militant unions in manufacturing sectors (Bramble 1994). Higher tariffs were also strongly supported by the manufacturing industry, but not by the peak lobby groups for the mining and

---

By 1975 the CPA had developed in a more general 'New Left' radical orientation (Catley 2005, 97–98; Siemensma 2012). By this time, the CPA viewed the strategy for socialism as one where the state would be transformed from the inside, by becoming 'the instrument for rule of the majority of people led by the working class', beginning to 'wither away because its function to ensure domination of one class over others disappears as class division, exploitation and human oppression are abolished' (CPA 1974, 3).

pastoral sectors. The ACTU was not consulted on the change in tariff policy (Leigh 2002, 493). Yet, despite labour movement alarm at the historic shift, unions did not publicly denounce the government's decision to decrease tariffs because of a concern to protect the new ALP administration (Singleton 1990, 18). This book argues that the proto-neoliberal stage becomes clearer from this tariff decision in 1974.

The ALP's policy orientation changed more dramatically in February 1975, at the Labor Party's biannual Federal Conference, where delegates debated how to address the economic crisis. The conference was held at Terrigal, north of Sydney, and is generally recognised as commencing a significant shift in the orientation of the ALP (Bramble and Kuhn 2011; Lavelle 2010, 2005; Singleton 1990; Kelly 1976). The conference adopted a fiscally conservative position that, in the absence of economic growth, the reform program on which the Whitlam government had been elected could not be continued and significant cuts would be needed. During the conference, Jim Cairns (1975, 3), Deputy Prime Minister and a key figure in the left of the ALP, argued:

> At present, the economy is a system that is determined by what happens in the private sector. The Government has some power to determine the general level of economic activity, but the main powers lie in the private sector. ... I am a socialist in that I believe in co-operation and equality, and I deplore avarice and aggressiveness. I know the capitalist system is exploitative and leaves many genuine desires of many people unfulfilled. I also know that the jobs of most of our people depend on private industry—much of it part of the multinational system. I know, therefore, that we must follow policies generally in the interests of the private sector.

The following day, Whitlam (1975, 4) argued that the party needed to rebuild private sector profitability in order to re-establish full employment. Whitlam (1975, 8) also stated that the government could not 'beat inflation or unemployment if there [were] wage increases'. At that time, most unions did not agree that wages should be lowered and were concerned that the government might withdraw support for wage indexation to compensate for inflation and productivity increases. Shortly before the ALP conference, ACTU Secretary Harold J Souter (1974) wrote to Whitlam to express concern at a Treasury Department briefing which argued against any increase to wages at the upcoming arbitration National Wage Case, despite significant rises in the cost of living.

Labor economic adviser Barry Hughes later called the Terrigal conference 'a pro-business orgy' (cited in Bramble and Kuhn 2011, 96). Similarly, journalist Allan Ashbolt (1976, 21) argued that 'Terrigal marked ... a declaration of non-independence from the demands of capital'. What the conference primarily signalled was a move within the Labor Party away from a particular set of state interventionist policies, as the key way in which to deal with an economic crisis. Even if the ALP was not strictly a 'Keynesian' party prior to the conference, its reformism and interventionist policy framework fitted with Keynesian principles related to managing aggregate demand. The ALP's previous approach to economic policy provided an acceptable framework that did not require the rejection of mainstream economics, even for the left of the party (Lavelle 2005, 762). The advent of stagflation and the perceived incapacity of Keynesian policies to address the crisis—in particular the inability to take advantage of the trade-off between unemployment and inflation—created an ideological and political vacuum the left was unable to fill.

While Terrigal was a watershed moment in the policy direction of the ALP, Carol Johnson (1989, 72) argued that the speeches by Whitlam and Cairns cannot simply be read as 'sell outs', but as sincere meditations on the deep problems facing a Labor government in a period of profound economic crisis. The dilemma for the Labor Party was that governing through the state requires efforts to ensure the conditions for the successful reproduction of capitalist social relations. In a crisis, securing successful accumulation could not be squared with the interests of the labour movement and the working class—a problem that would again arise in the Accord period.

Lavelle (2005, 761) has posited that the conference was 'the beginnings of a move to neoliberalism' and that this was evident in the defeat of a 'motion that sought the strengthening of the public sector in favour of a resolution emphasising the restoration of profits in the private sector'. Paul Strangio similarly argued that the 1975–1976 Bill Hayden austerity budget, following the Terrigal conference, 'heralded the arrival in Australia of neoliberal economic government' (cited in Lavelle 2005, 761). However, as Whitlam noted at the conference, the ALP had 'always recognised the relationship between the prosperity of the private sector' and the 'ability to carry out the [reform] program' (cited in Lavelle 2005, 761). Whitlam argued that the program, 'particularly in education, welfare, hospitals and cities, [could] only work successfully within the framework of strong uninterrupted growth' (ibid 2005, 761). Seeing Terrigal as simply the first step on a slope towards 'full neoliberalism' downplays the conscious collective effort that was required to successfully cohere and implement the vanguard neoliberal reforms of the 1980s.

The moments of tariff reduction and the Terrigal conference are important in understanding the proto-neoliberal stage. Tariff reduction (alongside 'free trade') is generally seen as a signal neoliberal reform, however there was no coherent tendency within the Whitlam Government to implement neoliberalism.

Further, understanding neoliberalism as commencing from the political shift at the Terrigal conference downplays the more complex and contingent process of constructing a hegemonic neoliberal project over the next decade. The Whitlam period is not characterised as proto-neoliberal just because Whitlam introduced progressive social reforms alongside certain regressive reforms. It is characterised in this manner, as is the Fraser period discussed below, because political society was struggling for a solution to the crisis but was not yet capable of cohering a hegemonic neoliberal project.

3.2.1 Whitlam Referendum on Prices and Incomes

Whitlam had argued that nothing would please him as much as being able to effect 'an income and price freeze for six months and then increase it', as Nixon had done in the US (cited in Catley and McFarlane 1974, 32). However, the Commonwealth Government did not (and still does not) have general powers to make legislation regarding prices or incomes. Union lobbying to ensure the 25 percent tariff cut would flow directly to a drop in real prices led the federal Labor Caucus to agree to hold a referendum to give the Commonwealth the power to control prices (Singleton 1990, 27–28; Rydon 1974).

This move provoked a larger debate on control over wages, and the referendum was expanded in scope to include giving the Commonwealth the power to control wages. The referendum in December 1973 was fought largely along party lines with the ALP urging a 'yes' vote on both questions—the right of the Commonwealth to legislate on wages and on prices—and the Liberal Party[2] a 'no' vote. The ACTU and many other unions, however, urged a 'yes' vote on powers to legislate on prices and a 'no' vote on wages (Rydon 1974, 22). Constitutional referendums rarely succeed in Australia and usually require bipartisan support to do so (Brent 1991). Both questions fell short of majority support.

The defeat of the referendum shifted the political focus from direct control over prices and wages to the development of a social contract with labour or capital (or both) in order to manage these issues on a voluntary basis.

---

2 The Australian Liberal Party is a descendent of a party formed in the first Australian parliaments of the early 1900s, out of a merger of free traders and protectionists. The party formed as a united opposition to the emergence of the Australian Labour Party in the 1890s. The Australian National Party is a minor party that has traditionally represented farmers, graziers and rural communities, and has for many years been in a (more or less) formal relationship of coalition with the Liberal Party. The National Party was formally known as the Australian Country Party and National Country Party. For the sake of brevity, this book refers to the Coalition as the 'Liberal Government' or 'Liberal Opposition'.

3.2.2 Social Contract Efforts under Whitlam

The Whitlam Government increasingly focused on wages as the source of inflation during its term in office. In mid-1973, Treasury urged the government to enact a 'short sharp shock' to reduce demand, which was refused by the government on the basis it would increase unemployment (Singleton 1990, 30). By mid-1974, Treasurer Frank Crean identified 'wage-push' as the foundation of the problem (ibid 1990, 31) and, in November, Whitlam made the shift complete in a Ministerial Statement on the Economy:

> The problems of the rapid rise in unemployment and continuing steep rise in prices and costs are interlocked. The rate of wage and salary increases has easily outstripped the rate of increase in prices. The consequential squeeze on profits has been sharp. This has in turn led to a loss of confidence by business in its ability to obtain an adequate return on capital in an inflationary environment. Employees can price themselves out of the market as effectively as business can. There are signs that this is happening. As the Treasurer said recently, in current circumstances: 'One man's larger pay packet may mean another man's job'
>
> Commonwealth Parliamentary Debates 1974, 3360.

Whitlam argued wage restraint would be an essential component of the government's economic management strategy. Adopting a national incomes policy also fitted with the OECD's recommendations at the time, which suggested the adoption of policies to hold down wages would have short term benefits, even if they were not confident of its long-term efficacy (Catley and McFarlane 1974, 25).

The ACTU and many affiliates initially maintained that wages were not the cause of inflation or unemployment, continuing to call for regulation of prices to protect workers. There is evidence that wage claims during much of the Whitlam government were similar to those before his election. It was not until 1974 that wages increased significantly, when the unions launched a wage push in response to high inflation and compromised living standards (O'Lincoln 1993, 236–237; Hughes 1979, 13–14). However, given the failure of the crisis to abate, the ACTU offered to moderate wage demands if the government agreed to a number of conditions on how indexation would work and to a number of policy initiatives—specifically tax cuts and inflation relief (Hagan and Castle 1986, 12; Unknown 1974). In September 1974, the ACTU convened a Special Conference and arrived at a highly-detailed position, including nine criteria that needed to be satisfied by the government (Singleton 1990, 36). The government, on the basis that the unions included too many conditions to ensure wages would be held down successfully, rejected the ACTU offer.

Singleton (1990, 35–37) has argued that the Special Conference saw a shift within the AMWU to support a social contract. However, analysis of archival and other material has indicated that this was not the case. The 1974 Biennial National Conference of the AMWU declared that the union would never accept any system of wages control (AMWSU 1980, 23). The union remained committed to industrial action rather than an agreement with the government—with 'most of the full-time union officials ... not only [attaching] importance to the equation militancy equals success, but [believing] their record [demonstrated] the validity of it' (Bentley 1974, 381). It would take further recessions and a deepening economic crisis for the AMWU to support a social contract over workplace-based action. This point is significant, as the proposition from Singleton that the AMWU had shifted its orientation from the early 1970s downplays the AMWU's more decisive shift to supporting the Accord in the early 1980s.

The closest the unions came to an agreement with the Labor Party in this period was in 1974, in discussions between then ACTU President Hawke, Whitlam and the ALP executive about how they would approach the next National Wage Case. Known as the 'Kirribilli Accord', the agreement sought to establish 'voluntary' wage moderation by unions and provide indexation only up to the maximum level of average weekly earnings (Singleton 1990, 41). This was a compromise on the part of the government, which had previously sought 'plateau' wage indexation—a full percentage increase to the level of average weekly earnings and a flat amount above that plateau (McGarvie 1976). It was also a compromise on the part of the ACTU, which had been seeking full indexation of the total wages bill. However, Hawke could not deliver the support of the ACTU executive. The ACTU (and the two smaller peak union bodies[3]) went on to argue for full indexation at the Commission's wage case.

In April 1975, the government successfully pressed the Commission to introduce wage indexation without union support. This sought to 'restore the profitability of business at the expense of workers' real living standards, because pay rises through indexation lagged behind prices', given they were applied retrospectively (Bramble and Kuhn 2010, 317). Coupled with budget austerity introduced under Treasurer Hayden in 1975, this signalled a sharp shift in the government's approach to wages and economic management. Labor had also

3 The Australian Council of Salaried and Professional Associations and the Council of Australian Government Employee Organisations did not merge with the ACTU until 1981 (Griffin and Giuca 1986).

effectively abandoned its commitment to full employment, with Hayden intentionally adopting policy to keep joblessness high, despite several months of wage indexation being in place as a 'fail-safe' to reduce inflation (Hughes 1979, 31). Any further developments were cut short by the removal of the Whitlam Government from office in November 1975 (discussed below).

3.3 *The Fraser Government*

The ability of a government to cohere a hegemonic neoliberal project within political society is a necessary factor in successfully implementing neoliberalism. This is not always possible if the balance of social forces isn't favourable to the government of the day, even if its ideological predisposition is supportive of neoliberal reform. The Dismissal of the Whitlam Government in an administrative coup impacted significantly on the ability of the incoming centre-right Fraser Government to both influence wages and industrial activity, and to enact wider economic reform. As such, Fraser was unable to cohere a political project to defeat the unions or to implement widespread structural adjustment.

Those who plotted Whitlam's Dismissal may have imagined that it would play to their advantage; but Australian vanguard neoliberalism could not be implemented under Fraser, even in circumstances of economic crisis, political upheaval and a commitment to a variety of neoliberal ideas—circumstances the dominant narrative implies are favourable to such a project. As will be explained below, these factors stood in the way of vanguard neoliberalism advancing. Instead, the project had to await the 1983 election of Hawke's social democratic and labourist government, preaching compromise and end to conflict in the form of the Accord.

This book argues that Whitlam and Fraser were both part of the proto-neoliberal period—not because they were comparable governments, but because they implemented pragmatic responses to the crisis and made some ideological shifts away from the previous Keynesian consensus. Both governments were constrained by the lack of political space and circumstances needed to implement a full suite of neoliberal policies, in order to execute a sharper break with the past. Those circumstances meant that various political reforms and decisions were rebuffed—eventually leading to Whitlam's government descending into chaos and the Dismissal, and to Fraser's being unable to effect a breakthrough against union power.

3.3.1 The Dismissal

Despite rapidly adopting an austerity budget and cutting public sector jobs, as well as attempting to come to an agreement with the ACTU to hold down wages to address inflation, the Whitlam Government was administratively removed from office after a political campaign attacking its economic policy failures and political agenda (Beilharz 1985, 212). Whitlam won elections in 1972 and 1974, but in neither parliament did he have a Senate majority to pass legislation and budget appropriation bills. In October 1975, the Liberal Party-led Opposition blocked 'supply' (finances needed to keep government running). About a month later, with no resolution to the situation, Governor General Sir John Kerr intervened by sacking Whitlam and appointing Fraser as interim Prime Minister. The Governor General is the British Crown's representative in the Commonwealth of Australia, with the authority to dismiss a democratically elected government. The Dismissal was a seismic event in Australian politics, deeply shaping the ALP, trade unions and the labour movement during the period of the Fraser Government and after.

Political narratives of the Dismissal have tended to focus on the actions of key individuals—in particular Whitlam, Fraser and Kerr (Whitlam 2006; Kelly 1995; Oakes 1976; Horne 1975). However, widespread strikes and demonstrations took place against the blocking of supply and in the wake of the government's removal. As soon as Whitlam's sacking was announced, tens of thousands of workers took strike action and the ACTU was pressured to call a general strike (Griffiths 1997). While Whitlam called on voters to 'maintain the rage', the ALP and ACTU leaderships worked hard to demobilise the anger in an effort to reassure business of their reliability as economic and political managers. The campaign that followed focused on questions of constitutional legitimacy and the 'unreasonableness' of the coup. Hawke campaigned within the union movement against the calls for a national strike and, when a national mobilisation did go ahead, his calls resulted in diminished numbers on the streets (Griffiths 1997). A general election was held on 13 December 1975 and the conservatives were elected to office in a landslide.

Whitlam had begun to address the economic crisis in terms largely favourable to capital, but was politically destroyed in extreme and controversial circumstances. The manner of his defeat created new and unexpected problems in implementing economic reform for the newly-elected Fraser government, which proved too politically weak to implement a coherent reform program addressing the economic malaise against labour movement opposition.

3.3.2 Fraser's Dilemma

The eight years of the Fraser Government 'created more dilemmas than it resolved' (O'Lincoln 1993, vii). In this period, business expected the conservatives to resolve the economic crisis and to quell industrial militancy and trade union power. However, Fraser was unable to use the political upheaval around the Dismissal to advance definitive crisis resolution and none of these expectations were met. Fraser's failure was tied up with how the social forces represented by the trade union leadership—and less directly by the ALP itself—were profoundly antagonistic to his administration. Fraser's perceived complicity in Whitlam's unprecedented method of defeat created political polarisation and prevented (in contrast to the Hawke government) any agreement on economic management based on wage suppression. Additionally, unlike Thatcher when she came to power in 1979, Fraser in this period faced a more powerful and confident labour movement—one that was able to break his attempts at wage fixation with relative ease—and not one that had already been 'softened up' by a period of corporatist sacrifice (such as through the British social contract of the mid to late-1970s, as discussed in Chapter 9).

Between 1975 and 1983 Fraser pursued a mix of monetarist and 'inflation-first' policies, austerity and a wage freeze (Odom 1992, 45; Stilwell 1986, 6–8; Berry 1977). The government was initially convinced that 'a combination of monetarist macroeconomic policies and a cut in real wages' would resolve the economic crisis by addressing inflationary pressures (Quiggin 1998, 77). Although Fraser had won in 1975 after campaigning on the basis he would grant full wage indexation and seek to restore permanent lines of contact with union leaders (Singleton 1990, 50–51), he immediately repudiated these commitments and implemented a number of policies without consultation. Wage indexation was meant to provide regular wage increases, but the government and the Arbitration Commission found ways to ensure rises were less frequent and lower than the inflation rate (Minns 1989, 7). Fraser argued, as Whitlam had, that wage increases were the cause of inflation and that it was essential the labour movement moderate its claims.

Pressure on living standards contributed to increased industrial action. Unions used militant tactics to win wage increases in a number of sectors, especially when the economy picked up with a resources boom at the turn of the decade (Hampson 1997, 545). Tom O'Lincoln (1993, 237) has argued that 'the union "wage push" during 1979–1982 was partly a response to exaggerated expectations around Fraser about the wonders of the resources boom'—rather than simply workers' greed—as the 'government had portrayed wage restraint as a temporary expedient until prosperity returned, so it was now boom time, why not claim the pay rise?' (see also Kelly 2011). Motivated by expectations of economic growth, 'sections of workers in the transport, building and communications industries broke through the indexation guidelines' and undermined the wage fixing system (Minns 1989, 7).

There was an effective collapse of centralised arbitration as a macroeconomic strategy to manage wages in this period. The government and business representatives labelled this a 'wages explosion'. However, despite the increases in wages, the picture was complex for workers as wage gains were undermined by cuts to social services. Also, it is important to note that some union leaders were uncomfortable about the breakdown of the structured system of wage management centred on the Commission given it undermined their role in settling claims through arbitration.

While there was a brief economic recovery with the extraction-led export boom of the early 1980s, this evaporated and the Australian economy was again pushed into recession. In 1982, Fraser turned to implementing a 12-month wage freeze, despite an unsuccessful 'voluntary' wage and price freeze in 1977 (Dabscheck and Kitay 1991). The unions quickly rendered the 1982 wages freeze ineffectual (O'Lincoln 1993; Stewart 1985, 26). These factors were key in shaping the eventual emergence of both vanguard neoliberalism and the Accord.

While much has been made of the general cuts to social welfare in this period, some argue that Fraser's 'bark was worse than his bite' when assessed in terms of total government expenditure (Hughes 1979, 40). However, this does not account for where reductions in expenditure occurred and the relative impact on different sections of Australian society. Budget cuts limited job growth and increased the financial burden on workers though various policy changes including: the abolition of the universal Medibank health care system (introduced by Whitlam); the introduction of a health insurance levy that disadvantaged low income earners; real reductions in education expenditure; and the decision to make most welfare payments taxable. Fraser targeted the social wage by placing greater conditions on those who could access government support—in particular unemployment benefits (ibid 1979, 36–37).

Political tensions between the government and the unions steadily intensified during this period. Fraser outlawed secondary boycotts by amending the *Trade Practices Act*, introduced anti-union legislation, and set up the Industrial Relations Bureau to intervene in union organisation. This provoked an increasingly combative approach on the part of organised workers in key sectors (Singleton 1990, 50–69; Jones 1979). In seeking to suppress real wages, Fraser also generated industrial conflict and contributed to growing disenchantment with the conservative government' (Langmore 2000a, 21).

It would be incorrect to view the Fraser Government as neoliberal. At the end of the 1970s and start of the 1980s, the Fraser cabinet was debating tariff policy and closely following the economic transformations occurring abroad (particularly those in the UK and US) for signals as to how to proceed locally. Yet, despite Fraser's admiration for Thatcher, he stood against the drive within the Liberal Party to implement a generalised neoliberal policy framework—even in a context of a state bureaucracy increasingly influenced by and committed to such policies (Pusey 1991). While 'advocating lowered protection, his enthusiasm was tempered by the electoral consequences of unemployment and industrial strife, and by the interests of rural manufacturers his coalition partner [the National Country Party] articulated' (Hampson 1997, 545). Additionally, although Fraser established the Campbell Committee of Inquiry into Australia's Financial System, which recommended extensive changes to regulation, he did not implement the findings—literally throwing the report in a bin in his office because he believed it could not be carried politically (Clark 2015). The proposals of the Campbell Committee would have to await the arrival of the first Hawke ALP cabinet to be realised, despite Fraser personally supporting them.

Before the 1975 election, the Liberals had called for a 'national conference between unions, employers and governments to develop a social contract' but this was not pursued in government (Hughes 1979, 38). Despite this, from the mid to late-1970s, Hawke (as ACTU leader) pursued an agreement with the government on economic management on behalf of the ACTU—only to be rebuffed by Fraser and certain powerful unions (Bramble and Kuhn 2011, 102; Singleton 1990, 74–79). A discussion paper released by the ACTU executive in 1978 argued that wage restraint might be necessary to protect employment—and also that real wage increases should be foregone in return for income tax cuts (Singleton 1990, 78). Many left unions, which maintained there should be no change to ACTU policy at that time, fought this position. They successfully argued the labour movement strategy should remain based on increasing wages in order to restore and maintain real disposable income for workers (ibid 1990, 78–79). The ACTU executive's position paper was rejected and the 1979 ACTU conference included a resolution stating wages were not responsible for inflation, instead blaming rising prices on the actions of the government and an 'unaccountable' business sector (ibid 1990, 78–79).

During the Fraser years, Hawke continued to argue for a consensual approach to incomes policy and economic management, at the same time preparing the ground for his move to federal politics. When Hawke delivered the Australian Broadcasting Council's Boyer Lectures on *The Resolution of Conflict* (1979), he argued for several policies that were later to become part of the Accord process—this included the streamlining of unions through amalgamation to reduce industrial disputation, a program of industrial democracy in order to reduce conflict and increase productivity, and an extended social wage (ibid 1979, 51–54).

The media, the ACTU and ALP politicians increasingly argued in the Fraser years that the failure to end the crisis lay mainly in local rather than global circumstances. As such, 'rising unemployment and slow growth were seen as the outcome of national economic failings rather than as a part of an economic crisis common to all developed countries' (Quiggin 1998, 77). The ACTU and

ALP argued living standards would decrease and that Australia needed a radical reorientation in order to deal with this. Such arguments helped to lay the basis for a new project to address the economic crisis, especially as (contrary to the dominant narrative of neoliberalism's origins) Australia's right was unable to cohere and implement a neoliberal reform project. Instead, that project was to be the signal achievement of the next ALP government through a pact between the industrial and political wings of the labour movement.

4 Vanguard Neoliberal Stage: 1983–1993

The election of the Hawke ALP Government, on a platform of implementing the Accord agreement with the trade unions, was the key moment in cohering the vanguard neoliberal project in Australia. It is uncontentious to argue that the election in 1983 signalled a sharp political-economic shift, but what is in dispute—even now—is the nature of that reorientation. In this section—and to a more detailed level in later chapters—I demonstrate that the advance of neoliberalism in Australia was only made possible by the election of the ALP government, preaching consensus and economic reform in the national interest, and by deepening corporatism through the introduction of a social contract. As the vanguard neoliberal stage is the focus of the remainder of the book, this section briefly analyses the transition into the vanguard period.

4.1 *The Impasse of the 1970s*

The failure to resolve the 1970s economic crisis provoked a search among progressive activists, trade unionists and labourist political organisations for an alternative strategy to address the economic turmoil and maintain living standards. In Australia this expressed itself in a number of ways. Many argued there had been a failure of Keynesian tools to deal with stagflation and that an alternative macroeconomic policy framework would need to be developed (Beilharz 2009, 53). Simultaneously, there was a rejection of the embryonic neoliberal policy direction of the New Right, which the ALP and labour movement believed would try to resolve the crisis in the interests of capital (Stilwell 1982). The moment of crisis also came to be viewed as an opportunity to attempt wider structural change to the political economy of Australia, especially by left trade unions (Dettmer 2013, 186; Stilwell 1982). This latter group believed the longer-term security of the working class could be achieved via comprehensive changes to taxation, pensions, social services and workplaces—codified in an agreement between the ALP and the trade unions (AMWSU 1977b, 1979,

1982). Some in the left unions also believed a social contract would be a path to socialism (Ross, O'Lincoln, and Willett 1986, 13).

It was in this context that the Accord emerged as the product of intersecting processes. The Accord was an economic program *from above*, promoted by politicians and their advisors inside the ALP and in the highest levels of leadership of the trade union movement. This included Hawke (who was transitioning from the ACTU into parliament), Willis (later Federal Treasurer), John Langmore (then advisor to Willis and later an ALP member of parliament) and ACTU Secretary Kelty. The social contract as envisaged from above was not one of radical transformation, but one intended to revive capital accumulation, end industrial conflict, and address inflation by holding down wages. This was a process that also included establishing the Accord as a way in which to improve the ALP's chances of re-election. It saw the industrial conflict of the 1970s not as a marker of working class strength, but as undesirable social division and a brake on economic restructuring. Moreover, the ALP largely saw Whitlam's demise in the constitutional sacking of the government as arising from his inability to be a good economic manager and bring industrial action under control, which had coloured perceptions of the ALP more generally.

The Accord was simultaneously influenced by processes *from below*, reflecting attempts by the labour movement, academics and parts of the left to promote and seek alternative economic solutions that would protect the working class in the crisis (Bramble 2000, 243 & 247; G. Campbell 2000; Stilwell 1986, 8, 1982). As will be discussed in Chapter 8, the AMWU promoted the alternative economic perspectives of thinkers like British economist and politician, Stuart Holland (1977), and produced and distributed booklets including *Australia Up-Rooted* (AMWSU 1977b) and *A People's Economic Program* (AMWSU 1977a). While initially opposed to an incomes policy in the 1970s, the ACTU explored social contracts at a number of conferences and, in 1981, carried a motion to establish an agreement (Bramble and Kuhn 2011, 102).

According to those negotiating the new Accord, militancy had only taken the labour movement so far in the economic downturn and a decade of struggle had not maintained workers' living standards. They argued that an exclusively industrial strategy would be insufficient to resolve the economic impasse, and that it was important to seek an alternative strategy in a concrete political project. Such efforts were largely conceived as placing pressure on and gaining influence within the state via a progressive government (Scalmer and Irving 1999, 73–75). This turn away from militancy was based on underplaying (and even dismissing) the way high levels of industrial struggle had shifted the political terrain, so that ideas about union involvement in government—and even the need for socialist transformation—could gain such a wide hearing inside the labour movement.

The failure of Whitlam and Hawke to establish a social contract influenced the process to secure the Accord in two ways. First, as Daren McDonald (1984, 57) argued, the experience of the Whitlam Dismissal was formative for Hawke and convinced him 'of the importance in securing a workable incomes agreement, to winning and maintaining government'—despite the difficulties in achieving this. Second, in order for the CPA unions to be brought firmly into the social contract, either the form of the agreement (as touted by Whitlam) or the political priorities of the unions had to change. The Accord architects needed to incorporate the militant unions into the Accord process—not only because of their ability to scuttle any agreement, but because of their capacity to promote the ideological argument in favour of the Accord within the wider labour movement.

Securing agreement for the Accord was also achieved through the efforts of Hawke and Keating in persuading the trade union movement that they had little choice but to assent to a social contract in the midst of such difficult economic times. As mentioned above, Whitlam had argued the ALP had always believed there was a productive relationship between the prosperity of the private sector and the ability that it gave government, through taxation, to implement a progressive reform program. Hawke and Keating pursued the position that the ALP was premised on a social harmony between labour and capital (Johnson 1989), and this was later wrapped up neatly in an economically 'rational' framework and ideas of trickle-down theory (Parker 2012; Frankel 1993).

In 1980, when Hawke left the ACTU for parliament, he had already been identified in opinion polls as the preferred Prime Minister over both Fraser and then ALP Opposition Leader Hayden (National Archives of Australia 2014). Once elected leader of the ALP, he argued that a social contract was the *only* way the political and industrial wings of labour could bring an end to the social conflict that had characterised the previous decade. Unions with less industrial strength also believed centralised indexation would provide their members with a better outcome than direct bargaining had. When the economy entered recession yet again in the early 1980s, and the Fraser Government successfully sought the sanction of the Commission to provide only partial indexation and subsequently a wage freeze (Odom 1992, 30), a crucial point had arrived for the more militant unions.

The Fraser government had demonstrated its determination to decrease real wages and the new downturn led to a fresh bout of redundancies in manufacturing. While 'many in the labour movement did "maintain the rage" [after the dismissal of Whitlam], seven years of strife brought only the exhaustion of the contending forces and the triumph of new political leaders preaching "national reconciliation"' (O'Lincoln 1993, vii). Thus the:

> … 1981/82 recession and the industrial problems that occurred in that period, structural changes and a rise in unemployment gave some needed impetus to the discussions about an Australian Accord—discussions that became more intense as the Fraser Government in 1982 offered the 'solution' of a six month wage freeze, voluntary price restraint and a curbing of what it termed unlawful union power. Labor's answer was to create a partnership between the unions and the alternative government—a high risk political strategy until the election of Bob Hawke as Labor leader just as the 1983 election was underway
>
> EASSON and FORREST 1994, 123–124.

In other words, neither the confrontational Fraser Government nor the historically militant labour movement had achieved a decisive victory. The moves towards an Accord, therefore, addressed an impasse in the left's strategy for the labour movement. In order to cohere the Accord, both the type of agreement (industry policy and the social wage became key components) and the outlook of the CPA unions (now willing to accept retrospective indexation and other compromises) shifted. The social contract was shaped as not only an industrial strategy—one that shifted the location of action and struggle from workplaces to the state—but as a more general political one, where unions gained influence directly in political society.

These shifts in the labour movement occurred slowly over the 1970s, at the same time as some economists were arguing that some form of indexation of wages and prices would give unions certainty about maintenance of real wages and eschew the necessity for industrial action. In some ways, such a proposal was controversial, as wage indexation had been blamed by many economists for inflation in the early 1950s (Beggs 2015, 207–208). However, given the arbitration system had failed to limit wage growth in the 1970s, there was a search for a new approach among key business advocates and sections of the state—including inside Treasury.

Politically, even though many employers were sceptical of a social contract, the reality of the Fraser years was that the natural party of business—the Liberal Party of Australia—had failed to resolve the private sector's economic problems with a strategy of confrontation. Indeed, by the early 1980s, the AMWU and key employers were making agreements outside Fraser's wage suppression policies in exchange for promises of industrial peace (O'Lincoln 1993, 231). These deals were effectively 'no further claims' agreements to limit militancy, which was central to the establishment of the Accord. Such deals signalled the exhaustion of Fraser's approach as one that could look after business interests, opening the way for employer acquiescence to, or engagement with, the Accord process under Labor.

In opposition in the Fraser period, the ALP was dominated by the belief that the Keynesian tools of monetary and budgetary policy were unable to address the crisis—despite the fact that Keynesian macroeconomics was not implemented fully and coherently in the Whitlam era. The more global argument that there was a fiscal crisis of the state became increasingly accepted (O'Connor 1973). The ALP felt unable to defend itself against the allegation that it had engaged in reckless spending in the Whitlam era and contributed to, rather than helped resolve, the economic crisis (Quiggin 1998, 77). As a result, subsequent Labor leaders 'were at pains to present themselves as responsible economic managers and to distance themselves, as much as possible, from Whitlam' (ibid 1998, 77).

4.2 *Developing the Accord*

From the late 1970s, the ALP and ACTU worked together to develop an agreement along several dimensions. A number of senior members of the ALP drafted discussion papers on a prices and incomes policy, which were discussed with the ACTU through the Australian Labor Advisory Council (ALAC) (Langmore 2000b; Willis 1979). In addition, various union officials and politicians studied corporatist arrangements and visited the UK, Sweden[4] and other locations, in order to design a social contract—or alternative economic strategy—for the Australian context (Scott 2006). They included Keating, who visited Britain in the late 1970s as Shadow Minister for Minerals and Energy and was influenced by the then Callaghan Labour Government's ideas on strategic intervention (Scott 2000, 218). As mentioned above, the ACTU also internally discussed the possibility of, and content of, a social contract. And, importantly, the AMWU increasingly debated alternative economic plans and increased centralised economic planning as a way to achieve socialist reform (AMWSU 1977a).

In the late 1970s and in the lead-up to the 1983 election, work towards an incomes policy proceeded quickly. In September 1978, Langmore, then parliamentary advisor to Willis (the Shadow Minister for Industrial Relations, Economic Affairs and Treasury) wrote the first paper proposing a prices and incomes policy for internal ALP consumption (2000b). Support for the initial paper from the ALP caucus and the party executive led to informal discussions with leaders and staff of the ACTU (Langmore 2000a, 20). The ALAC, the standing consultative committee between the ACTU and the ALP, had met only

4 It is important to note that some believed that the character of Australian unions, institutions and government compared with those of Sweden, meant any replication of a Swedish model (as pursued through Australia Reconstructed) was impossible (Kriesler and Halevi 1997; Jones 1997, 34).

twice during the period of the Whitlam Government, but it now became a central forum in which to craft the Accord (Langmore 2000a, 19).

In April 1979, Willis (1979) penned a document titled 'The Case for a Co-operative Prices and Incomes Policy under a Labor Government' and presented it to the ALAC. It stated that a formal agreement would be 'of great assistance in the election of a Federal Labor Government', but that essential to retaining office was the successful implementation of an agreed policy package 'in respect to prices and incomes ... with the purpose of restraining inflation and equitably redistributing income, wealth, and economic power' (ibid 1979). Soon after, in May 1979, Willis delivered a key speech at the Labor Economists' Conference on the 'Role of Incomes Policy'. Willis argued that 'full employment would not be obtainable if each side of the Labor movement simply [went] on "doing its own thing" as was very much the case when Labor was last in government' under Whitlam (cited in Langmore 2000a, 20). Willis emphasised that:

> ... an essential aspect of a viable prices and incomes policy must be that it has a redistributive element—that a basic aim of the policy is to bring about a more equitable distribution of income, wealth and power (ibid 2000a, 20).

In sync with the private discussions at the ALAC, a number of unions were calling publicly for 'cooperation not confrontation' as a solution to the economic turbulence. ACTU Secretary Peter Nolan (1979, 2) argued in an address on 'The Challenge of the 1980s' that the ACTU:

> ... has suggested, advocated, even preached at time[s], that there should be national conferences of governments (we seem to be blessed with several) – employers, unions and even financial institutions to allow their points of view or policies to be expressed and debated. Hopefully a broadly based consensus of how well we deal with the day to day problems of this country, let alone what we may be doing next month, will emerge. It might, such a national conference, if we ever got to it, lead to some sort of national economic planning.

There was a rhetorical element to this call, with the unions seeking to paint themselves as seeking consensus and the government painted as the leading edge of militancy. However, there was also real desire for a new political strategy. The new approach was focused on high-level negotiations with the government, rather than workplace strategies exercising industrial muscle—despite the relative historic strength of the unions at that point in time.

Formal negotiations between the ALP and ACTU, when Bill Hayden was leader of the Party, produced the Accord agreement. The agreement was signed in principle by the ACTU Executive and announced publicly on 20 August 1982, about six months before the federal election (Singleton 1990, 142). ACTU delegates overwhelmingly sanctioned the Accord at a special conference on 21 February 1983, during the election campaign.[5] In his statement to the ACTU conference, President Cliff Dolan outlined the Accord's 'fundamental consideration' as follows:

> First, it accepts the need for more expansionary economic policies to generate sustained growth and generate employment.
> Second, there is agreement that a centralised wage fixation system based on equity and egalitarian precincts will be supported.
> Third, [it implements] consensus between major participants in the economy—governments, unions and employers. The ongoing policy is premised on accord not discord, cooperation not confrontation
>
> ACTU 1983.

Hawke replaced Hayden as ALP leader only weeks before the ACTU special conference, and went on to win the federal election and establish the Accord as government policy. The ALP was able to present itself as not so close to the unions politically as to be controlled by them, but close enough to ensure it was the only party that could address industrial unrest. The electoral victory on 5 March 1983 was a landslide and the political victory was decisive. For the first time in Australian history, the unions entered into a formal social contract with a federal government.

Once elected, the ALP moved to address both the economic crisis and the longer-term structural issues in the economy, especially in manufacturing, through economic structural adjustment. By this time, virtually every major union in the country was backing the Accord and its agenda of suppression of real wages and industrial action—although the parties didn't describe it in those terms. There was also widespread consensus within the ALP and the union movement that higher wages had resulted in lower profits and prolonged economic slump (O'Lincoln 1993, 236).

Australian crisis management parallels Panitch's (1976, 3) description of the UK in the 1970s where:

5 I note, however, that Michael Rizzo (1991) argued—based on his interviews with union leaders during the Accord period—that some did not take the Accord process seriously, as they did not think it would amount to more than election propaganda.

> ... in an attempt to control price inflation in the context of managing a predominantly private enterprise economy, both [Labour and conservative] governments turned toward securing ... 'in the national interest' ... wage restraint from the trade unions.

Both sides of politics in Australia argued that (to resolve the crisis) wage growth had to be suppressed in the 'national interest', although in practice this was implementing the state's own interests in managing economic crisis through securing stable accumulation. The labour movement's incorporation into that hegemonic project was a key objective of the Accord, as the central mechanism of a wider restructuring program to address the crisis.

In practice, the Accord was a series of agreements (Mark I to Mark VIII) between the ALP and the ACTU, commencing with the original agreement voted on by ACTU Special Conference, in February 1983, just prior to the federal election. The content of the agreement is set out in the next chapter, and the implementation of it and its successors is detailed in the remainder of the book. The Accord was implemented by five successive ALP governments, from 1983 to 1996, under the leadership of Prime Minsters Hawke and Keating. Over its lifetime, the Accord proved to be a particularly flexible, adaptive and lasting framework, despite constant warnings of its impending demise (Stilwell 1986, 148).

Over time, the Accord involved a protracted assimilation of the unions and their members into the Australian state's neoliberal imperatives. Despite the unions claiming they would only continue to support the Accord if it delivered for their members, the left unions entered the social contract with no clear exit strategy if the stipulations of the document were not implemented. As the Accord period progressed, the 'contrast between [its] policy commitments and [its] policy in practice' was stark (Stilwell 1986, 109). Ultimately very little was achieved by the Accord and wages policy was 'integrated into a quite different program of austerity and regressive distribution' (Stilwell 1993, 84).

At the same time, the Hawke and Keating Governments implemented many of the reforms that are considered paradigmatic of neoliberalism. As discussed in the following chapters, these 'vanguard' reforms included: floating the Australian dollar and abolition of exchange controls; entry of foreign banks; fiscal austerity; inflation-targeting monetary policy; general reductions in tariffs; privatisation and corporatisation of public assets and agencies; promotion of free trade; competition policy; welfare 'targeting'; and direct attacks on dissident trade unions. For example, by the time of the defeat of ALP in 1996, it had implemented many policies that had been advocated in the fundamentalist neoliberal document produced by New Right ideologues in the Fraser era—*Australia at the Crossroads* (Kasper, Blandy, and Freebairn 1980). John Quiggin (1998, 78) has argued that in many areas the ALP actually went further than the authors of *Crossroads* proposed.

Despite this, the Accord's legacy remains hotly debated and 'there is little evidence that the fundamentally anti-labour character of [the] economic policy orientation has been acknowledged' (Stilwell 1993, 84). While commentators have sometimes presented the shift in economic policy as somewhat problematic, or done only out of necessity, it is important to recall that the vanguard neoliberal period's reforms were openly and publicly 'presented as a break with the dogmas of the past' (Quiggin 1998, 80). The government prosecuted an argument for structural adjustment and the 'opening up of the economy', on the basis that all sections of society would benefit in the longer term from such efforts. In this way, the economic restructuring was presented as a positive collaborative project of reconciliation centred on the Accord (Keating 2012; Kelty 2012; Megalogenis 2012, 41–51).

In Davidson's description of the vanguard phase, the weakening of the trade unions was a decisive and necessary component in that it allowed for the successful implementation of 'all the other components of the neoliberal repertoire' (Davidson 2013). Basing his analysis primarily on the UK and US examples, Davidson mapped out three chronologically overlapping strategies that delivered the 'successful onslaught on the labour movement': mass unemployment; set-piece confrontations with key groups of state workers; and promotion of new, un-unionised industries (ibid 2013). The hobbling of the trade unions was also necessary in Australia, but took a radically different form—a corporatist social contract that unions willingly signed but which weakened and disorganised them as the full panoply of the neoliberal economic program was driven through by 'their' government. How this occurred is explored in the following three chapters.

5 Piecemeal Neoliberalisation Stage: 1993–2008

This section argues that the piecemeal neoliberalisation stage involved the latter years of the Accord period, and the term of the Howard government. Given, the content of this book on the relationship of the Accord to neoliberalism, this section focuses on the transition out of the vanguard neoliberal stage in the middle of the Accord years and the final of the years of the Accord.

While the period 1983–1993 was dominated by public advocacy for neoliberal reforms and open calls for sacrifice in order to address economic problems, by the end of Labor's first decade in office there was a shift from the vanguard phase to one of piecemeal neoliberalisation. The project moved from being a *positive* project framed around collective sacrifice and involving landmark reforms, to one that involved ongoing smaller-scale changes within a less coherent political framework. It is not that neoliberal reform ceased, or became unimportant, but that vanguard reforms could not be implemented as easily because of a growing rejection of the neoliberal agenda in the electorate (although without large-scale social movement and industrial activity of the sort that characterised the 1970s). Davidson (2010, 47) usefully characterised the similar shift in Britain as a move from a 'regime of reorientation' (meaning vanguard neoliberalism) to a 'regime of consolidation'.

The Hawke-Keating Government's reform program in the 1980s had not decisively corrected high unemployment, relatively high inflation and high interest rates. This undermined the political class's ability to argue for more restructuring on the basis of sacrifice. Further, after eight years of difficult economic reform—in which there was economic growth alongside declining real wages and increasing inequality (Frijters and Gregory 2006)—the recession of 1991 rendered the government and its policy agenda deeply unpopular. The failure of Hawke to recognise the impact of the recession, the worst since the Great Depression, and to shift his focus from social consensus around the Accord and neoliberal reform, were major factors in the exhaustion of his Prime Ministership. There was increasing talk of Keating (Treasurer and Deputy Prime Minister at the time) challenging Hawke in order to replace him, which he did successfully in December 1991. While there was a brief rise in the approval rating for the Prime Minister after Keating won the leadership of the parliamentary party from Hawke, it quickly declined until the 1993 election (see Figure 5.2).

The 1993 election was fought around the Liberal Party opposition leader John Hewson's *Fightback!* program. His election platform was premised on leveraging voters' anger at the government, in the wake of the 1991 recession, into support for an even more radical set of neoliberal reforms, including: further changes to the industrial relations system; a partial dismantling of the new health system (Medicare); and the introduction of a flat consumption tax (GST). In reality, the package was a logical extension of many Hawke-Keating era reforms and, in the case of the GST, something Keating had himself once proposed. Initially, Hewson was well ahead of Keating in the polls, even after the release of *Fightback!*. The key turning point was the election of Jeff Kennett's Liberal Party state government in Victoria (1992–1999) on a platform of similarly aggressive neoliberal reform.[6] However, Kennett immediately broke

6 The John Cain Victorian ALP state government (1982–1992), which preceded Kennett, had also been pushing in a neoliberal direction during the Accord era.

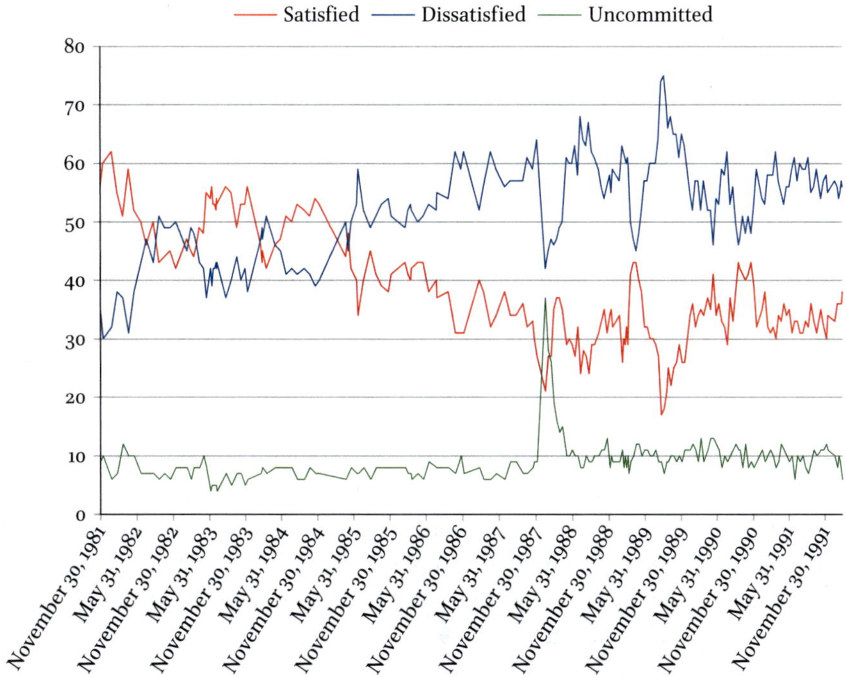

FIGURE 5.2 Australian Prime Minister approval rating (%), 1981–1991
Note: Newspoll was established in 1985 and data commences from that date. The data used to produce this graph was publically available at newspoll.com.au, until end of June 2015.
SOURCE: NEWSPOLL

a pre-election promise to not cut workers' penalty rates and there were mass trade union protests across the state (Megalogenis 2006, 802). This increased concern across the country that Hewson would replicate Kennett's unpopular attacks nationally. Hewson and others credit these events as key to his declining popularity and eventual defeat (Megalogenis 2006, loc 1403).

Popular opinion suggested that the 1993 election was 'unwinnable' for the ALP, in the wake of the 1991 recession and alongside a tide of sentiment against the government's economic reform program. Keating grasped that Labor could not win the election either by simply warning of the 'threat' from *Fightback!*, given the ALP's record in government, or by campaigning on a positive espousal of the neoliberal agenda. Keating, for practical purposes, decided to run *against* his own neoliberal record and oriented the election campaign on a more traditional social democratic agenda around job creation and tax cuts for workers. Keating's *One Nation* (1992) speech emphasised a more traditional objective for the ALP: the need to deal with unemployment and a promise to create 800,000 jobs in four years. He was able to create sufficient distance between the 'social democracy' of the ALP and the 'free-market' agenda of the Liberal Party, despite Labor's clearly neoliberal agenda up to that time.

Hewson's campaign lost ground in the days before the election and the ALP was returned for an historic fifth term with an increased majority. Keating (1993) began his victory speech by saying 'this is a victory for the true believers, the people who in difficult times have kept the faith' acknowledging that 'the Australian people [were] going through hard times'. The speech was a general call to the party faithful—the traditional base of the party in the trade unions and in working-class electorates—attempting to draw together the fractured Labor project.

The election honeymoon did not last long and a brief surge in approval for the Prime Minister fell away (see earlier Figure 5.1). In August 1993, Keating's treasurer John Dawkins delivered a regressive budget that the ACTU called 'indefensible' (Keane 2014). The Dawkins Budget was so unpopular in the electorate that it provoked an unprecedented caucus revolt (Peake 1993). Alongside this, Keating introduced enterprise bargaining, with the backing of the unions (Briggs 2001), thereby ending elements of the centralised industrial relations system that had been the cornerstone of the ALP's platform for a century and further advancing neoliberal re-regulation of the labour market. This policy change resulted from a complex set of circumstances and was supported by the union bureaucracy, because of the negative impact of the Accord on real wages (discussed in detail in Chapters 6 and 8). The horror Budget and the workplace reforms 'killed the Australian public's enthusiasm for the Keating government, consigning the Labor Party to the electoral gallows' (Carney 2002). Keating subsequently pursued an increasingly incoherent mishmash of initiatives to try to revive his fortunes, but when faced with a reinvented New Right Liberal Party leader in John Howard—now promising a 'relaxed and comfortable' nation after 13 years of frenetic reform—the government was defeated in a landslide in March 1996.

5.1 *Howard's Piecemeal Neoliberalism*

Howard, a well-known admirer of the Thatcher revolution, proved unable to carry out the radical reforms for which many in his party and the New Right had been waiting. The pattern of rapid and large-scale reforms of the vanguard neoliberal era had come to an end. For example, while the government was able to remodel the higher education sector (by expanding the deferred fees program put in place by the ALP and extracting industrial changes on campuses from university administrations), it was unable to enact desired components of the New Right agenda. Similarly, while further privatisation occurred under Howard, the government was unable to privatise key targets such as Medicare directly (although there was a more passive undermining through the extension of private health coverage). In short, pet proposals of hard-line neoliberals—such as education vouchers and dismantling public health—were sidelined.

While Howard did enact some significant neoliberal reforms, in particular around workplace relations and free trade agreements, the initial phase of his incumbency saw a significant percentage of the Liberal and National party bases peel off to the right, in support of the anti-globalisation and racist One Nation party of former Liberal candidate Pauline Hanson (Brett 1998). Howard's later *WorkChoices* industrial reforms, introduced in a fit of hubris after an unexpectedly strong re-election victory in 2004, were strongly opposed by trade unions, non-government organisations and some churches. The proposed reforms also received a lukewarm response from the business sector they were designed to serve, causing Howard to hesitate and water down the legislation (although it was still regressive).

Lacking a clear policy agenda, the Liberal Government was defeated by a reinvigorated ALP in 2007. So decisive was the Labor victory under the leadership of Kevin Rudd, that Howard lost his own (formally safe conservative) seat—only the second time a prime minister had done this.[7] Paul Kelly (2009, 75), a veteran political commentator, cut through the revisionist claim that Howard presided over the highpoint of neoliberal reform in Australia when he stated:

> [The 1993 election] … extinguished more than John Hewson's dreams—it terminated the neoliberal political experiment. This was the conclusion of both Paul Keating and John Howard and they operated on this assumption. 'Big bang' liberalism was finished as an ideology and a strategy for the Liberal Party. … The claim won its greatest traction in early 2009 when Prime Minister Rudd, in a significant analysis, accused the Liberal Party of being 'the political home of neoliberalism in Australia' and attacked the Howard government for being the local champion of the neoliberal philosophy that had brought the world to the financial precipice. Such claims generated a political bandwagon. But they cannot be sustained by the story of Australian public policy. It is tempting for Labor to depict the demise of Australian neoliberalism in 2007 with Howard's fall but the only tenable location for such an event is the 1993 poll.

Kelly was correct to identify the shifts that took place in the early 1990s as crucial. However, the end of the vanguard period was not something that simply

7 The first being when ALP Prime Minister Scullin lost his seat in the midst of the Great Depression

occurred at the level of political rhetoric or ideology, as he implied. It was the result of deepening resentment toward neoliberal restructuring within the electorate, ending the possibility of politicians being able to win government by campaigning openly on a reform agenda.

6 Crisis Stage: 2008 Onwards

Piecemeal neoliberalisation reached its endpoint with the global economic crisis of 2008. Originating in the US housing market and the complex system of debt-related derivatives surrounding it, then flowing onto other sections of the North American and international economic systems, the global financial crisis signalled the collapse of any remaining practical coherence in the neoliberal political project in Australia. In order to 'save capitalism from itself' (Rudd 2009), governments at the centre of neoliberalism did what many would have considered unthinkable: pump-primed national economies; nationalised banks; and bailed out financial institutions while undertaking economic activity previously carried out exclusively by the private sector. While such efforts were not unheard of in the neoliberal era prior to the crisis, they intensified and were generalised across the advanced capitalist countries.

In Australia, the Rudd Labor government implemented a stimulus package that focused on securing bank deposits; stimulated the at-risk construction and retail sectors (through building school capital works and placing $900 cash in the hands of every tax payer); and engaged in medium-term infrastructure works (the home insulation program) (Parker 2013). More recently, governments and supra-national bodies have used varying combinations of austerity and stimulus, in an effort to restore stable accumulation and minimise economic costs to the capitalist class. These policy responses have generally been pragmatic and often contradictory crisis management responses, rather than a coherent new hegemonic project. Indeed, the post-2008 period has been accompanied by growing political crisis and upheaval, most spectacularly in the 'peripheral' countries of the Eurozone.

The responses to the current crisis have generated debates over whether this is a decisive crisis of the neoliberal project, or just one crisis within its continuing logic—in effect asking whether this is a crisis 'in' or 'of' neoliberalism (Saad-Filho 2010). Alternatively, some have argued that, after some hiccups, the crisis has seen neoliberalism re-emerge stronger than ever (Davidson 2015; Mirowski 2013). One useful way to think about neoliberalism's 'crisis' may be to see it as a crisis *through* neoliberalism. This focuses attention on how neoliberalism's internal contradictions have forced change and adaptation, often of a kind that results in public policies that diverge greatly from those traditionally associated with neoliberalism. However, it is not a period in which neoliberal ideas have been eradicated from public life, given that: neoliberal ideology still circulates; various neoliberal practices continue; and past neoliberal reforms remain embedded in political-economic structures.

7 Conclusion

Periodisation is a process of differentiating between historical periods in order to highlight continuities and discontinuities. The genesis of vanguard neoliberalism in Australia was located in the failure of crisis responses by the Whitlam and Fraser governments, plus the coming together of tendencies within the industrial and political wings of the labour movement to mount a more coherent political project. Both the Whitlam and Fraser Governments were unable to curb wage growth and industrial militancy. The attempted political resolution to the economic crisis by conservative forces—through the destruction of the ALP government via the constitutional sacking of Whitlam—can be contrasted with the ensuing failure by Fraser to develop a hegemonic project to successfully address the economic difficulties.

The conservatives also provoked significant social resistance and the government's strategy was quickly exhausted when the labour movement successfully withstood a number of the regressive policies including a wage freeze. With recession returning in the early 1980s, the Fraser government was unable to develop an approach to ensure the re-establishment of successful accumulation. At the same time, the trade union movement and the left were at an impasse, with industrial action failing to maintain living standards. It was these circumstances, alongside efforts inside the ALP and trade unions, which cohered the Accord. The Accord tied the labour movement to political society and the state, at the very moment the new ALP Government would implement widespread political-economic change. In this way, the Accord facilitated the advance of the vanguard neoliberal project in Australia.

Following the recession of 1991, the ability of political society to continue mobilising civil society support for neoliberal reform was greatly diminished. At one level, as has been argued in this chapter, this was due to widespread public concern at the considerable social costs and limited social benefits of the vanguard reform era. This eroded hegemony resulted in the piecemeal neoliberalisation phase.

This periodisation can help explain why, in Australia, the political right failed to drive through vanguard neoliberal reforms, and how the election of the ALP Government in 1983 brought together the social forces needed to cohere a state-centred hegemonic neoliberal political project. The following chapters will expand on how the suppression and disorganisation of the labour movement were chiefly achieved through consensual agreement, rather than outright confrontation, as it had been in other spatial locations.

Contrary to Rudd's (2009) assertion that the 'political home of neoliberalism in Australia is, of course, the Liberal Party', the account of neoliberalism developed in this chapter demonstrates that it was in fact the election of a Labor government in 1983 that was the harbinger of neoliberal restructuring. Subsequent chapters will concretely explain how the nominally 'Keynesian' or 'social democratic' corporatism of the Accord was actually central to the Australian vanguard neoliberal period. It is to the content of the Accord specifically, and to the suppression of real wages, I now turn.

CHAPTER 6

The Disorganisation of Labour

> The parties to this accord are aware of the difficulties which abound in finding solutions which meet the social and economic goals to which both are committed. We state this difficulty not by way of apology but to indicate the understanding we share of the difficult task ahead, and the consequential importance of the shared commitment to facing those difficulties through humane policies based on consensus.
>
> ALP and ACTU, 1983, *Statement of Accord*

1 Introduction

The protracted economic crisis of the 1970s led to increased support, in both the political and industrial wings of the labour movement, for a social contract that would limit wage growth to the level of inflation. In return for wage restraint on the part of the trade union movement, the social contract agreed to the moderation of prices, an expanded social wage and tax relief. However, over the life of Accord, the agreement narrowed from the broad focus of the original statement to concentrate primarily on wages policy—a focus which was, in effect, on real wage suppression. This chapter examines the content of the Accord and how the main component—wages policy—was implemented over the eight editions.

While the initial Accord was a document that fitted with the 'ALP in opposition' and a broadly progressive social democratic framework, the Accord was adjusted to fit the neoliberal reform focus of the 'ALP in government' after the 1983 election (Quiggin 1998, 79). The introduction of the agreement and its content shifts in relation to wages cannot be understood outside of either the prolonged economic malaise that persisted until the early 1990s or the advance of the vanguard neoliberal project in Australia.

The first section of this chapter outlines the content of the original Accord statement, and the second section outlines the shifts in wages policy under the Accord—from Mark I to Mark VIII. The third section outlines and demonstrates the scope of wage suppression, then commences the consideration of how the income policy component of the Accord contributed to the disorganisation of the labour movement in Australia (which is continued in the

 | DOI:10.1163/9789004383463_007

following chapters). While this chapter focuses explicitly on wages policy, the two following chapters examine the other policy divergences from the original agreement—including the suppression of industrial action and the re-regulation of the industrial relations system with the introduction of enterprise bargaining.

2 The Accord Agreement

The Hawke Government was elected on a platform of implementing the Accord, and the agreement sought to address stagflation by tackling upward wage pressure. In return for the labour movement voluntarily holding down wages, the government agreed to a number of policies including full wage indexation, industry policy, tax concessions and an expanded social wage.

The 'social wage' is generally understood as non-wage 'benefits in cash and in kind received by workers from state expenditures minus the total taxes paid by those workers to the state' (Maniatis 2014, 16). In the context of the Accord, the planned non-wage benefits included expanded public health, tax concessions and increased social security payments. In relation to the Accord, the social wage is generally also understood to include the expanded compulsory superannuation system—even though these privately managed retirement pension contributions are employer-payed (rather than part of state expenditure), other than the forgone tax receipts on that component of a person's income.

The social contract set out a broad and comprehensive economic plan, with the stated aim of ensuring:

> … living standards of wage and salary earners and non-income earning sectors of the population requiring protection [were] maintained and through time increased with movements in national productivity.
>
> ALP & ACTU 1986, 162–163

Importantly, the Accord also returned the Australian industrial relations system to centralised wage fixing with full indexation, after its breakdown during the Fraser Government wage freeze. The parties agreed that 'government policy should be applied to prices and all income groups, rather than, as has often been the case, to wages alone' (ibid 1986, 163). The agreement established a process of continuous consultation between the ALP and the ACTU, to be embedded and supported at all levels of government. The agreement established 'a representative tripartite body [with business which had] responsibility for advising on the prices and incomes policy and for monitoring and discussing problems associated with the implementation' (ibid 1986, 175).

The Accord consisted of four sections: an introduction setting out the general political-economic context; a statement on the nature of incomes and prices policies; a brief section on the elements of such policies; plus a longer section in overview of the policy details agreed between the parties. Wages policy was one aspect of the agreement, alongside a more general economic management program related to price control, targeting of non-wage incomes, taxation, migration, government employment and government expenditure. The agreement explicitly committed the government to 'an equitable and clearly discernible redistribution of income' (ibid 1986, 163).

The introduction opened by acknowledging the depths of the economic crisis and stated that a radical new approach was needed in order to ensure economic recovery. On the one hand, the agreement blamed overseas economic factors for the inability to return to full employment. On the other hand, it argued that the Fraser Government was specifically culpable for domestic factors. The statement stated that stagflation, unpredicted by economists internationally, meant the crisis was unable to be addressed by 'conventional economic weapons of fiscal, monetary and exchange rate policy, however varied and applied' (ibid 1986, 159).

The introduction stated that the severity of the crisis had been made worse by Fraser's recourse to monetarism, 'leading universally to spiralling unemployment and interest rates, low or negative economic growth, stagnant or declining living standards and continuing high inflation' (ibid 1986, 160). The Accord argued it was 'abhorrent' to use unemployment to control inflation. The agreement stated that Fraser's macroeconomic approach had led to 'negative growth, double digit unemployment, double digit inflation and no sign of recovery'(ibid 1986, 160). The ALP and ACTU argued that:

> … economic recovery [would] soon lead to increased inflation, thus forcing the Government to adopt contractionary anti-inflation policies which [would] truncate the recovery and prevent any restoration of full, or even near-full employment (ibid 1986, 159).

The introduction argued that no economic program would be able to meet the objective of full employment in the short term. While the parties stated the goal of full employment remained the prime objective (positioning it as distant from Fraser's 'inflation first' strategy), this signalled an important shift in the orientation of the ALP and ACTU. Ultimately, the Accord was a document that accepted 'the imperative of price stability: there [was] no notion of exploiting the trade-off between unemployment and inflation' (Beggs 2015, 262). The importance of this statement was that, while the Accord sought to draw distance between the social contract and an 'inflation first' strategy, in practice it prioritised bringing down inflation over reducing unemployment. The document claimed that an Accord strategy was more likely than any other to result in prolonged growth, reduced unemployment, and an increase in living standards without increasing inflation. Thus, the parties argued that the Accord would provide for the 'resolution of conflicting income claims at lower levels of inflation than would otherwise be the case' (ALP & ACTU 1986, 160).

The Accord was posited against the Frazer wage freeze and suppression as a long-term strategy for economic recovery and the maintenance of living standards, which the document argued was unlikely to be successful and would result in depressed living standards (ibid 1986, 161). Moreover, it fashioned the argument in class terms, by arguing that Fraser had been willing to reduce the wages of low and middle-income earners but not the incomes of non-wage earners—because no action has been taken on prices. The agreement argued that the approach of the Fraser Government was unfair, increased inequality, provoked industrial confrontation, and could not provide a cure for stagflation. The final paragraphs of the introduction underlined the view of the ALP and ACTU that:

> ... for policies based on incomes and prices to work, within a framework of policy measures directed at alleviating unemployment and redistributing income and wealth to the less well-off, ... a greater understanding of the complexity of the economy by key participants—governments, employers, and unions—[would] be required for the policy approach to realise its full potential (ibid 1986, 161).

Thus, although the agreement was only signed by the ALP and the ACTU, it contained the foundations for a strategy involving the state, labour and capital.

Section two of the agreement detailed the nature of the prices and incomes components. It stated that improvements to living standards could only be achieved through processes other than money wage increases, given the persistence of high inflation (ibid 1986, 162). The parties insisted that any new process must be consensual, and apply to wage and salary earners, as well as non-income earning groups. In short, they committed to a new decision-making process that would be comprehensive and equitable, based on co-operation rather than confrontation. The Accord also stated it would aim to eliminate poverty (Sonder 1984, 155).

Section three diminished certainty regarding the implementation of the agreed components. It stated that both parties agreed that 'policies must remain flexible to some degree', although new policies would need to abide by various 'fundamental features' including the protection of living standards, and not be restricted to wages only (ALP & ACTU 1986, 162–163). This position was also clear in union statements in the early period of the Accord, when leading officials argued there was 'a mutual understanding that the … terms of the Accord [were] not immutable and there [might] be the need for refinement or alteration over time' (Dolan 1984). This is important in understanding how some in the Accord process could take the view that the components of the agreement were quite firm, while others saw the agreement as providing more general parameters that may need to be revised in response to changes in the economy.

Section four of the Accord set out the specific components of the policies. These were, in turn: wages and working conditions; non-wage incomes; taxation and government expenditure; industrial relations; industry development; industry protection; change adjustment; migration; social security; occupational health and safety; education; health; government employment; and implementation mechanics. The policies following this related to: full wage indexation; appropriate sharing of increased productivity by wage and salary earners; legislative action on prices and non-wage incomes; progressive tax reform; industrial relations reform; increased social spending on social security, education and health; industry development policy; tripartite industry councils; and migration policy with an emphasis on family reunion and refugee intake.

While the agreement—taken as a whole—was broad and covered a range of policy areas, at it heart it focused on wage restraint in order to: reduce inflation; increase growth; decrease industrial action; and address unemployment (but not with the aim of restoring full employment in the short term). Its central goal was to ensure that the next period of growth did not lead to a 'wages explosion'.

3 Wages and the Accord

While wage suppression is not unique to neoliberalism (and, as discussed in Chapter 3, is a focus of many social democratic corporatist arrangements) it was central to vanguard neoliberalism in Australia for three reasons. First, after the failure of 'Keynesian' strategies to resolve the crisis in the 1970s, a proactive union leadership became committed to a solution based on offering up organised labour—and its ability to increase its own exploitation by accepting 'wage restraint' on a national basis—as a critical tool of macroeconomic policy. The arbitration system had always been an instrument directed, in part, at moderating labour incomes. The failure of arbitration to maintain wage relativities (real wages and wage share of GDP) in the 1970s resulted in the state being unable to impose such constraints through the usual mechanism (Beggs 2015, 202). The Fraser years had also proven that labour resistance to measures directly imposed by government could easily be broken by militancy. Thus, the ALP in government gained the *voluntary* cooperation of the unions on wages (and sought that of capital on prices) in order to achieve those ends.

Second, it has been more generally argued that 'the "disorganisation" of working class organisation, in unions and political parties, [was] one of the central objectives of neoliberalism' (Albo 2009, 121; see also Cahill 2002, 227). While implemented consensually—and only possible because of the size, strong organisation and centralised nature of the Australian union movement—the suppression of wages through the Accord was indispensable to the industrial disorganisation of labour that took place in the 1980s and 1990s.

Third, as Harvey (2005) argues, the shift in national income from wages to profits was a key feature of the neoliberal period. As detailed below, this was successfully implemented in Australia through the centralised wage setting of the Accord.

3.1 *The First Accord (1983)*

Prior to being elected in 1983, the ALP in opposition was already managing expectations about whether it would support fully the Accord's wage indexation component. Three days after the press conference announcing the Accord, and prior to Hawke becoming ALP leader, it was reported that the:

> …[opposition] spokesman on industrial relations, Mr Hawke, [had] conceded that under the prices and incomes policy, there would be circumstances in which a Labor Government would want workers to get less than full wage indexation.
>
> WEST 1982, 4

After the election, and less than two months after the Accord was passed by the ACTU Special Conference, Hawke again dampened expectations that full indexation would be delivered. Hawke announced that Fraser's price freeze would remain in place until after the April Economic Summit (a national meeting between the government, unions, business and others) and subsequently extended the freeze until later in the year. Thus, the 'six month wages freeze enacted by the Fraser Government in 1982 was de facto extended by a further six prior to full indexation at a National Wage Case' in 1983 (Easson and Forrest 1994, 129).

In September 1983, the IRC heard the submissions of the government, unions and business at the first National Wage Case. The Commission agreed to the broad scope of the Accord, reintroducing indexation of wages, salaries and over-award payments based on Consumer Price Index (CPI) movements in the previous two quarters. The Commission in the first year ordered two wage increases of 4.3 percent and 4.4 percent. The IRC deferred consideration of the unions' claim for a productivity increase until after 1985 and rejected claims to reduce the working week below 38 hours (Willis and Wilson 2000, 2). Certain unions also sought a 9.1 percent catch-up pay rise for the period of the wage freeze, but this was refused. Those unions which continued to pursue it directly with employers were policed and pressured to desist by the Government, the ACTU and employers in a number of ways—as will be discussed in Chapter 8.

In 1984, the first indexation decision was deferred 'for the impact of the Medicare Levy on the CPI in September' (Easson and Forrest 1994, 129). The government and the IRC argued that 'real' inflation had been negative in that period. The second increase, September–December, was at the full indexation of 2.7 percent (Stilwell 1986, 42). Thus, there was no full indexation of wages under the first Accord.

Table 6.1 summarises the Accord Mark I determinations and the subsequent decisions and Accord revisions discussed in the rest of this chapter.

Wage developments in 1984 took place alongside what was known as 'the Trilogy' commitment—a fiscal approach announced in the lead-up to the 1984 election. The Trilogy commitment was that the government would not increase: (1) total taxation as a percentage of GDP; (2) total government expenditure as a percentage of GDP; or (3) the size of the budget deficit as a percentage of GDP (Odom 1992, 53; Scott 2000, 219). Within a short space of time, the government had moved to a severely constrained fiscal policy stance, undermining its ability to deliver on the expansionary policies of the original Accord (Scott 2000, 219). While the government initially increased social spending, the level of expenditure quickly dropped to the same as, or lower than, that of the previous Fraser Government (Johnson 1989, 101). The government was, in effect, shifting to implement an 'inflation first' strategy (Kuhn 1993, 26). This is because the government routinely prioritised policies to bring down inflation, even if they increased unemployment or had other negative consequences for the working class.

TABLE 6.1 National Wage Case decisions under the Accord

Accord	Calendar year	CPI increase	National wage case increases	Operative date
Mark I	1983	4.3%	4.3%	6 October 1983
		4.1%	4.1%	6 April 1984
	1984	−0.2%	Deferred	
		2.7%	2.6%	6 April 1985
Mark II	1985	3.8%	3.8%	
		4.3%	2.3% (2% discounted due to fall in $)	4 November 1985 1 July 1986
Mark III	1986	6.7%	$10 Tier One flat increase, plus possible 4% (Tier Two)	10 March 1987
	1987	9.3%	$6 flat increase	5 February 1988
Mark IV	1988	7.3%	3% plus $10 (award restructuring: SEP) after 6 months (approx. 5.2% in total)	Available from 1 September 1988 and 1 March 1989
Mark V	1989	7.3%	$20–$30 in two instalments (approx. 6.0% in total) (SEP)	Available from August 1989
Mark VI	1990	8.0%	2.5% (SEP)	
	1991		Enterprise bargaining commences	
Mark VII	1993		Safety net adjustment of $8, with three further increases of $8 scheduled for 1994	

Source: Reproduced, with small additions, from Bramble 2008 (p. 138), published by Cambridge Univeristy Press.

3.2 *Accord Mark II (1985–1987)*

In 1985, the Accord was renegotiated between June and September, as a result of an exchange rate crisis for the Australian dollar (Easson and Forrest 1994, 129). The Mark II agreement included a recommitment by the parties to the Accord for a further two years, and stated that 'adjustment to wages policy is more appropriately achieved through a combination of reduced wage indexation increases and deferral of the productivity award' (ALP & ACTU 2000a, 309–310). Mark II was a narrower agreement than the original statement, concerned almost exclusively with wage and superannuation policies. While it made mention of fairer tax reform, prices, industry development and Accord decision-making processes, there was little concrete detail and no new specific measures were proposed in these domains.

The detailed policy content of the first agreement was increasingly being relegated in practice by the time of Mark II, through decisions at the National Economic Summit; the failure to implement price control; and the re-regulation of the financial sector—as will be demonstrated in further chapters. With the unions increasingly tied into the Accord process, the social contract was progressively more of a vehicle to support the government's priorities of neoliberal structural adjustment. By the time of the Mark II agreement, and as detailed in Chapter 6, the government had already floated the Australian dollar; re-regulated the banking and finance sectors along neoliberal lines; and signed a free trade agreement with NZ. These new concerns were reflected in the new agreement, which stated that:

> ... given the trade union movement's strong record of compliance with undertakings within the Prices and Incomes Accord, this Agreement establishes a basis for the continuation of low industrial disputation, international competitiveness, strong economic growth and moderating inflation.
>
> ALP & ACTU 2000a, 311–312

As part of Mark II, the IRC also modified its decision-making principles in relation to setting workers' wages, giving increased weight to economic conditions (rather than, for example, the cost of living for workers).

While the April 1985 wage case granted full indexation, the September case resulted in a discounted indexation—a move advocated by both the government and the ACTU. Partial indexation sought to isolate the depreciating dollar from the wage system (ibid 1986, 43), as:

> ... a rapidly falling exchange rate ran the risk of an inflation-depreciation spiral, as higher import prices fed into the cost of living, and from there into money-wage inflation, price inflation and a further fall in the currency.
>
> BEGGS 2015, 268

In return for the ACTU agreeing to discounted indexation, the government granted compensatory tax cuts—equivalent to the 2 percent discount—and sought from the Commission superannuation increases of 3 percent for Australian workers. However, although the IRC agreed to the 2 percent discounted wage claim, it rejected the superannuation claim. The IRC also rejected the union productivity claim, held over from 1983, and accepted the government's argument to hold only one national wage case the following year.

The agreement stated that unemployment would be reduced by stimulating growth, not through direct job creation. In this period Hawke (1986) argued that the working class would have 'to accept reduced standards of living' and the Accord partners would have 'to obtain a lower wage outcome than anticipated when the Accord was renegotiated in 1985'. Government rhetoric had, by this point, shifted quickly and markedly from the original framing of the Accord as a process to protect living standards. Restraint by labour and lowering inflation remained at the centre of the Accord framework, but the social wage and price moderation were consigned to the margins. The government also announced in the August 1986 budget that it would no longer formally support full wage indexation (Easson and Forrest 1994, 130). As with Accord Mark I, wages were not able to maintain their real value under Accord Mark II (see Figure 6.2 on page 125).

3.3 *Accord Mark III (1986–1987)*

A continued falling exchange rate in 1986 ensured the government continued to promote 'a sense of crisis to encourage the unions to make further sacrifices' (Beggs 2015, 269). The depreciation of the Australian dollar was 'widely perceived as requiring a reduction of real wages' (Hancock 1999, 40). Accord Mark III was not a formally negotiated document, but took the form of the National Wage Case heard in late 1986 and early 1987.

While the unions initially applied for full indexation of 6.7 percent, they were aware that the government would not support this and proposed a fallback position of two flat increases. On 23 December 1986, the IRC rejected the ACTU's 6.7 percent claim, directing the parties to continue discussions to resolve their differences and thereby further delaying a wage rise (Willis and Wilson 2000, 4). The ACTU continued to seek greater increases than the federal government would accede to and, on 10 March 1987, the IRC established a two-tier wage increase system along the lines pursued by the ALP government. In March 1987, workers received a flat increase of $10 per week under Tier One. This could be supplemented by up to a 4 percent wage increase based on efficiency outcomes under Tier Two, negotiated with employers at the level of the individual firm (B. Mitchell 2000a, 319; Willis and Wilson 2000, 3–6; ALP & ACTU 2000b).

Accord Mark III was a shift towards productivity-based wage rises, but most Tier Two negotiations emphasised raw cost cutting and, in practice, little such bargaining occurred—and not all workers could gain rises (B. Mitchell 2000a). The IRC also introduced a new Restructuring and Efficiency Principle, which identified the possible areas of productivity improvement including: 'eliminating restrictive work and management practices; multi-skilling and broad basing; and reducing demarcation barriers' (Willis and Wilson 2000, 2). Tier Two increases were expected to be cost neutral for employers. The 1987 decision under Mark III was the effective abandonment of indexation and the consensual submission of the unions to significant real wage suppression, given they did not break with the Accord.

In February 1988, the IRC awarded a flat rate $6 increase—lower than both the $7 pursued by the ACTU and the $6.60 pursued by the federal government. However, the two-tier system opened up a pressure valve in light of growing dissatisfaction with the direction of wages policy. This allowed stronger unions to pursue enterprise level gains (still capped to a centrally-mandated ceiling), while providing some protection for less well-organised workers via the flat increases (Singleton 1990b, 166–171). The build-up of this pressure within the wage setting process will be discussed in detail in Chapter 8, in the context of the eventual re-regulation of industrial relations through the adoption of enterprise bargaining—an outcome actively sought by the unions. However, despite the introduction of the two-tier system, increases to award wages below the level of inflation resulted in continued wage suppression, as indicated in Figure 6.1.

By 1988, significant cuts to the federal budget were also made to improve Australia's current account standing, in what was called the 'return to surplus' budget (Collett 2014). This occurred alongside declining real wages and high inflation, meaning that the working class was under significant financial strain. The original Accord architects were understandably 'coy' about its agenda to suppress real wages (Stilwell 2000, 278) and, although this had not been made explicit in the original document, many unions began to understand the agreement in those terms and were—by the end of Accord Mark II—accepting the economic decline of the constituency they represented. ACTU leader Kelty later admitted that 'once you move away from indexation inexorably it will lead to a reduction in living standards' (cited in Oliver and Collins 1993).

3.4 *Accord Mark IV (1988–1989), V (1989–1990) & VI (1990–1993)*

The Accord partners had difficulty in reaching agreement when Accord Mark IV was negotiated. For this reason, there is no 'official' Accord statement—with 'Mark IV' being predominantly a media label (Easson and Forrest 1994, 131). The August 1988 and October 1989 National Wage Case decisions, based around a new 'Structural Efficiency Principle' (SEP), delivered increases subject to the

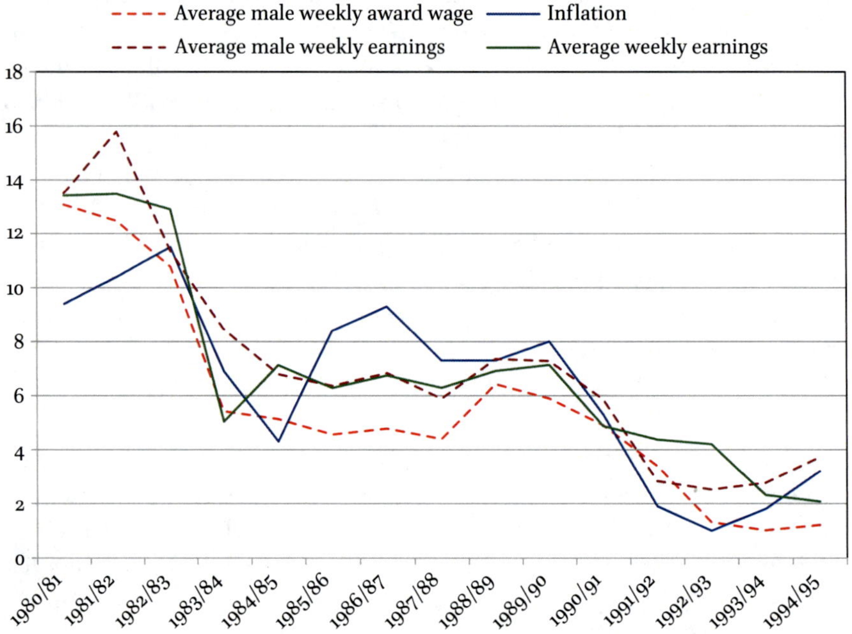

FIGURE 6.1 Inflation, average weekly earnings, and average male award wage in Australia, 1980–1995
SOURCE: BEGGS 2015 (P. 270); FOSTER 1996 (P. 207, 257)
NOTE: SHOWS INFLATION AND REAL WAGES AS A % CHANGE.

delivery of productivity improvements. Wage increases of up to 6 percent were permitted—3 percent in Tier One from September 1998 and $10 a week in Tier Two in March 1989. These wage increases/decisions signalled a move away from cost cutting to genuine efficiency gains, given that efficiency wage increases could only be claimed on the basis of changes such as:

> ... establishing skill related career paths; eliminating impediments to multi-skilling and broad-banding; creating appropriate wage relativities; and enhancing flexibility of working arrangements.
>
> B. MITCHELL 2000b, 331

The mid to late-1980s were marked by moderate economic growth alongside declining real wages and increasing inequality (Frijters and Gregory 2006; Leigh 2005). Treasurer Keating was explicit about the Accord's agenda when he said that 'increasing the profit share was the name of the game' (Stilwell 2000, 278). Similarly, Keating (1993a, 27) went on to note in the later years of the Accord that 'wage restraint was a major factor in lifting the corporate profit share to high levels around 17 percent, after it had fallen to a low of 12.4 percent' just prior to the election of the ALP government in 1983.

Accord Mark V took the form of a draft (unfinalised) agreement that continued the 'no extra claims' framework. During this period, there were increasing calls for flexibility in the wages system from both unions and employers (Hancock 1999, 39). The SEP continued to be applied to wage cases and, in April 1989, the Accord parties agreed that the unions would not make a claim for any across-the-board pay increases during 1989–1990 (Willis and Wilson 2000, 6). As a result, wage gains were linked to the implementation of award restructuring—changes to the wages, conditions and structures of legislated entitlements—apart from some adjustments to the minimum rates in the awards of low paid workers. Many workers had not received increases under the Tier Two components of Accords Mark III and IV and, in 1989, the Government 'indicated that tax cuts would be delivered [which] took some pressure off the union wage push' (B. Mitchell 2000c). In August, the Commission allowed wage increases to proceed, if the SEP tasks were agreed to (first increase) and properly implemented (second increase).

The trajectory of wages policy reached its logical conclusion in Accord Mark VI (1990–1993), with the parties seeking to re-regulate industrial relations and introduce enterprise bargaining. The capitulation of the ACTU to the state imperative of wage suppression led to growing resentment among better-organised unions. This antipathy towards the ACTU's strategy precipitated the ACTU's exit from centralised wage setting, in an attempt to recover some of the ground workers had lost, but not the Accord itself. Sections of the trade union movement leadership believed dissatisfaction with the Accord would spill over into open revolt in some unions (Briggs 2001).

Initially the ACTU 'started pushing for a Phillips curve model of wage setting focusing on price expectations rather than indexation in retrospect' (B. Mitchell 2000d, 341). However, this push was scuppered by the advent of recession in 1990–1991—the worst since the Great Depression. The ACTU leadership, in an effort to protect the government, sought to exit the centralised wage framework—by seeking the introduction of enterprise bargaining—but to remain within the Accord. The IRC rejected the initial request at its April 1991 National Wage Case, citing lack of progress on productivity improvements and fears of a wages breakout. The Commission instead imposed a selective and qualified 2.5 percent wage increase (Willis and Wilson 2000, 9). Enterprise bargaining was only introduced in October 1991, when the IRC acquiesced to the ACTU and government demands (Bramble 2008, 161, see Chapter 8 for a detailed discussion of this question).

The wage components of the Mark VI agreement between the Labor Government and ACTU were rejected by the IRC, but the agreement also set out: tax cuts; a superannuation increase of 3 percent; a 'social wage' commitment in the form of a promise to be attentive to families and childcare; and (once again) an acknowledgement of the vital role of industry policy. As following chapters will demonstrate, there was no shift in government direction away from its neoliberal imperatives.

While much was made by the Accord parties of the small change in take-home pay from tax cuts (ALP & ACTU 2000c, 353), this has to be seen in the wider context of the severe recession in 1991 (Gruen 2000, 2). GDP fell by 1.7 percent and unemployment pushed into double digits in 1991—rising sharply from around 6.75 percent in mid-1990 to peak at over 11 percent (Gruen and Stevens 2000, 32; see also Figure 5.1 in the previous chapter). While the early years of the Accord saw unemployment decrease:

> ... following a shift to very tight monetary policy and fiscal contraction, unemployment in Australia rose sharply, to even higher levels than in Britain (and in most other OECD nations) in the early to mid-1990s.
>
> SCOTT 2000, 220

The period also included: falling government expenditure from 1985 until the 1991 recession, in terms of nominal payments as a percent of GDP and real government expenditure (Laurie and McDonald 2008); a declining public spending base through the personal income and business profits tax cuts (Stilwell 1986); and other political-economic changes that shifted costs on to workers, including increasing fees for university students (McKinnon 1990). Occurring in the wake of 14 to 17.5 percent interest rates between January and August 1990 (Beggs 2015, 271), the recession was harsh. Unemployment was allowed to remain high as a strategy to address persistently high inflation, with Treasurer Keating ultimately arguing that the recession was one Australia 'had to have' in order to deal with inflation once and for all. This was an approach that had been specifically labelled 'abhorrent' in the original Accord. And, despite this political-economic context, business and public sector elites continued to call for more belt tightening, because of 'the excesses of the 1980s' (McFarlane 2006).

3.5 *Accord Mark VII (1993) & VIII (Draft Only)*

The government response to the 1991 recession and its aftermath took the form of the 1993 Accord Mark VII and the 1994 *Working Nation* statement.

The new edition of the Accord, entitled 'Putting Jobs First', agreed to increase employment by a minimum of 500,000 net additional jobs over three years. The agreement implemented enterprise bargaining, which shifted responsibility for wage setting away from the IRC to the level of the firm. This was a historic downgrading of arbitration and the introduction of a new industrial relations regulatory framework. While wage suppression had been central to neoliberalism in a variety of ways, enterprise bargaining signalled a more comprehensive 'neoliberalisation' of the industrial relations system—and one actively supported by the unions (discussed in greater detail in Chapter 8).

The Accord Mark VII agreed to safety net increases, directed at low paid workers, of $8 in 1993 and $24 in 1994 (B. Mitchell 2000e, 355). By that time—given that enterprise bargaining was effectively the mechanism for wage setting—the award system became 'more and more a set of minimum wages, of less relevance to the average worker' (Beggs 2015, 272). *Working Nation* was a statement on employment and, at first sight, appeared to return ALP policy to a traditional labourist focus and break from the neoliberal direction of the government. However, although the main objective of the agreement was to reduce unemployment, it included a 'reaffirmation of the commitment to maintain an inflation rate consistent with that of our major trading partners' (Willis and Wilson 2000, 12). This underscored the continued centrality of 'inflation first' strategy. In the end, the government's response to the recession involved no significant revision of policy priorities and delivered a further shift 'towards the agenda of international competitiveness' (Rafferty 1997, 102). The government 'continued along the neoliberal trajectory that had been established from the mid-1980s, albeit one latterly travelled with a softer rhetoric' (Ramsay and Battin 2005, 1). The government was increasingly unpopular in this period, as was discussed in Chapter 5. Although Keating began to move ideologically against neoliberalism in public statements, in practice little changed.

Accord Mark VIII was negotiated in June 1995, but was not implemented because the ALP lost the 1996 election. Mark VIII, as a hypothetical map of ALP and ACTU intentions, was effectively a continuation of enterprise bargaining with award safety net increases. The agreement set an inflation target of 2 to 3 percent over the economic cycle and included vague commitments to: promote 'public expenditure [in order] to enhance the living standards of Australians'; develop 'a forward looking industry policy'; and seek 'a closer integration of trade and industry policies' (ALP & ACTU 2000d). Such statements were, ironically, echoes of the original social contact, yet over the 13 years of ALP rule many of these 'new' aims had not been implemented (see further discussion in Chapters 7 and 8).

Hawke-Keating government budgets throughout the Accord era resulted in virtually no increase in government spending from the 1984–1985 to 1987–1988 budgets. There was a fall in spending in the 1988–1989 and 1989–1990 budgets, with a spending increase again from 1991—partly on the basis of rising expenditure on government payments as unemployment climbed into double digits (via automatic stabilisers) (Laurie and McDonald 2008). In the first five years of the Hawke government, in the midst of economic turmoil, the ALP turned a budget deficit of $5.7 billion into a $5.5 billion surplus (Minns 1989, 4). As Langmore later recollected, the work of the Accord architects was discarded and policy initiatives promised in the election campaign abandoned—a personally shattering and disillusioning experience (Oliver and Collins 1993).

4 Wage Suppression

As Figure 6.1 shows, the Accord had an immediate impact on nominal award wages and average weekly earnings, which slowed from the 1983–84 financial year. Wages growth between 1985 and 1987 was well below CPI and continued declining until the 1991–1992 financial year. Michael Beggs (2015, 270) has noted that 'it should not be taken for granted that the Accord was entirely responsible for this restraint—it was also, after all, a period of historically high unemployment'. In terms of the identifiable contribution of the Accord to wage suppression, however, the:

> ... consensus of a number of econometric studies—based on both estimating a counterfactual non-Accord comparison case on the basis of parameters from historical data, and on using a dummy variable—is that the Accord had substantial effects on the rate of growth of both nominal and real wages (ibid 2015, 270).

Similarly, ALP advisor and economist, Bruce Chapman, noted that:

> ... the move to a consensual incomes policy has been argued (conservatively) to have ... decreased wage inflation by three percentage points per year, and real wage levels by ten percent for 1983–89 (or 1.67 percent per year on average), *ceteris paribus* [all other things being equal].
>
> cited in Beggs 2015, 270

The Accord helped to reduce the average real level of wages, which did not recover to their pre-Accord levels until the final year of the Accord—as shown in Figure 6.2 below.

The trend line in Figure 6.2 projects mean wages based on their level in the long boom and, although data is only available from 1960, it is generally accepted that the 1960s trend applied to the 1950s also (Frijters and Gregory 2006, 206). The graph demonstrates that, even though the labour wage push in the mid-1970s drove wages above the 'golden age' trend line, the push in the early 1980s—which heralded calls of 'real wage overhang'—only resulted in mean wages recovering to the level of the trend line after they were suppressed under the Fraser Government.

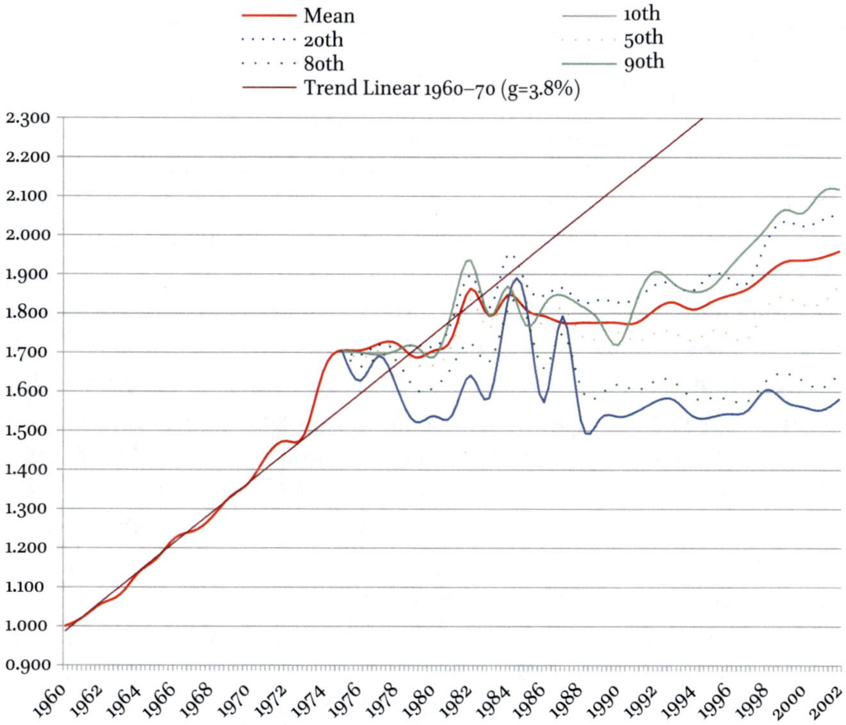

FIGURE 6.2 Real total compensation per employee in Australia, 1960–2002
NOTE: Straight rising line is a trend line, based on the 1960–1970 mean. Adult male full-time weekly earnings, indexed to 1.0 in 1960, including 10th, 20th, 50th, 80th and 90th deciles. For 1996, there is no series and values are linearly interpolated from 1995 and 1997 data. For 1995, the 90th decile was incalculable and derived in the same way from 1994 and 1997 data.
SOURCE: ABS 6310.0

Paul Frijters and Bob Gregory noted in their detailed study of labour market outcomes between the long boom and the turn of the 21st century (in which they provided a similar wage suppression graph to that of Figure 6.2[1]) that:

> The golden age is clear. Real wages were growing at about 2–3 percent per annum during the 1960s and early 1970s. Then, after an above average real wage increase during the mid-1970s, real wages stayed more or less constant for the next 15–20 years. The deviation from a linear projection of the golden age trend ... is remarkable. By 1995, real wages are about 30 percent to 50 percent less than they might have been if the golden age had continued.
>
> FRIJTERS and GREGORY 2006, 208–209

Crucially, Figure 6.2 also shows that the decline in real wages during the Accord was not uniform across the population, with the wages of lowest paid workers falling further and taking longer to recover than those in the higher deciles. Thus, the decline in real wages had a disproportionate impact on those on lower incomes. Further, indexation (even if it had been fully implemented) was always going to freeze certain wage differentials—such as gender wage inequality in Australia—while it was in place, hitting those already disadvantaged[2] (Stilwell 1986, 32; Yates 1996). The real wages of all workers were negatively impacted by the Accord, but many who began the period already disadvantaged became more so, comparatively, over the 13 years.

Wage suppression also contributed to the growth of the profit share of GDP in both the Accord and post-Accord periods. Figure 6.3, overleaf, shows a significant shift from wages to profits over the Accord period. As Bruce Chapman (2000) argued, the aim of the agreement was to decrease the wages share of national output. It is important to restate that this suppression was not accidental, but resulted from the deliberate efforts of the government and ACTU embedded within the Accord framework.

Beggs (2015, 273) has usefully focused attention on how the Accord was able transform the arbitration system into an instrument of macroeconomic policy, realising a 'long held dream of Australian macroeconomists'. The agreement achieved the suppression of real wages, which had 'proven impossible to impose from above ... due to the nature of the arbitration system—part of the

1 Their calculations use OECD data, which for the mean series is identical, but indexed to 1.0 in 1976. The deciles vary slightly from those in Figure 6.2, although follow the same general shape.

2 Percentage-based wage increases tend to increase wage differentials (as higher income earners gain higher increases), while flat wage increases tend to decrease wage differentials—all other things being equal.

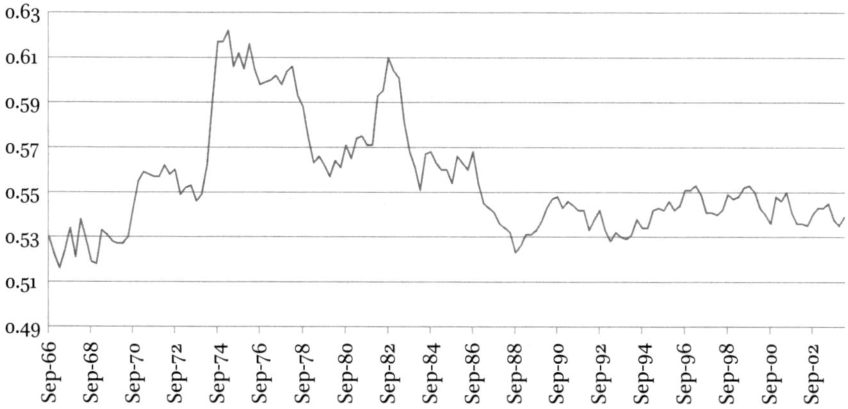

FIGURE 6.3 Total labour share (%) of national income in Australia, 1970–2006
NOTE: WAGE RATES: WAGE SHARE OF GROSS DOMESTIC PRODUCT AT FACTOR COST. RAW DATA PROVIDED BY PAUL FRIJTERS AND BOB GREGORY.
SOURCE: ECONOMIC OUTLOOK, OECD, DX DATABASE, MARCH 2005

state, but not under the control of the government or policy makers' (ibid 2015, 273). Thus, the import of the Accord was that it voluntarily drew the unions into wage suppression, enwrapping them in the state's priorities in the vanguard neoliberal era and enacted that through the arbitration process.

Centralised wage setting was the mechanism through which workers' interests were discarded by the ALP and ACTU in the Accord period, especially given the privileged position of government submissions in the National Wage Cases—where the government, like the tribunal itself, purported to represent the interests of all (ibid 2015, 273). Thus, although government views and IRC decisions could and did diverge—given the general direction of arbitration (including the prioritisation of national economic factors over workers' cost of living) and the direction of the ALP (in implementing vanguard neoliberalism in the national interest)—they were moving in the same direction and against the interests of wage earners. Even the interests of the IRC (in maintaining its fundamental role in centralised arbitration and as evidenced in decisions like initially rejecting the introduction of enterprise bargaining) were ultimately overcome by the efforts of the ALP and trade union leadership to move away from the centralised system.

4.1 *Labour Disorganisation*

The Accord's wages and bargaining trajectory must also be understood as a key element in labour disorganisation, which directly contributed to the neoliberal project for two reasons. First, the shift from workplace-based organising in the pre-Accord period—which previously had provided coherence to the labour movement—to a centrally arbitrated process disorganised the labour movement at the rank-and-file level. Second, real wage suppression necessitated the inhibition of industrial activity. Both of these issues are discussed further in Chapters 7 and 8. Wages policy under the Accord represented, therefore, a simultaneous deepening of corporatism and advance of neoliberalism—achieved by undermining labour remuneration, conditions and organisation. That is, the Accord and neoliberalism were not distinct policy frameworks, pulling in opposite directions, but intertwined components of the same agenda.

The suppression of wages and wage share—as well as the related disorganisation of labour and subdual of industrial activity—was achieved differently in Australia from the countries which have influenced the construction of the dominant narrative of neoliberalism's construction, and from those with which Australia is often compared (in particular the UK,[3] US and NZ). Unlike those locations, the processes of wage and industrial action suppression in Australia were primarily *voluntary*. These objectives were organised by the trade union movement, through the reinvigoration of a centralised wages system that significantly reduced the need for rank-and-file involvement in wage bargaining and trade unions more generally. This process allowed wages policy to be directed by the ALP Government and saw the ACTU offer up organised labour—and its ability to accede to increased exploitation—as part of a macroeconomic policy framework that also sat at the heart of the advance of neoliberalism. Kelty stated in 1993 that the ACTU leadership developed the Accord because they had 'made a mess' of wage rates in relation to the economy under Whitlam—that they did not look back on the era (where labour increased its share of national wealth) with any sense of pride (Oliver and Collins 1993). Kelty, in effect, argued that a key achievement of the trade union movement in the 1970s—a greater wages share of national income—was an error, and that wages policy under the Accord would need to take a different path. While the dominant narrative of neoliberalism's origins constructs vanguard neoliberalism as something imposed non-consensually, against the wishes of organised labour, the Accord's consensual corporatist framework was central to the neoliberal objectives of suppressing real wages and industrial activity in Australia.

Some theorists have tended to emphasise the 'break' from the past in the economic perspectives developed by the Hawke-Keating Governments. It is true that the ALP did move further right than predecessor Labor governments in the areas of wages, industrial relations regulation and public sector cuts in

3 Real wages did not fall under Thatcher, but during the social contract implemented by the preceding British Labour Party government. Nevertheless, the wages share of UK national income did decline under Thatcher.

the vanguard neoliberal era (Johnson 1989, 95). However, there was also significant continuity—in particular the belief that improved socio-economic standards would be delivered through a stable economy and profitability, even if there needed to be sacrifices. For example, the Curtin (1941–1945), Chifley (1945–1949) and Whitlam (1972–1975) Governments had all emphasised the need for wage restraint (ibid 1989, 75). The ALP was also in government during the two most important economic crises prior to 1983, with James Scullin elected Prime Minister only days before the 1929 stock market crash and Whitlam in power when the crisis of the 1970s ended the post-war boom. Each time the ALP cut public spending and sought to suppress the wages of certain segments of the population (Millmow 2004).

Thus, the Labor Party had a history of developing austerity and wage restraint as prescriptions to address economic crises. Yet, while previous ALP governments had taken similar action during crises, the Hawke-Keating government, through the Accord, pushed wage restraint further and ultimately re-regulated wage setting with the implementation of enterprise bargaining. This was a process of both continuity (as a party historically committed to managing capitalist crisis by attacking working class living standards) and break (in its historic dismantling of centralised wage determination and adoption of neoliberalism).

In the conjuncture of the economic and political crisis of the 1970s and early 1980s, it was the Labor Party and the trade unions that stepped forward with an alternative strategy. Central to the political-economic solution developed by the ALP, both in terms of winning the electoral vote at the March 1983 election and as a plan to tackle the economic problems confronting Australia, was the Accord and its agenda of wage moderation and reducing industrial disputation. For the state and capital, the Accord was 'fit for purpose' in a period of failing profitability and high levels of industrial struggle. For the labour movement, including the militant blue-collar unions (whose members were bearing the brunt of mass retrenchments), it held out the promise of resolving the crisis and delivering progressive social wage reforms for their members. In practice, the interests of the state and capital won out.

5 Conclusion

The political and industrial wings of the labour movement came together through the Accord process to institute a corporatist social contract centred on wage suppression, on the basis of a common strategy between the state, capital and labour in the (so-called) national interest. This was posited as an alternative to the New Right policies being implemented at that time in the UK and US. As Hawke said in the early months of the agreement:

> ... sustained economic recovery ... will not be possible without a greater sense of common purpose ... [and] unless the benefits of growth, and the inevitable costs, are shared equitably.
>
> HAWKE 1983b

As this chapter has demonstrated, however, the outcome of wages policy in the Accord was not shared equally.

The wages of the working class were significantly curtailed under the Accord; with the lowest wage brackets having their wages suppressed the most. Wage inequality also increased under the Accord, with a growing gap between the wages of those in the highest and lowest deciles. Also, the profit share of national income grew at the expense of working class wages. Given the historical role of the male wage and full employment as the backbone of the welfare state in Australia, wage suppression also resulted in an undermining of the primary source of social security—any moderate increases in other social wage entitlements under the Hawke-Keating governments aside. As Michael Pusey (1991, 223) argued, these are the reasons that 'welfare' in Australia was more vulnerable than 'in Britain, or other European countries, where welfare *entitlements* still stood, *as such*, even in the fire of Mrs Thatcher's breath'.

In a 2007 interview, Keating described his role in economic management in the Accord era as being 'the guy who had to get the ACTU in a headlock and pull its teeth out with a pair of pliers ... administering [and] pulling a set of rotten teeth' (2007). While Keating is known for his rhetorical flourish, there is no doubt that the ALP leadership viewed the Accord process as a way to draw the labour movement into supporting (or at least not campaigning against) its agenda of significant wage suppression—and, simultaneously, neoliberal policy transformation. Thus, while the election of the Hawke Government in 1983 has been referred to as 'the year of national reconciliation' (Beilharz and Watts 1983, 27), it was a key step in cohering a hegemonic neoliberal project and the political effort to suppress the wages and standard of living of the working class.

Centralised arbitration in Australia was recast through the Accord process. Initially, the Accord reincorporated the trade unions (after the Dismissal and confrontational Fraser period) into a state project to use labour exploitation to address the economic crisis. This was a process of deepening corporatism. The Accord, however, also laid the ground for the eventual decline of arbitration itself through the introduction of decentralised wage setting in the form of enterprise bargaining. This was one element in the process of advancing neoliberalism. The reincorporation of the labour movement into the priorities of political society also muted industrial action and facilitated the advance of other neoliberal policy objectives, including financial re-regulation, privatisation and competition policy—issues which are considered in the next chapter.

CHAPTER 7

An Integral State

> Between the economic structure and the state with its legislation and its coercion stands civil society, and it is this latter which has to be radically transformed, in concrete terms and not just as it appears in statutes and learned books. The state is the instrument for bringing civil society into line with the economic structure, but the state has to 'want' to do that ...
>
> GRAMSCI, *Prison Notebooks*, Q10II §15

1 Introduction

The next two chapters will demonstrate that the advance of neoliberalism in Australia occurred through a simultaneous deepening of corporatism, as co-terminal aspects of a unitary process of state-led class rule. While the claim that neoliberalism and the Accord are deeply entwined directly contradicts many analyses of the social contract, in fact the development of neoliberalism everywhere took place 'among its others' and necessarily encompassed a mix of geographically-specific 'non-neoliberal' features (Peck, Theodore, and Brenner 2009b, 103; see also Jessop 2002). While various authors have suggested how neoliberalisation 'among its others' occurred in general, this chapter and the next examine the specific and concrete unfolding of this process in Australia. In the following I develop an account of how neoliberalism's origins were embedded in the Accord process, as well as highlighting how the Australian case might destabilise the 'dominant narrative' of neoliberalism's advance internationally.

Following on from the discussion of wages and bargaining in the previous chapter, the focus here is on how the social contract was shaped—and reshaped—to be 'fit for purpose' within the vanguard neoliberal project. This chapter emphasises how the Accord in practice diverged from the originally agreed terms of the social contract. It details how policies related to prices and trade were moulded to align with the wider neoliberal transformations of the Hawke-Keating era.

The first section of the chapter explores deviations from the original Accord statement, including the outcomes of the 1983 National Economic Summit, prices policy and trade liberalisation policies. These are placed in the context

 | DOI:10.1163/9789004383463_008

of wider government reforms that advanced neoliberalism in this period, such as the 'big bang' financial reforms in the early 1980s and privatisations. The discussion explores how these policies reflected and facilitated the shifting priorities of the ALP government.

The 'social wage' components of the Accord are analysed in the second section, in particular the expansion of compulsory superannuation and the introduction of the Medicare universal health system. Social wage reform is often held up as evidence of the overall benefits of the Accord to the working class, even among analysts critical of the regressive wage and industrial policy outcomes of the period. The progressive credentials of superannuation and Medicare are critically assessed, and how they were related to neoliberalism is examined.

The third section considers how the overarching relationship between the Accord and neoliberalism should be understood. The section outlines problems with how this connection has been articulated, with the Accord usually posited as a policy framework counterposed to neoliberalism. Building on earlier chapters, the analysis demonstrates how the relationship is best understood as one of enwrapment of the social sphere by the political sphere. The Accord is argued to represent a high point of successful integration of key civil society subaltern groups by the state, as well as the assimilation of the organised labour movement into the reorganisation of class rule after the economic and political turmoil of the 1970s. This enwrapment—or *involucro*—incorporated formerly oppositional civil society actors into the process of state rule. The section concludes by critiquing the concept of the 'informal Accord'—developed by Bramble and Kuhn (1999) and extended by Cahill (2008, 326)—by way of considering whether it adequately explains this process of enwrapment. The informal Accord concept is argued to be incomplete. It is transcended by the application of Gramsci's concept of the integral state; a concept which allows a more nuanced delineation of the concord between the corporatist and neoliberal projects.

2 Accord Divergences

2.1 *The National Economic Summit and Communiqué*

Immediately after the 1983 election, the direction of economic policy began to move away from the framework outlined in the original Accord statement. Only a month after taking office, Hawke convened the 1983 National Economic Summit, from 11–14 April, at the Commonwealth Parliament House. Hawke (1979, 43) had long argued for a forum that involved the:

> ... convening, by Government, of a national summit conference of major employer organisations, trade unions and other relevant bodies, [as] an essential pre-condition for creating the greater degree of positive co-operation which [would] be necessary for us to meet these challenges and the conflict they are already generating.

This nationally televised event occurred prior to the first sitting of the newly elected Parliament. Consequently, Hawke's first speech in Parliament House as Prime Minister was not to politicians, but to leading civil society representatives. The Summit included invitees from government, trade unions, business organisations and social welfare organisations. The event culminated in the release of the Summit's Communiqué (Commonwealth of Australia 1983), which set out an agreed political-economic agenda. Hawke's (1983a, 4) cabinet submission, endorsing the outcomes of the Summit, stated the event and agreement were a central part of 'a more open and cooperative approach to economic management'.

Business was not formally a party to the Accord, but the agreement's content (such as decisions making structures) effectively brought sections of capital inside its framework (Thornthwaite and Sheldon 1996; Singleton 1990a, 171). The Summit extended this by establishing tripartite bodies to negotiate and implement industry policy, and by gaining a general sanction from the business representatives at the forum to move back to the centralised arbitration of wages. The Summit, in part, *post facto* secured the consent of business to the Accord (Beilharz 1985, 215)—a consent to be understood in a dual sense of incorporating capital into the social contract *and* the priorities of the state. Stilwell (1986, 11–14) argued that the significance of the meeting was that it moved politics on from the Accord agreement, to something more economically moderate and agreeable to business. Stilwell argued the process was one of bringing business to the table, although not in a form as clearly organised as the trade unions, and thereby facilitating its involvement in decision-making processes.

The Summit was strictly managed, with discussion framed around three proposals distributed prior to the event. One proposal generally reflected a stance favoured by the union leadership, while another reflected business's preferred approach—despite internal disagreement in both camps.[1]

1 The business community was not homogenous at the Summit, as the negotiations over the Communiqué highlighted tensions within and between various representative bodies (Hagan and Castle 1986, 13; McEachern 1986). Similarly, the Summit created some tension between the right and left unions over the content of the Communiqué (Rizzo 1991), although this did not spill over into public debate to any significant extent.

An intermediate proposal was backed by the government and positioned as the 'compromise', ultimately receiving what was effectively unanimous support[2]. While the Accord was prominent at the Summit, the final Communiqué was not consistent with the spirit of the social contract. The Government and business effectively treated the Accord as an ambit claim within the process, destined to be watered down with capital now at the table (Beggs 2015, 266).

NSW Labor Premier, Neville Wran, argued that the Summit was about three issues—'jobs, jobs, jobs'—but it was, in reality, about wage restraint (Stilwell 1986, 12; Rizzo 1991, 88). The Summit established ground for the narrowing of the Accord (over its subsequent editions) to focus almost exclusively on wages, as was explored in the previous chapter. Other shifts between the Accord and the Communiqué were obvious, if at times subtle. For example, while:

> ... the Accord [had] stressed protecting and enhancing living standards and the reduction of unemployment, the Communiqué was more guarded, tying increased real incomes to productivity movements and a decrease in unemployment to a simultaneous reduction in inflation.
>
> SONDER 1984, 157

There was also a 'move away from the social reform tenor of the Accord to a more qualified, more conservative economic language' around prices, wages, non-wage-incomes, taxation and government expenditure (ibid 1984, 157). As Tom Bramble (2008, 127) argued, the Summit made:

> ... clear that the proposed redistribution of income [in the original Accord] was, if anything, to be in favour of business and the wealthy, and that 'collective restraint' was to weigh disproportionately on workers.

Other divergences from the Accord included: a watering down of action on prices; changed wording about wages so that it did not necessarily support cost-of-living adjustments; a greater focus on questions of productivity; limitations over the control of incomes not subject to determination by industrial tribunals (i.e. voluntary restraint for non-wage incomes); and a less candid discussion of taxation and government expenditure (Sonder 1984, 156–157). The Communiqué resulted in employer representatives acceding to a return to centralised wage fixing, but only on the basis that: if 'profitability increased, real wages would be restrained and only increased "over time", while sectional claims were to be suppressed' (Rizzo 1991, 90). Tom McDonald,

2 The official Communiqué was not signed by the idiosyncratic Queensland Premier, Joh Bjelke Petersen (B. Jones 2006, 338).

Assistant National Secretary of the BWIU, summarised the differences in noting that the Accord's main purpose was 'towards protecting living standards and the Communiqué's main [purpose was] to restore profitability' (cited in Rizzo 1991, 91).

While the ACTU leadership were content with the Communiqué, some left unions were not. These unions attacked the elements of the Communiqué that parted ways with the Accord on the basis that the Summit document was non-binding, while the Accord was. The AMWU stated in internal documents that while the Summit:

> ... embraced a number of policy objectives set out in the Accord, the Communiqué from the Summit does not in any way modify the Accord or any of its policy objectives.
>
> AMFSU 1983c, 7

Similarly, John Halfpenny, Victorian State Secretary of the AMWU, stated:

> The Accord is the only agreement between the Trade Union Movement and the Labor Government. The Summit was something different [and] where the Summit Communiqué is consistent with the Accord, then we welcome that additional support. Some of the differences are quite obvious, for example, on wages. ... On the other hand, the Accord, by agreement between the Unions and the Government supports a centralised wages system, but also says that [the] system must maintain real wages on regular cost of living adjustments. Because the Summit Communiqué represents consensus about very little more than shadows, it has of course receded well into the background of life in this country. On the other hand, because the Accord deals with policies of substance, it will become increasingly important for the Trade Union Movement to insist that those policies be implemented. ... Reasonable progress has been made towards implementing the priority policy objectives in the Accord, but much more needs to be done and the next 12 months or so will test the credibility of the agreement.
>
> HALFPENNY 1984a, 9–10

Halfpenny's comments illuminate the paradox in the approach of left unions in this period. His statement articulates a concern about the failure of the government to defend the letter and spirit of the Accord so soon after the election, yet also expresses confidence that the Accord (rather than the Communiqué) will be the central and lasting document—notwithstanding the general acknowledgement of tripartite 'consensus' around the Summit agreement. Furthermore, Halfpenny's faith in the Accord is also in spite of the regressive impact of early Labor Government reforms, such as the 1983 budget decision to increase and index many indirect taxes. This was in contrast to the 'well established view in the Labor Movement that indirect taxes are inequitable and impose greater burden on low income earners than they do on high income earners' (Halfpenny 1984a, 1–2), and the Accord statement committing the ALP to a discernible redistribution of income and a more progressive taxation system. As detailed below, this was not the only shift away from the Accord framework and it was far from the only reason for disquiet in the union movement so early in the Accord period.

Although the Summit was a process of drawing business into the Accord, it must also be understood as more firmly tying the labour movement into the government's agenda—'cementing' the unions further into the social contract (Rizzo 1991, 90). The Summit was used to demonstrate to business that the ALP 'was more capable than the Liberal-Country Party coalition of serving the interests of capital' and that this, in conjunction with the Accord itself, offered 'a foundation to discipline the trade union movement' (Thompson 1984, 9). Ross Garnaut, leading proponent of trade liberalisation and Hawke economic advisor, argued that the Summit was one of the early 'instruments of public education, helping to prepare a climate of public opinion that expected and favoured trade liberalisation' (Garnaut 2002). This education of the public was directed at the civil society organisations participating in the Summit, as much as the broader public outside it—but was particularly directed at the union and labour movement in both cases. Kelty later stated that the Summit 'forced the unions to come to terms with process of government very early' (cited in Oliver and Collins 1993). Thus, the Summit began to 'educate' the unions about what would be possible under the Accord—educating consent for the emerging neoliberal project, through civil society organisations (Gramsci 2011a, 153–154; Q1 §47).

The Summit strengthened the corporatist framework in a manner Panitch had foreshadowed, with cooperative interaction at the leadership level sitting alongside a political agenda of social control at the mass level (1977b, 66; 1981, 24). The scholarly literature tends to assume that parties in the social contract process had equivalent power because the Accord and the Summit's Communiqué were mutually agreed to. However, in practice, the public display of the Summit made it more difficult for the unions to take a public position against the new government, in case they might be seen to destabilise it politically. In this way, the Summit should be viewed as a successful moment in enwrapping the unions into the Accord process, while at the same time shifting economic policy away from the letter of the Accord itself.

2.2 *Prices*

In reading historical assessments of the Accord, one could be mistaken for thinking that prices were not a central component of the agreement nor taken seriously by the parties. Yet price (and thus non-wage income) control was a core plank of the initial agreement. In an indication of the perceived importance of price control at the time, prices policy appears before wages policy in the original Accord statement (ALP & ACTU 1986, 163–164). The failure to take concerted action the prices component of the agreement is rarely discussed in detail by scholars, with analysis instead emphasising wages policy and select elements of the social wage promises.

There were two main reasons that no serious price control occurred: the legal barriers preventing direct government intervention; and the failure of the government to seek voluntary price suppression. As was discussed in Chapter 5, the unsuccessful 1973 referendum to provide the Commonwealth with powers to manage wages and prices shifted the labour movement's focus from government-legislated control to a voluntary agreement. On prices, however, the government did not genuinely seek capital's involvement in controls, although it was not likely that the business sector would have agreed even if it had. The replacement for the Prices Justification Tribunal (PJT), which was established under Whitlam in 1973 and which lasted until 1981, was the Prices Surveillance Authority (PSA)—introduced by Hawke in 1983. Despite the Accord stating it would establish a regulatory body, the PSA had 'no powers to enforce its observations'—it could simply object publicly to unreasonable price rises and ask the firm to reconsider (Gibson 1984, 5). The PSA, in practice, had even less power of enforcement than its predecessor (Johnson 1989, 102). As a result, the focus in the Accord period remained on indirect action such as price monitoring.

Early in the Accord era, unions expressed strong reservations about the likely effectiveness of the PSA as it had been constructed, arguing it would not have the ability to meet the obligations of the social contract (Halfpenny 1984b, 2). Left unions threatened that, unless the letter of the Accord was implemented, they would take industrial or political action. Halfpenny (1984b, 6–7) stated there was a conflict between the government insisting that the 'price' of wages was 'to be restrained by a variety of enforcement mechanisms including the Arbitration Commission', yet there being 'no similar mechanism to ensure that the corporate sector exercise[d] restraint'. Halfpenny (1984b, 6–7) added that the 'existence of this conflict or contradiction...need not be damaging to the Accord providing the Trade Union Movement is prepared and able to force restraint onto the corporate sector'.

Yet, rather than publicly mobilising to try to force real regulation by the government or capital, the AMWU and other unions established a community price monitoring program (Halfpenny 1984a). The justification for establishing this system was that in collecting information on prices through a phone-in service, the unions would gather a comprehensive picture of price rises and act as a grass roots 'watchdog' over the PSA, retail chains and supermarkets. While the unions did not believe such activities could change 'the course of history', they did believe they could assist implementation of the prices component of the Accord (Halfpenny 1984b, 6). With the ALP in power, and with formal union involvement in economic policy at a senior level, it is telling that the central mechanism developed to deal with prices was a community-based price watch process that had no agenda of political mobilisation. The process of 'price watching' likely acted to channel anger about price rises within the unions and ALP branches into an acceptable project, thereby limiting the likelihood of an alternative strategy coming to the fore.

Apart from community monitoring, union action was confined to raising the failure to act on prices with the government and moving motions at union meetings and conferences. The 1986 AMWU national conference carried a motion seeking serious and concerted action on controlling prices (AMWU 1986a), and the ACTU wrote to the government arguing that recent CPI figures raised 'continuing doubts as to the existence of any restraint on the part of price fixers' (Crean 1986). Such efforts were in vain, however, and action on prices was not significant—with the 1980s being dominated by both relatively high inflation (see Figure 6.1) and real wage suppression (see Figure 6.2).

More generally, constraining prices through government policy conflicted with the government's objective of increasing economic growth to resolve unemployment, and hence its desire to protect profits by reducing wages relative to inflation. Further, the agreement to act on prices was difficult to implement directly, because prices are generally harder to suppress than wages. As Beggs argues:

> ... prices and profit margins they incorporate depend on a number of firm and industry-specific factors as well as macroeconomic conditions: for example, the state of demand for the product, the competitive structure of the industry, the vintage of the means of production. This is why price control cannot work effectively on the basis of standard rule, but calls for a case-by-case consideration. ... [T]his is not to say leaving it to companies' pricing policies necessarily leads to more rational outcomes, especially given the vagaries of imperfect competition. But a pricing authority

> with real power was always going to cut against the grain of capitalism, especially in the deregulatory atmosphere of the 1980s (2015, 265).

The failure by the ALP government to act on pricing, in the midst of the vanguard neoliberal period, was underscored by statements such as Keating's claim that market competition was the most efficient way to control prices (Stilwell 1986, 39–40). Ultimately, there was neither serious effort nor desire on the part of the government to control prices in a similar way to wages (i.e. by direct suppression).

Further, given that the lack of federal government power to act easily on prices was known before the Accord was signed, it suggests the prices element of the Accord was always unlikely to be effected—even though union archival documents make clear that the left unions firmly *believed* it would be implemented (AMFSU 1983a). Importantly, given that the wages of many professionals are the price paid by consumers, wage earners received lower wages under the Accord but 'paid' for the comparatively higher incomes of those who drew their income directly from service fees—in circumstances where prices did not fall for other reasons.

2.3 *'Big Bang' and Other Neoliberal Reforms*

The term 'big bang' has been used to describe financial re-regulation[3] undertaken by the Thatcher Government in 1986. While some argued that this approach was ignored in favour of a slower change process in Australia (Battellino 2007), important 'big bang' reforms were enacted in the early years of the Hawke Government. In his seminal account of the 1980s in Australia, Kelly (1992, 387) argued that there were broadly four key areas of policy change: labour market deregulation (discussed in Chapters 6 and 8); financial deregulation; the reduction of protection; and market pricing and privatisation (all discussed below).

On 9 December 1983, when the Australian dollar came under speculative pressure, the government closed the stock market for a day, floated the currency (to allow the market and not the Australian government to set the rate), and abolished exchange controls (to re-regulate investment, lending and borrowing). As a result, 'instead of tightening controls on capital flows, as the Whitlam Labor government had done in similar circumstances, the government' chose deregulation and 'market discipline' (Quiggin 1998, 79). This move

3 The changes in the neoliberal era are not usefully described as 'deregulation' given the process did not involve in less government intervention (Wacquant 2012). The changes are better understood as a re-regulation of economic frameworks and social relationships on new lines (Anderson 1999).

began a process of wider reform 'with the deregulation of the financial sector [occurring] ahead of the real economy, and the external ahead of the domestic economy' (Garnaut 2002). This sequencing of reform drove a reorientation of the domestic economy. It 'placed Hawke and Keating firmly on the side of the movement towards liberalised and globalised financial systems that swept the world from the late 1970s onwards' (Quiggin 2010, 33). Crucially, the shift of policy towards removing barriers to international competitive pressures was used to discipline union and sectional business resistance to domestic restructuring through microeconomic reform. By 1984, *Euromoney Magazine* had named Keating 'Finance Minister of the Year' for undertaking these reforms, leading to his being nicknamed 'World's Best Treasurer' in the midst of the vanguard neoliberal era (Oliver and Collins 1993).

A raft of further neoliberal policies was enacted by the Labor Government. These reforms included privatisation, corporatisation of government agencies, implementation of 'user-pays', industry re-regulation and competition policy. Such changes were often directly against the spirit of the Accord agreement, or developed in a way that made implementing the Accord more difficult. The neoliberal policy direction formed part of a new rationale for national economic policy, based on international competitiveness and market competition (Bryan 1995, 2; Stilwell 1986, 39–40). In most cases these policy decisions were taken unilaterally and against the spirit of the Accord, in circumstances where the trade unions believed they should have been consulted under the terms of the social contract. Some unions were scathing of Keating's running of Treasury during the early years of the Accord, arguing that his approach was in contradiction to the letter of the agreement—in particular the Accord's commitments to protect Australian industry and assist the manufacturing and metals sectors (AMFSU 1984a, 9–10). Left unions argued that the Accord could not be implemented alongside neoliberal re-regulation and greater international integration, with criticism accelerating after the first financial reforms.

However, a close reading of the Accord statement suggests that the obligation to consult with the unions can be read more narrowly, as applying only to matters related to incomes, prices and industry protection. The early to mid-1980s reforms brought to the fore the lack of specificity of the Accord and the multiple interpretations it allowed—despite high-profile union leaders arguing that the Accord was 'not just a statement of positions, but ... a set of precise policy objectives' (Halfpenny 1984a).

The unions tended to express their views on the direction of economic policy privately to the government, but occasionally they took a more public stand. In July 1984, 50 labour officials from unions that had backed the Accord released a joint statement to delegates at the ALP National Conference. The document reiterated support for the Accord and noted general satisfaction with it, but raised concerns over differences emerging between the unions and the government. In particular, it raised disquiet over the policy direction in 'the metals manufacturing sector', with regard to 'deregulation and internationalisation of the financial system' and 'public sector resource allocation' (i.e. implementation of the social wage) (AMFSU and others 1984). But unlike in the Fraser years, the unions did not mobilise rank-and-file members to defeat policy changes or to force the government to implement the 'full' social contract.

2.4 *Trade Liberalisation*

From the early 1970s, trade liberalisation and tariff reduction began to alter Australia's highly protected economy. Between 1970 and 2001 'the average level of industry assistance [through tariffs] fell from over thirty percent to under five percent' (Leigh 2002, 487). Since World War II, there were three significant decisions to reduce industry assistance in Australia and ALP governments—in 1973, 1988 and 1991—made all of them. As outlined in Chapter 5, Whitlam reduced tariffs by 25 percent soon after his election in 1973. However, because of other factors, there was no change in the average effective protection levels for manufacturing. The 1988 and 1991 tariff reductions under Hawke and Keating significantly reduced protection of industry, and the 'reform of manufacturing protection in Australia in the 1980s was accompanied by the removal of most agricultural assistance' (Garnaut 2002). Such moves were directly counter to the letter of the Accord, which argued there was:

> ... no economic sense in reducing protection levels in the midst of high unemployment [and] that neither current economic conditions, expected future trends, nor balance of payments constraints [justified] reduction in protection in the foreseeable future.
>
> ALP & ACTU 1986, 168–169

Any changes to protection were supposed to be determined through the industry planning mechanism of the Accord, and to entail significant consultation with unions and business. Such consultation and consensus decision-making did not take place.

While agreements centred on national reciprocity were limited in the Hawke-Keating era, the government increasingly engaged in international discussions seeking to enhance trade liberalisation. The most significant moves in this regard were the central role Australia played in forming the Asia-Pacific Economic Cooperation (APEC)—with Hawke convening its first meeting in 1989 in Canberra—and in the process leading to APEC's 1994 Bogor Declaration on free trade in the region (Garnaut 2002).

However, an early decision that troubled the AMWU was the signing of a free trade agreement with NZ—the Australia and NZ Closer Economic Relations Trade Agreement (ANZCERTA or CER). In the lead-up to the 1983 election, the AMWU had received assurances from the ALP that the treaty would not be finalised (Carmichael 1983b). Despite this guarantee—and the AMWU's belief that a new ALP government might re-negotiate the terms of the CER to better reflect the priorities of the Accord—the inner cabinet signed it without consulting the unions (Carmichael 1983a). The CER's aims were to reduce tariffs and other barriers to trade with New Zealand, promote competition, and eliminate 'market distortions' (Commonwealth of Australia 2014). There was a pointed shift in tone from AMWU correspondence on the CER over these events. On the day of the 1983 election, in a letter to its sister union in NZ, Carmichael (1983a) noted that the Accord opened 'up many avenues ... to blast International Capital'. Carmichael's (1983b) letter only a month later to Robert Reid, a delegate in same union, noted that the 'new bloody Government signed the CER agreement' after the union thought it had been halted.

In government Labor was committed to trade liberalisation and believed 'closer integration into the international economy, through trade liberalisation and other means, was a necessary element of economic reform to build a modern economy in Australia' (ibid 2002). Although this was not a feature of the Hawke election platform—and counter to the Accord itself—'Hawke's consistent public position from the early days of his government was that sustained economic growth in Australia required reductions in protection' (Leigh 2002). Within the Hawke-Keating Cabinets:

> ... as the voice of those advocating tariff cuts was becoming louder, the direct opposition to cuts was becoming more muted ... [and] those provisions in the Accord that ostensibly limited tariff cuts were ... effectively ignored.
>
> LEIGH 2002, 503

The unions did little to interrupt this trajectory in practice.

3 Privatisation

The 1980s and 1990s saw momentous change in the Australian public sector, including significant privatisations at the three levels of government—federal, state and local. Privatisation is 'the transfer of ownership of an asset or function from the public to the private sector' (Fairbrother, Svensen, and Teicher 1997, 2). It involves three interrelated initiatives:

1. The partial or complete sale of equity in a public enterprise to private investors or companies.
2. The contracting-out of services formerly performed within the public sector to the private sector.
3. The approval of privately built and operated public infrastructure projects, eg. tollways, prisons and hospitals (ibid 1997, 2).

During the Accord, the Commonwealth Government completed the sale of various assets, including: the Australian Industry Development Corporation (1990); AUSSAT National Satellite Company (1991); Commonwealth Bank (1991–1996); Commonwealth Serum Laboratories (1994); Moomba to Sydney gas pipeline (1994); Qantas (1995) and Aerospace Technologies of Australia (1995). The ALP also commenced processes of privatisation that were finalised under the following conservative Howard government, including the Australian National Line (1998) and the national telecommunications carrier Telecom (later Telstra, 1997–2006).

While there was 'minimal public debate about the rationale for these changes and the likely effect on the role of the public sector in contemporary society' (Walker and Con Walker 2006, 1), neoliberal ideological claims that government should be about 'steering not rowing' were often advanced (E S Savas quoted in ibid 2006, 150). Garnaut (2002) reasoned that unions, the general community and business increasingly accepted that the government was inefficient at running certain agencies. This underpinned the:

> … conditions for widespread deregulation and privatisation in transport, communications, energy, banking, efficiency-raising taxation and general regulatory report, and the beginnings of labour market arrangements.
> ibid 2002, 149–150

While Garnaut may have overstated the level of consensus, as some unions were opposed to privatisation, there is no doubt that in the 1980s neoliberalism and privatisation were spoken about openly and positively. Moreover, it was increasingly difficult to challenge the processes of neoliberalism and privatisation within the political sphere in circumstances where the trade unions were moderating any public criticism of the government. Critics have noted that 'the ACTU did little to oppose the privatisations that occurred under the ALP' (Schulman 2015, 85).

Walker and Con Walker's (2006, 9) detailed examination of privatisation concluded that in Australia the process, commenced in the Accord era and continued under subsequent governments, produced a massive transfer of wealth from the state to those within the capitalist class who could afford to hold significant shares in listed companies. Further, that privatisation processes often led to a loss of essential services, which demonstrated that claims about savings to the taxpayer were spurious (ibid 2006, 9). Quiggin's (1995, 41) analysis, for example, suggested that the fiscal stability of the state is likely to be improved over the long term by reforms that do not involve privatisation, despite the ongoing desire by governments to seek reform through privatisation. Others have criticised privatisation on the basis that it: has consequences for transgenerational equity; results in less effective service delivery; necessitates loss of revenues which negatively impact on the fiscal position of the state; undermines working conditions across the economy through the loss of public sector jobs; and reduces the capacity of unions to defend and advance the interests of workers (Fairbrother, Svensen, and Teicher 1997, 3).

The first and only political split over the Accord, in the left of ALP, broke out in 1991 in relation to the privatisation of public assets—forming 'over the Accord and the neoliberal agenda of small government through privatisation of public assets' (Timmerman 2013). A group of unions 'pledged to oppose privatisation' (the Victorian Pledge unions) and publicly attacked the Accord, most specifically the privatisation agendas of the Commonwealth and Victorian Labor governments (Timmerman 2013; see also Boyle 1991). While this split was confined to the Victorian Branch of the ALP and involved only a small number of unions—who simply broke in to a new faction rather than leaving the ALP itself—it demonstrated the depth of concern within some left unions at the overall direction of economic policy, even if there was limited wider public resistance the ALP's neoliberal agenda.

Competition policy also became a key feature of the government's agenda, with Keating instituting a national policy review in 1992. The final statement—the 'Hilmer Report' (Hilmer 1993)—was delivered the following year. The government adopted recommendations to encourage 'microeconomic reform' and productivity growth in the public sector, by bringing competitive market pressures to bear on the functions of the state and state-owned entities (Keating 1993c). The report 'definitively sanctioned "competition policy" as the principal rationale underpinning economic reform in Australia and as the centrepiece of Australian public policy' (Beeson and Firth 1998, 223).

4 Social Wage and Contested Understandings

The first two sections of this chapter demonstrated that, in both wages and other economic policy areas, there was early—and then increasing—divergence from the letter and spirit of the original Accord agreement. Yet notwithstanding sporadic, fragmentary and generally low-level dissent or resistance to such deviations (which included the introduction of a raft of classically 'neoliberal' reforms) the unions clung to their alliance with the government. Before explaining why this was the case, I look at whether the introduction of 'social wage' measures in the Accord era could provide justification—like that given by union leaders and in much of the scholarly literature—for the maintenance of the government-union social contact arrangement.

Analysis of the role of the trade unions in the Accord mostly argues that the social contract must be considered a positive advance for the labour movement and a buffer against neoliberalism, because the working class in other locations fared worse in the era (Spies-Butcher 2012; Ahlquist 2011; Castles, Gerritsen, and Vowles 1996; Quiggin 1998). This view is prosecuted on the basis that the Accord implemented elements of an expanded 'social wage'—a new public health system, universal superannuation, increased family payments, and unemployment benefits—and that these reforms represented 'a significant legacy' which 'alter[ed] the course of future social provision' (Vidler and Coates 2004, 9).

In *Australia on the Rack* (AMWSU 1982), it was reported that 'between 1975–1976 and 1981–1982 an average metal tradesman (sic) had effectively lost $53.50 per week due to direct and indirect tax increases and reductions in the social wage' (Sonder 1984, 153–154; AMWSU 1982). It was this reality that resulted in the AMWU, and then the ACTU, proselytising the virtues of an expanded social wage and pursuing this through the Accord process.

Two key elements of the social wage are often cited as the signal reforms won by the labour movement through the Accord: the reintroduction of universal health care in the form of Medicare; and, the implementation of superannuation across the paid workforce. It is important to examine how these policies related to wider neoliberal restructuring, and particularly the issue of risk in relation to the new pension system. We also need to question the way these reforms are presented as sufficient to compensate for the raft of regressive measures introduced via the corporatist process.

Apart from Medicare and superannuation, there were many other elements (to the social wage implemented through the Accord) that had problematic content. These included family income improvements (sole parents received only derisory help); moderate increases to the unemployment benefit (which still remained low in the very difficult economic climate that persisted well into the 1990s[4]); tax relief (which, as discussed previously, undermined public revenue and expenditure); and increased childcare fee relief (subsidising

4 The unemployment benefit (as a proportion of average full-time earnings) increased from just below 20 percent in 1983 to just below 25 percent in 1991, before falling slightly by 1996. As a proportion of the full-time *minimum* wage, it rose from about 32 percent in 1983 to about 43 percent in 1991, then to just over 45 percent when the ALP lost office in 1996 (Cowgill 2013).

private provision) (McLelland 2000, 52–53). Leading feminist scholar, Anna Yeatman (1990, 93), described the latter childcare reforms as looking 'like welfare rationing and [being] welfare rationing ... predicated on a principle of privatisation'. There was also a streamlining of welfare state spending no longer deemed to be appropriate (1990, ibid; Parker 2013). Other retreats from the social wage agenda included overall fiscal restraint, the abolition of free tertiary education, and the regressive nature of 'bracket creep' (where workers' wage increases pushed their taxable income into a higher tax bracket) (McLelland 2000, 53).

4.1 *Medicare*

In April 1981, the Fraser Liberal Government abolished the Medibank universal healthcare system—a program established in 1975 by Whitlam. While many assume that the reintroduction of universal health care was inevitable under Labor, given the program aligned closely with aspects of traditional ALP ideology, this was not the case (Boxall and Gillespie 2013, 114). The ALP's support for a universal health scheme had diminished while it was in opposition, and the trade union movement made the issue a core demand in the Accord negotiations (ibid 2013, 120–121). The ALP only fully committed to replace Medibank in 1982, doing so on a pragmatic basis—in that 'Labor needed union support for wage restraint, and that support was contingent on the restoration of universal health insurance' (ibid 2013, 115). While a significant budget deficit during its first term meant that much of Labor's election spending program was abolished or delayed, Medicare was so central to union backing of the social contract that the government moved to introduce it in 1984. Although some in the ALP 'hankered after more radical transformations of the way medicine was practised' (ibid 2013, 141), the Medicare model was chosen because the institutional framework needed for it was already in place and its cost was achievable—allowing the restoration of universal health cover to occur relatively quickly (ibid 2013, 118).

In considering the social wage gains of the Accord, there has been a tendency to view the outcomes as a case of 'anything is better than nothing'. Yet, as Johnson (1989, 101) argued, the introduction of Medicare was not without contradictions and the ALP in general 'subordinated welfare policies to their wider economic' priorities. Free access to health care was limited in various ways under Medicare. While public hospital inpatient and emergency treatment was made free and was generally government funded, it was private doctors (reimbursed by government) who performed most general and specialist medical outpatient treatments. Medicare was effectively 'a new version of Whitlam's Medibank and, like its predecessor, subsidise[d] rather than challenge[d] private medicine' (ibid 1989, 101). Private doctors could charge 'gap' fees over what the government would subsidise; and certain areas of healthcare including most dental, physiotherapy and psychology were not provided for in the public system. Further, doctor-ordered medications continued to be only partly subsidised. Thus, although Medicare is often described as a 'universal' system, it has significant gaps in its coverage.

Funding for the new program was obtained through a one percent levy on top of ordinary income taxes, although the costs of the system significantly exceeded the revenue from the new budget stream (Quiggin 2010, 34). The percentage to be paid was increased to 1.25 percent in the 1986–1987 Budget (Jericho 2014a), and was further increased to 1.4 percent and then 1.5 percent by July 1995 (Biggs 2003). The impact of the levy was claimed to have been offset by tax cuts, so that an average metal worker's salary increased by the equivalent of an $11 to $12 a week wage rise—an amount considered to be greater than the levy at that time (AMWU 1986b).

'While the social wage elements of this reform process often fell short of initial expectations' (Spies-Butcher 2014, 84), it is clear that Medicare represented an important advance in social welfare policy and did not follow a particularly 'neoliberal' model (at least in the Accord years). At the same time, however, Medicare entrenched private medicine. Fully universal healthcare was never Labor's intention, as was made clear early in the Accord period when the NSW and Commonwealth ALP governments gave a written commitment during the 1984–1985 doctors' dispute that 'it was not the intention of the Labor Party now or in the future to nationalise medicine' (AMA 2014). At best, Medicare was the clawing back of past gains that had been lost, although at a greater cost to workers than before as they were required to accept a reduction in take-home pay in order to gain this social wage benefit. A benefit abolished by Fraser only three years earlier.

4.2 *Superannuation*

Alongside Medicare, superannuation is seen as the other key progressive social reform of the Accord era. Superannuation had been available to limited sections of the private and public workforces for many years, including some blue-collar workers who had won the entitlement through industrial struggle. In 1980, less than half the workforce had access to superannuation, with coverage concentrated amongst higher paid workers, members of the defence forces and employees of large private sector companies such as airlines (Sheehan and Jennings 2010, 148). Compulsory superannuation (the 'Superannuation Guarantee') was introduced in 1992 by the Keating Government, to support the living standards of the working class in retirement and to raise national savings (Bryan 2004). Its development was seen as a crucial part of social security and it was campaigned for by the unions for many years (AMFSU 1984b, 2).

The Australian retirement system now consists of a compulsory, universal employer-funded and privately-managed superannuation 'pension' system, supplemented by a limited and means-tested public pension (Coates, Vidler, and Stilwell 2004). The compulsory employer contributions commenced at 3 percent of income and were increased to 6 percent before the ALP lost office in 1996. Contributions have increased over time to the current 9.5 percent, with a planned increase to 12 percent by 2025. Employees can make voluntary contributions, while the state makes a payment in kind by forgoing certain taxes on contributions. Some industries have won higher employer contributions through industry bargaining, such as the higher education sector where the rate is 17 percent.

The ALP and many union leaders argued that superannuation would be a national savings plan to reinvigorate investment in manufacturing without additional foreign borrowing and that it would promote the socialisation of investment (Ramsay 2004; Stilwell 2000, 270). To some extent this was rhetoric to draw militant unions into the social contract, as the CPA-aligned unions and others had campaigned for superannuation to be the basis of a national development fund. This fund was to:

> … provide cheap loans to, or equity in, Australian industry and cheap housing loans. Priority [was to be] given to investments which replace imports, increase exports and modernise industry.
>
> AMWU and others 1989

Such investment planning did not eventuate (Vidler and Coates 2004, 12–13, 15). Unsurprisingly, investments in superannuation funds have worked largely in the same manner as other capital in the neoliberal era—i.e. to maximise returns in the stock market, rather than bring investment decisions under 'social' control.

Superannuation assets have steadily increased since the system was introduced and at the end of the June 2017 quarter totalled $2.3 trillion (ASFA 2017). Industry and public sector funds, the boards of which include key representation from union officials, account for a majority and increasing proportion of all superannuation capital (APRA 2013). Former ACTU official and ALP minister, Greg Combet (2004, 24), who works in the superannuation industry, has pointed out that the role of those managing superannuation is limited and there is little scope to pursue 'social' ends (as was envisaged by some involved in the Accord process):

> I'm a trustee, and we have a sole responsibility to the members of the fund to maximise benefits for them. That means you have to make

> investment decisions, on the basis of your best judgement and information available, to maximise returns to the members over time. This is your sole purpose as a trustee and we have been meticulous in making sure we meet that goal. It means that a lot of these rhetorical flourishes about national development funds have to be tested as investments, in terms of returns and risk in comparison with other forms of investment. That's a discipline that we must be very conscious of.

Ordinary union members are, therefore, unable to direct fund investment strategy.

Although this book is largely concerned with events up to the end of the Accord, on the question of superannuation it is also important to evaluate the longer-term trajectory of the pension system and its associated risk for the working class. Superannuation has long been held up as 'an industrial achievement of the labour movement, specifically the unions' (Combet 2004, 17; see also Pierson 2002). However, its legacy is paradoxical. Quiggin (2010, 36) has argued that the social wage policies 'of the Hawke-Keating government had mixed effects on the social allocation of risk', with Medicare reducing private risk while superannuation increased it for workers and households in the last years of the Keating government. In the latter years of the Accord, superannuation shifted from:

> ... 'defined benefits', meaning workers would be guaranteed a pension based on their final salary, [to] new schemes [which were] 'defined contribution', meaning the contributions into the scheme are set, but the end payment is dependent on the performance of the fund, making workers more dependent on market conditions.
>
> SPIES-BUTCHER 2014, 88–89

The global trend in the neoliberal period has been to shift risk for retirement on to individuals and decrease government responsibility (Orenstein 2009; 2008). Achieving this was a key motivation for the ALP government and sections of capital in supporting the introduction of superannuation (Bryan 2004). The business organisation Australian National Industries put it bluntly when, at the 1983 National Economic Summit, it nominated topics to be discussed and argued that superannuation should be run by the private sector and expanded to 'take pressure off the welfare bill' (Leard 1983). The universal adoption of the system constituted a fundamental policy shift away from government to privately funded retirement. In the process, the ALP 'institutionalised the role of the private sector' and the primary emphasis shifted 'to funding future retirement incomes with compulsory earnings-related savings accumulated in decentralised private funds' (Gallery, Brown, and Gallery 1996, 99). The public pension was simultaneously relegated to a secondary status, underpinning the main retirement system and with access based on means testing (Combet 2004, 22).

In seeking a 'fix' for the growing reliance on public monies for retirement, in a period when the labour movement and ALP were delivering cuts in both personal and business taxation, the unions did not appear to seriously consider the consequences of shifting retirement risk onto workers. A few years before the 2008 crisis, and while he was still a senior ACTU official, Combet (2004, 19) argued that the union movement did not view the risk for workers as problematic and that unions:

> ... had confidence that smart asset allocation in interest securities and equities would be able to return consistently decent outcomes for the membership with acceptable risk. And that has been the experience. [Superannuation is] about collectivising, having a collective system of retirement savings that was secure and which was collected in large funds.

While superannuation gains were made until the financial crisis of 2008, the losses to pension funds through speculation in Australia were the worst in the world—apart from the very particular case of Iceland (David 2012). Bryan (2004, 103) has argued that the promotion of superannuation as a 'solution' to government expenditure pressures was based on the idea of 'self-perpetuating wealth creation in capital markets' embedded in neoliberal policy. Bryan asked:

> ... how would private saving (via superannuation) avert the crisis so apparent in the projected reliance [of retirement] on the public purse? Where would the private revenues come from? The answer was never far away from a neo-liberal, idealised view of markets.
>
> ibid 2004, 103

The role of superannuation in neoliberal financialisation in Australia delivered 'one of the most highly exposed pension investment structures to the equity market' in the world (Rafferty 2011). Financialisation, in this instance, is understood as the absorption of households into financial markets through the speculation of workers retirement incomes (Lapavitsas 2011).

The superannuation system has also been expensive to manage, having among the highest operational costs of any pension system in the OECD (Martin 2014). Tax arrangements have also diverted state subsidy of superannuation to high-income earners, because tax concessions for payments (including extra contributions made by workers) mean the rate of subsidy increases with personal income. The:

> ... cost of tax concessions for superannuation now rival[s] total spending on the old age pension, yet the bulk of these benefits go to those on the highest incomes, with low paid workers receiving very little.
>
> SPIES-BUTCHER 2014, 90

Superannuation has also been criticised for its failure to deal with issues of equity. Given that the scheme is based on lifetime earnings, those without access to the workforce (and those who receive less remuneration in general) are disadvantaged. Thus, in general, women, people with a disability, migrants and those who have been underemployed have reduced superannuation reserves to rely on (O'Brien and Burgess 2004; Olsberg 2004). The wealthy also benefit given the low tax rate on superannuation contributions and the tax-free status of income from super funds (Bramble and Kuhn 2011, 148). While superannuation exists alongside a limited 'safety net' pension, this does not undo the fact that existing disadvantages segment the workforce and these are exacerbated by a system based on lifetime earnings.

Critics of superannuation have also argued that there is a vested interest for senior union officials in maintaining the system, given their legislated role on the boards of industry and public sector funds. From the left, Bramble and Kuhn (2011, 171) noted that involvement in managing industry superannuation funds has become a new area of employment for union officials. Similarly, conservative politician Paul Fletcher (2013) argued in a speech to a neoliberal think tank, that 'the structure and governance of today's superannuation system suits the interests of ... union officials, very nicely'. Both point out the social interest of union officials in maintaining the present system and show how union leaders were incorporated into maintaining a privatised pension system—despite its poor returns for certain segments of the population and the risk involved for workers reliant on the system. This is pertinent in light of the argument made by Estelle James and Sarah Brooks (2001, 157)—in a World Bank publication examining pension reform in Argentina, Poland and Hungary—that resistance to pension 'reform can overcome the opposition of unions by giving them a role to playin the new system'.

4.3 *Worth the Cost?*

There are two main ways that defenders of the 'social wage justification' for the Accord have made their case in the scholarly literature. Firstly, they have argued that despite the failure to fully implement the original Accord statement, the project delivered key social wage policy reforms and was therefore on the whole of benefit to working people. Secondly, they have claimed that the negative aspects of the Accord were reasonable consequences, because Australia fared far better than other advanced capitalist countries that developed in a neoliberal direction in the same period, *but* without a social contract (eg. the UK, US and NZ).

In calculating the outcomes of the Accord era, Chris Pierson (2002, 184) argued that although the 'reputation of the ALP under Hawke and Keating [was] as the first neoliberal labour government', this judgement is 'too straightforward'. For Pierson (2002, 184), while 'Canberra's policy making and opinion formation did come increasingly under the direction of economic rationalism', there was not the 'wholesale assault upon welfare provision that marked out neoliberal governments (at least in aspiration) elsewhere'. Pierson (2002, 184) pointed to 'the introduction of Medicare, the introduction of rent assistance for the unemployed, and the maintenance of the old age pension' in particular. Similarly, Singleton (2000, 85) viewed the defeat of the Labor Government's consumption tax proposal in 1985 as proof that the Accord partners did not exercise complete hegemony over the other parts of the community, as social welfare and church groups exercised influence alongside the unions to achieve this defeat.

Deploying a balance sheet of progressive and regressive reforms in this way effectively reads history backwards. Such positions argue that even if the overall outcome in the Accord era was negative, entering an alliance with the government based on sacrifice in the national interest produced a better result than elsewhere. Such an approach presumes the inevitability of harsh neoliberal restructuring under any alternative hypothetical scenario. Furthermore, it is an approach that interprets small wins within wider and deeper losses parallel to the process of neoliberalisation—rather than as concessions or 'sweeteners', designed to smooth the incorporation of the labour movement and disadvantaged social groups into the restructuring process itself (as part of gaining their consent for going against their own social interests). This separation obscures the role of the union movement within the state's political project and in actively constructing neoliberalism.

5 The Concord of Neoliberalism and the Accord

The preceding section challenged the claim in the literature and by union leaders that the re-establishment of Medicare, the expansion of superannuation, and a series of other 'social wage' reforms were unequivocally progressive outcomes of the Accord. Furthermore, it argued that the Accord cannot be usefully evaluated by examining a list of policy positives and negatives for the labour movement or workers, as such an approach detaches limited positive aspects of policies from the wider state-led hegemonic project of the era.

Such an approach conceals the overall trajectory of neoliberalism, which in all locations has varied (to a greater or lesser extent) from an idealised and ideologically pure suite of policies. Neoliberalism is path dependent—the result of local factors related to class conflict, institutional forms and historical settings. Neoliberalisation cannot be viewed as a single road along which all states travel, only to arrive at a 'full' neoliberal endpoint. In this way:

> ... actually existing neoliberalism ... both exploits and produces socio-spatial difference [and its uneven] development does not signal some transitory stage, or interruption, on the path to 'full' neoliberalisation; it represents a coevolving and co-dependent facet of the neoliberalisation process itself.
>
> PECK, THEODORE, and BRENNER 2009a, 53

Moreover, analyses of the Accord era that see social wage advances as being a result of a (beneficent) corporatist policy framework, while reforms such as privatisation and financial re-regulation are seen as part of a (destructive) neoliberal project, obscure the internal connection between corporatism and vanguard neoliberalism in this period. This obfuscation allows authors to remove the simultaneous diminution of workers' organised power and social conditions within that project from rigorous examination. Analysis combining a Marxist critique of the nature of corporatist arrangements, with an understanding of neoliberalism as a state-led hegemonic political project of class rule, can lay the basis for theorising the exact nature of the relationship between the Accord and the vanguard phase of neoliberalism in Australia. That analysis is the focus of the rest of this chapter.

5.1 *A Brace against Neoliberalism?*

The fact that neoliberal reorganisation in Australia occurred at the same time as the Accord is not sufficient evidence to conclude that the two were internally-related aspects of state-led class rule during the Hawke and Keating governments. While there was a strong temporal overlap—and many accept some policy commonality between the Accord and vanguard neoliberalism—this book argues more strongly that there was a deeper correspondence between these projects. The concordance between the Accord and neoliberalism is not accepted in most of the scholarly literature, even that which is critical of the Accord. They are usually seen as *opposed* policy agendas, where the social contract provided a brace against (or moderation of) the advance of neoliberalism, at a time of protracted economic stagnation in which resistance to restructuring was not possible or could not realistically succeed (Ahlquist 2011; Spies-Butcher 2012). The Accord has also been seen as a framework that limited the growth of inequality compared with other nations implementing neoliberalism at the same time—in particular NZ, the US and UK (Spies-Butcher 2012; Ahlquist 2011; Langmore 2000a; Singleton 1990b).

Hampson (1997, 540) posits neoliberalism as something external or additional to the corporatist process and, in a general sense, standing opposed to it:

> The [Accord] arrangements were unstable because they imposed too much of the burden of industrial adjustment on workers, through wage restraint and work reorganisation. At the same time, the policies lifted constraints on capital, increased profits and permitted chronic misallocation of investment. They contradicted the documentary basis of … the Accord … which actually sketched a diametrically opposed policy stance, involving interventionist industry policy and economic expansion. The tensions between these policy stances undermined the democratic element in Australian corporatism, causing it to assume more and more authoritarian forms.

In this approach, corporatism and neoliberalism are seen as conflicting 'policy stances', with the latter ultimately undermining the former. Similarly, David Peetz (2013) has argued that corporatism was an alternative policy regime (and challenge) to Thatcherism, Reaganomics and Rogernomics in NZ, in that it:

> … brought about a period in which the government worked under contesting ideas. There was no uniformity of thought. When these two big ideas were in contest—market liberalism and the modified Keynesianism of the Accord—sometimes one idea won out, sometimes the other idea did.

Spies-Butcher (2012) has argued that the Accord was a process whereby different views on economic management were reconciled, in that it allowed for the interests of all parties to be protected through the collective management of the macro economy (see also earlier similar arguments by Singleton 2000; Willis and Wilson 2000). Thus collaboration combined with a realistic approach to macroeconomic management allowed the ALP to achieve 'a pragmatic accommodation between markets and equity' (Spies-Butcher 2012, 208). Such an approach frames the corporatist agreement in relatively neutral terms, despite an acknowledgement that there were negative consequences in terms of declining union strength and the failure to deliver many aspects of the agreement. While emphasising the positive outcomes of the era, the negative outcomes are relegated as second order issues on the basis that a period of crisis cannot deliver on all desires—and Spies-Butcher (2012, 222) concluded his analysis with a call for a 'new compact'.

Spies-Butcher (2012, 211) also posited that the Accord allowed the involvement of social movement actors, in particular feminists and environmentalists, in setting public policy. This interprets the process of assimilation of unions and other civil society organisations into the Accord framework optimistically, whereby:

> ... the ability to integrate social movements through collaborative and consultative processes not only helped to integrate these groups directly, but also modified the program of restructuring ... [whereas in] Britain and New Zealand Labour parties saw splits, with particularly devastating consequences in Britain due to first-past-the-post voting.
>
> ibid 2012, 211

Spies-Butcher's approach is problematic in that it presumes that disruption of politics (or at least of its left-wing variants) is always undesirable, because centre-left party stability is necessarily a defence against regressive outcomes. By way of contrast, if the Accord is understood critically as a state-led process of rule to implement the hegemonic project of the dominant class—in this instance neoliberalism—then party breakdowns in the UK and NZ are better viewed as, at the very least, a breakdown of the political structures that drove attacks on subaltern civil society groups in the vanguard neoliberal era. Spies-Butcher, in a general sense, deploys an understanding of corporatism that was criticised in Chapter 3, one which tends to presume a neutral or absent centre to the social contract framework—with the political content filled by the will of the parties. While the state is not considered neutral or passive, such analysis is silent on the question of what interests liberal corporatism serves and fails to question the design behind various Accord outcomes.

As noted, many authors favour comparing the Australian situation with NZ, arguing that the outcomes for the working class and labour movement under the NZ Labour Party were 'worse' and therefore the 'better' Australian result must be attributable to the Accord (Quiggin 1998; Castles, Gerritsen, and Vowles 1996; Ahlquist 2011). Such an approach rests on the claim that the process in NZ was less consensual and that 'a similar history and economy had given way to a much more radical experiment' with greater negative consequences (Spies-Butcher 2012, 206). Yet, as Jane Kelsey (2014) argued, the relative success of each restructuring project cannot be judged solely on the basis of how radical or extensive it was at the time, but must also consider how fully and stably neoliberalism was entrenched in each country. Kelsey (2014, 169) examined the implementation in both nations and concluded that 'Australia's consensus building pragmatism and reliance on institutions has created a more deeply embedded regime than New Zealand's' (discussed further in Chapter 9).

Another example of using international comparisons in the Accord's favour can be seen regarding the question of inequality in the Accord era, as debated in the scholarly literature (Spies-Butcher 2012; Pierson 2002, 188). Standard measures of income inequality, such as the Gini coefficient, universally show rising inequality during the Accord era, despite initial belief that it would reduce wealth disparity through redistributive measures (Leigh 2005). A 2013 report looking at long-term trends in the distribution of both income and expenditure 'found that the economy was on a steady descent towards greater inequality between 1983 and 1993' (Valenzuela, Lean, and Athanasopoulos 2014), in the period this book argues to be the vanguard stage. And it is generally accepted that Australian inequality 'declined between the 1950s and the late 1970s, before increasing again in the 1980s' in the vanguard neoliberal era (Whiteford 2014). Peter Saunders, leading expert on poverty and income distribution, argued that:

> ... income inequality increased in Australia between 1981–82 and 1989–90, whether it is measured before tax among income units or after tax among individuals, whether account is taken of differences in need or not, and whether ranking and weighting is based on individuals or income units. These results suggest that not only the distribution of income, but also the distribution of economic well-being has become less equal since 1981–82.
>
> SAUNDERS 1993, 364

In response, progressive defenders of the Accord simply claim that even if this were the case, at least inequality did not grow as fast as in other Anglophone countries such as the US, UK and NZ (Spies-Butcher 2012; Ahlquist 2011). Such a position seems manifestly insufficient and presumes that any alternate hypothetical scenario would have both mirrored those locations and led to even greater inequality.

Most analysis of the Accord also rests on the assumption that the original agreement was relatively clear, and that the program to be undertaken was transparent from the outset. However, the Accord was both imprecise and contradictory. The document failed to offer the clear alternative economic program imagined by many of its participants and, according to Beilharz (1985, 214), it is a 'masterpiece of ambiguity: it offers all things'. Therefore, arguments about the Accord often return to the question of its imputed potential, as opposed to the actuality of what occurred.

Beilharz (1985, 214) argued that very early in the Accord process many left unions believed that, although the ALP government was 'up to the same old tricks, the Accord itself offer[ed] new and real possibilities for socialist politics'. This clarifies why many involved in the Accord, or in analysing it in retrospect, are supportive of it as a political strategy—*despite* its categorical failure to deliver its core aims on wages and prices, even in the early years (Beggs 2015; Spies-Butcher 2012; Stilwell 2000). Hence, such authors are critical of the failure of the Accord to be implemented 'properly' and at the 'neoliberal' direction of government policy. They seek to separate the Accord and neoliberalism in order to emphasise the Accord as a project in competition with neoliberalism (or, at the very least, *potentially* opposed to it). An emphasis on potentiality is particularly problematic given that left unions were seeking a 'grand change' in macroeconomic terms, and given they were willing to set aside previous modes of relating to both ALP and conservative governments.

It has become clear, subsequently, that the left unions had no strategy for how to proceed once the ALP was in government and failing to implement the agreement. The Accord's sanctioning by the left unions, in particular the powerful and large AMWU, was a necessity for the Accord to proceed. Yet implementing the social contract meant these militant unions had to first 'give up' the very strategy that had allowed them to obtain a powerful enough bargaining position to be included in such an agreement. Union militancy, and the strong civil society workers' organisations it helped to build, meant the ALP needed the Accord to deal with the unions in a very direct manner, but the Accord itself forbade the unions using that weapon once they were in that position. In light of the rise of neoliberalism, this throws emphasis back on the impasse of the left within the Accord process and draws emphasis away from portraying it as simply a victim of the strength of the New Right.

This focus on the New Right threat has held back analysis of why the Accord process turned out the way it did. For example, Hampson (1997), whose work is on the whole extremely perceptive about the process and content of the Accord, failed to interrogate the assumptions behind corporatist frameworks as they relate to the advance of vanguard neoliberalism. Hampson (1997, 562) stated:

> Australia's version of corporatism was from the outset impaled on the contradiction between an economic liberal approach to policy and the interests of its own constituency. The union leadership could not

> enforce policies which better reflected union interests, and did not resolve the contradiction by ending the Accord, for reasons that remain to be analysed fully. This necessarily caused the nature of the corporatism to become increasingly less democratic and more authoritarian.

While Hampson identified that the Accord failed, he did not see this as a problem arising from corporatist agreements in general. Rather, he posited the problem as the Australian social contract being in competition with the advance of an 'economic liberal' framework—in other words, neoliberalism. Such analysis, although critical of the Accord's outcomes, is silent on the class nature of corporatism and instead attributes the failures of the Accord process and the associated rise of neoliberalism to various factors external to the Accord itself—be they international (eg. the global economy) or domestic (eg. parties or sections of the state being won over to neoliberal policies).

5.2 *Theorising the Corporatism–neoliberalism Connection*

The Accord framework was responsible for key changes to union structures and activity, which allowed various political and economic objectives of the period to be pursued in a manner that systematically favoured capital (discussed in the next chapter). Neoliberalisation in Australia—the ongoing political project of social and economic transformation through various stages of the periodisation in this book—was only possible after a curtailing of union power and working class resistance in the vanguard phase. This weakening of the power of labour was necessary for a medium-term project of restructuring, and the Accord was the central strategic plank towards this objective. That the process in Australia was mainly consensual—involving the agreement of the unions from the start—was secondary to the effect of the process, and should not divert attention from its intention to effect labour disorganisation, in keeping with neoliberal restructuring elsewhere.

Marxists have usefully—despite employing differing emphases—analysed neoliberalism as a form of, and/or process of, class rule (Davidson 2013; Saad-Filho 2010; Duménil and Lévy 2012; Harvey 2005; Albo 2002). This appreciation of the class nature of neoliberalism has also been used to analyse Australia, where it was seen as the triumph of the interests of the capitalist class over those of the labour movement and the working class (Bramble 2014; Bramble and Kuhn 2011; Cottle and Collins 2008; Lavelle 2005). Nevertheless, while some of the Marxist scholars examining Australia have contradicted mainstream claims of the Accord and neoliberalism being at odds with each other, arguing that the Accord helped facilitate the introduction of neoliberalism by curtailing union strength, certain questions remain insufficiently explored.

The social content of corporatism is rarely considered in the Marxist literature. Despite Panitch's development of a sophisticated critique of corporatism as a political project oriented on increasing labour exploitation, no radical or Marxist analysis of the Australian case has interrogated the character of corporatism in this way—instead focusing on more general and timeless questions as to the nature of the trade union bureaucracy and labourism. While those issues are important, they cannot explain why corporatism was the method of crisis management at that particular time. This failure also means the claim in the scholarly literature that the Accord was a consensual process has remained mostly unproblematised in the Marxist literature. Further, Marxist accounts have generally seen the defeat of the working class in the Accord period as the product of a process of class struggle and so cannot satisfactorily answer the question of why workers and their organisations participated (sometimes actively and enthusiastically) in that process. Following from this, Marxist analysis has generally failed to consider how the Accord formed part of a very specific moment of class rule within the neoliberal project. This is despite authors being explicit about corporatism and neoliberal structural adjustment occurring simultaneously. The pursuit of the Accord by the labour leadership thus tends to be viewed somewhat ahistorically.

For Bramble and Kuhn (2011, 105–110), the pursuit of the Accord as a strategy by union officials was a logical consequence of the social position of those officials in society, as mediators between capital and labour (including their influence over union delegates) and as a result of the ties between the unions and the ALP (including the labour movement's nationalism). While the role of union officials is an important component of the story and can assist us in understanding part of the dynamic, an approach that also focuses on the interconnection between the social contract and neoliberalism can better account for why both were successfully implemented *at that particular time* and *in that manner*. This then facilitates a clearer appreciation of how the labour movement was incorporated into a project of capitalist restructuring and increased exploitation so soon after one of its most militant phases.

Such a reappraisal of the Accord must be embedded in a materialist analysis that considers the nature of corporatism as framed in Chapter 3, so as to better understand the social interests behind the process and how it was ultimately tied closely to the advance of neoliberalism. In a situation of industrial militancy and severe weakness in the economy, the ALP utilised its integrative role within the Australian political system. While Labor did seek to protect working class living standards to an extent—and ALP politicians firmly believed they had the interests of all Australians at heart—this was within a framework of strengthening the national economy and the position of capital. The ALP's integrative role was connected to labourism's focus on the nation state as the site of political activity in the pursuit of social change.

The specific aim of the Accord was, as was the case with the earlier UK social contract:

> ... to infuse the working class with national consideration at that level where economic class considerations had persisted most stubbornly—at the level of trade union wage bargaining.
>
> PANITCH 1976, 5

In order to undertake significant restructuring of the economy, the government needed to project a national interest and the Accord was central to that mission. The corporatist agreement re-enveloped the unions under the direction of the ALP in government (therefore within the parameters of the capitalist state) and thus underpinned the advance of the vanguard phase of neoliberalism. Implicit in the framing of the social contract—and explicit in its implementation—was an effort to increase the exploitation of labour in order to address stagnant accumulation and recurrent crises. Over time, this purpose above all others came to the fore.

In Australia, it was in the deepening of corporatism, through the Accord, that the neoliberal political project advanced. Corporatism and neoliberalism were interconnected and mutually supporting elements of class rule. When corporatism is understood as a (ruling) class project of incorporation and subordination of the working class, via its labour movement structures and ties, then the apparent tension between a social contract and the neoliberal project dissolves in terms of its potential and actual outcomes. As will be seen in discussion of the concept of the informal Accord below, neoliberalism is best understood as emerging through the explicit parameters of the Accord in a *coterminal* relationship.

5.3 *An 'Informal Accord'?*

Why did the unions remain part of the Accord process after it was clear that the agreement was not going to be implemented? Most commentators have argued that union leaders and their rank and file calculated—rightly or wrongly—that the benefits of the agreement outweighed its costs. Some Marxists posit, however, that there was a more specific dynamic involved, where the trade union leadership tied the labour movement into the priorities of the government through an 'informal Accord'. Bramble and Kuhn (1999), followed later by Cahill (2008), developed and elaborated the concept of the informal Accord. They argued that the formal Accord (the provisions set out in the social contract) was supplemented by an ongoing commitment by the unions that the ALP should govern regardless of whether the formal agreement was implemented as initially intended. The informal Accord was thus an effort 'to manage the neo-liberal transformation of state and economy by tying the leadership of the labour movement to this process' (Cahill 2008, 326).

Such a framework has the strength of rejecting attempts to portray the social contract and neoliberal transformation as counterposed. Rather, the informal Accord allowed the introduction of neoliberalism because it meant that the unions were willing to compromise significantly their own political and economic objectives, to ensure 'their' government remained in power. In the words of Accord architect, Bill Kelty, the:

> ... Accord was at one end of the spectrum simply an expression of support for the Labor Party to govern. At the other end of the spectrum it was a working partnership.
>
> Cited in CAHILL 2008, 326

The informal Accord framework helps to clarify why the ACTU (and even some more radical unions) continued to support the ALP despite their concern at the direction of government policy. The framework logically implies that the arrangement helped facilitate the introduction of neoliberalism, by dulling dissent and providing support for the ALP government. However, framing the connection between the Accord and neoliberal economic transformation in terms of an informal arrangement implies there was something outside the formal agreement—a hidden centre—that was essential to the relationship between corporatism and vanguard neoliberalism. Yet the central motivation and key achievement of the Accord was its agenda of wage restraint and suppression of militancy. These primary objectives, of increasing the rate of exploitation and quashing industrial struggle to resolve problems of capital accumulation, also sit at the heart of neoliberalism. It is not that neoliberalism was possible because of an informal agreement to allow the ALP to do it, but because increasing the rate of exploitation and suppressing labour movement militancy were core objectives of *both* the corporatist and neoliberal projects. The notion of an informal Accord can, therefore, risk diverting analytical attention from the very direct way in which neoliberalism was implemented through the Accord.

The formal aspects of the Accord provided a set of political structures tying labour to the state, allowing informal understandings about the survival of the ALP government to have the importance they did. This integration of labour was mediated by the participation of trade union officials and activists operating in a set of highly-organised, institutionalised, state-centric political relationships with representatives of political society, the state bureaucracy and business elites. The unions supported 'their' ALP governments before and after the Accord, but in no other situation were the stakes involved in maintaining or withdrawing support so high. This is because in no other situation did the unions find themselves tied so directly to the inner workings of the government and its political-economic reform program. As highlighted in Chapter 3, such a process raises 'the basic dilemma of corporatism—coercion in the name of harmony' (Panitch 1976, 247). The formality of the corporatist agreement, about which Panitch theorises in general, was therefore crucial to the specific success of the vanguard phase of neoliberalism in Australia. The ability of the ALP to introduce neoliberal reform was a direct result of the formal components of the agreement, especially the inclusion of the unions within state processes and structures.

Although the concept of the informal Accord provides a way to consider how elements outside the formal Accord statement might be relevant, understanding the direct relationship between the formal Accord and neoliberalism as coterminal has greater explanatory power.

5.4 *The Accord as* Involucro

Chapter 2 drew on the work of Marx and Gramsci on the state in order to explore the relationship between the state and civil society, while Chapter 3 drew on Leo Panitch's class-based critique of corporatism. It is now possible to theorise that the Accord was the high point of successful integration of civil society into a new state-led political project amid the economic turmoil following the end of the post-war boom. This enwrapment of civil society by the state tied the labour movement into the process of economic restructuring and, unlike the UK example, the social contract did not result in the rank and file of the labour movement pushing back against the union hierarchy and forcing the agreement's breakdown. The remainder of this section will attempt to theorise the concord between the corporatist and neoliberal projects—described and analysed above—utilising Gramsci's concept of the integral state.

Summarising the argument to this point, Gramsci developed a particular understanding of the relationship between the social and political spheres in modern capitalism, especially the enwrapment of civil society by the state. The integral state—'conceived of as a dialectical unity of civil society and political society' (Thomas 2009a, 29)—'presents the image of "political society" as a "container" of civil society, surrounding or enmeshing and fundamentally reshaping it' (Thomas 2009b, 189). This concentrates attention on how civil society becomes incorporated into processes of political class rule. Panitch's framework for understanding corporatism stressed its nature as a class project, with the objective at the centre of the Accord being the suppression of wages and labour movement activity in the midst of economic crisis. Understanding the Accord in this way cuts through the mainstream narrative that the Accord was a consensual project in the interest of all, positing instead that corporatism involved the translation of 'working class loyalty to its party [and unions] into loyalty to the nation' (Panitch 1976, 247).

The Accord was the high point of such efforts at corporatist integration and provided the framework for the simultaneous advance of neoliberalism in Australia. This process substituted a project of national interest for the particular interests of the unions or their members and drew a militant labour movement inside the state's project—enwrapping its interests with those of the dominant class. Although political responses to the crises and contradictions afflicting Australian society in the 1970s and early 1980s came both 'from above' and 'from below', the latter responses ended up integrating subaltern groups into state imperatives—regardless of the fact that those imperatives directly undermined those groups' social interests.

The state does not simply rule coercively through the parliament, legislature, military and police, but through a process of hegemony. Thus, the state must be understood, according to Gramsci (2011b; Q6 §155), in its 'full sense: dictatorship + hegemony'. The integral state is, in this understanding:

> ... a network of social relations for the production of consent, for the integration of the subaltern classes into the expansive project of historical development of the leading social group.
>
> THOMAS 2009: 143

Because the capitalist class does not rule directly, but through a political state separate to the social existence of its members, it is this state and the political society around it that intergrates civil society groups into a wider project to maintain capitalist domination.

Gramsci's heuristic helps to delineate the changing relations between state, political society and civil society in the Accord era. Changes in the political economy were facilitated by the Accord, via the leading role of the state, with a Labor government in power. It was through the Accord process that the neoliberal political project transformed civil society, including the economy, with the labour movement acting as the ultimate tool of macroeconomic policy by voluntarily acceding to an increased rate of exploitation in the form of wage suppression. This was a process of political society enwrapping civil society, in order to enable neoliberal transformation. As highlighted in opening this chapter, Gramsci (1995, 167; Q10II §15) explained that:

> Between the economic structure and the state with its legislation and its coercion stands civil society, and it is this latter which has to be radically transformed, in concrete terms and not just as it appears in statutes and learned books. The state is the instrument for bringing civil society into line with the economic structure, but the state has to 'want' to do that....

While Gramsci was talking about periods of active or passive revolution in an epoch of early capitalist modernisation—and not simply any period of capitalist restructuring—it is not a large step to suggest that, even once capitalism is established, the state continues to operate in this way, with political society (through the state) concretely transforming civil society. This is clear in the neoliberal period in Australia, where the state sought to reincorporate the union movement into a stable mode of rule after the Fraser years. As discussed in Chapter 2, the Australian labour movement was heavily enmeshed in the state through the process of centralised arbitration from early in the 20th century. However, a consequence of both the dismissal of the Whitlam Government and the open industrial and political conflict of the Fraser years, was the effective partial exclusion of the labour movement from its privileged political position within statal structures and processes.

The social contract was a way to ensure that the labour movement could once again be an allied subaltern group in the bourgeoisie's political dominance over the working class, via the nation state and its associated political class. That is, workers and unions could 'once again' be incorporated into the normal patterns of governance after a period of being somewhat outside these and in direct conflict with Fraser, who was therefore unable to pull the unions into any attempt at reform. As argued in the periodisation laid out in Chapter 5, moves towards a neoliberal trajectory could not become hegemonic in the Fraser years and it took the re-incorporation of the union movement through the Accord for this to become possible.

The Accord's success as a process of assimilation is evidenced by the fact trade unions did not break with the social contract. Nor did the rank and file of the trade union movement effectively push back against the union officials centrally facilitating the agreement. On the basis of this dynamic, the Accord cannot be separated from its neoliberal 'other'. Rather, the stability of the Accord was central to the ALP Government's successful neoliberal restructuring of Australian society.

6 Conclusion

As this chapter has described, the Accord and neoliberalism have mostly been analysed as separate phenomena in the scholarly literature—including by most Marxist writers. Such an approach obfuscates the conscious direction of the ALP and the unions at the time, especially the failure of the left unions to offer an independent political strategy to protect the interests of labour once the unions were tied into the state project. Not only did unions fail to break with the Accord when it was not implemented, but many union officials were incorporated further into the state's strategies around reviving accumulation and 'modernising' the Australian economy. The 'molecular transformation' of CPA-aligned officials was particularly stark (and is considered in the next chapter), in that they shifted from arguing that the Accord would be a pathway to socialism to defending its most regressive aspects—including declining real wages—on the basis of the national interest.

This chapter and the last focused on how various Accord elements were implemented, and concluded that they are best understood as part of a process incorporating the labour movement into the state's priorities around economic restructuring and suppression of labour interests. The Accord was fashioned and reshaped over time to facilitate this structural adjustment. Importantly, the Accord also facilitated the enwrapment of civil society by political society and the state, in order to ensure particular policy ends could be achieved. The policy process and economic restructuring under the Hawke-Keating governments were the result of the Accord being coterminal with the implementation of vanguard neoliberalism, in a process of *simultaneously deepening corporatism and advancing neoliberalism.*

In the following chapter, this line of inquiry is continued, although the focus shifts to explore how the labour movement's participation in the Accord led it to: manage internal dissent; disorganise union structures; assist industrial restructuring; and eventually dismantle the central tenets of the centralised wage-fixing system. These changes force consideration of the Accord as a project of concurrent incorporation and destabilisation, with the subordination of workers' social interests to the revival of capital accumulation leading also to the hollowing out of the powerful union organisations that provided the Accord with its main lever to drive down wages.

CHAPTER 8

How Labour Made Neoliberalism

> Government by consent of the governed, but an organised consent, not the vague and generic kind which is declared at the time of elections: the state has and demands consent, but it also 'educates' this consent through political and trade-union associations which, however, are private organisms, left to the private initiative of the ruling class.
>
> ANTONIO GRAMSCI, *The Prison Notebooks*, Q1 §47

1 Introduction

Approaches that posit the Accord as exogenous to neoliberalism can shield from close examination the labour movement's role in political-economic transformation. This method limits understanding of both the Accord process and its connection to the neoliberal project, as well as the reasons for the labour movement's difficulties in the decades following the end of the social contract. This chapter demonstrates how the labour movement helped to build neoliberalism in Australia. It concludes the argument of how the construction of Australian neoliberalism diverged from the dominant narrative of neoliberalism's advance globally—an account that emphasises the role of a coercive state and the agenda of the New Right. The chapter casts the labour movement as not just an object of neoliberal change, but an active constructor.

The last two chapters have detailed empirically the regressive (anti-working class) nature of both the Accord and neoliberalism, as parts of a hegemonic political project carried out by the 1983–1996 ALP Government. This chapter furthers that analysis, by detailing the manner in which the institutions of labour actively constructed aspects of neoliberalism and thereby played a role in disorganising their own social power. This incorporation is understood not in a passive sense, but as an organised consent directly involving the unions in the building of a new hegemonic project. I also continue an elaboration and reinterpretation of Gramsci's concepts of hegemony and the integral state, and considers how these have applicability (or otherwise) beyond Gramsci's original work.

The first section analyses the move from workplace-based union organising to the centralised Accord. It argues that the growing belief that central planning offered the greatest chance of resolving the economic crisis in the interests of the labour movement was central to cohering the Accord. In order to be successful, the Accord also needed to bring key militant unions inside

 | DOI:10.1163/9789004383463_009

its framework. For this reason, analysis focuses on the drawing into the social contract of the largest union at that time—the AMWU—through the augmentation of industry policy within the agreement (E. Jones 1997, 20). This section also analyses the development and implementation of *Australia Reconstructed*, an initiative begun in 1986 to extend the corporatism of the Accord 'against' the neoliberal trajectory of the Hawke Government.

The second section considers the suppression of industrial struggle, particularly the roles of the ACTU and labour movement in policing unions that sought to go outside the Accord's 'no further claims' framework. The analysis also explores early attempts by dissident unions to seek wage increases outside the Accord—focusing on disputes at the Mudginberri meatworks (1983–1985) and Dollar Sweets (1985)—and the use of civil legal action by the New Right to undermine these struggles. The section analyses the successful deregistration of the radical Builders Labourers' Federation (BLF) in 1986, which nominally occurred over corruption. It also details the 1989 pilots' dispute, which resulted in the ALP government using the military as strikebreakers. The book argues that the suppression of industrial struggle under the banner of the Accord, in part through these confrontations, was central to how the social contract disorganised the working class and trade union movement.

The third section explores the implementation of enterprise bargaining, and thus a re-regulated industrial relations system that undermined centralised bargaining, as an outcome actively sought by the labour movement. This ended the historically centralised wage determination system in Australia. The analysis of enterprise bargaining underlines the argument that the Accord was highly successful in disorganising labour, and in preventing the labour movement from exercising its own social weight—a social weight that had earlier required the Accord to be established. The section explores some of the contradictions of the Accord, in particular how the process hollowed out the social weight of the ALP and the trade unions. It considers Gramsci's concepts of hegemony and the integral state in relation to these antinomies. The analysis asks whether the concept of the integral state has been increasingly historically demarcated because hegemony—of the sort Gramsci describes as organised and occurring through civil society organisations—has been undermined by changes in civil society since the end of the long boom.

2 From Worker Agency to State Agency

The Accord was a consensual project that brought about a shift in the locus of labour organisation from one level to another, with profound implications. Labour organising moved from the level of workplaces and rank-and-file workers to that of high-level negotiations and central planning. While worker agency had been central to the labour movement's gains in the long boom and, partially, in the decade after the boom ended, the shift to state agency from 1983 delivered a sharp curtailment of labour's interests.

The failure of the left unions' strategy of industrial militancy and mobilisation to resolve the crisis in favour of labour (in the 1970s and early 1980s), resulted in these unions seeking a political solution through central state planning, and, thus, being brought inside the state and political society. The role of the AMWU in the Accord process demonstrates how the social contract incorporated a militant union into the new political project centred on reviving accumulation and 'modernising' the Australian economy. Central to neoliberal restructuring was the participation of unions in industry structural adjustment and efforts to increase productivity, which proceeded alongside the attempted reorienting of the Accord in the 1986–1987 *Australia Reconstructed* initiative. The shift from a workplace-focused strategy to a corporatist one facilitated the enwrapment of labour and the trade union leadership by political society and its priorities.

2.1 *The Shift to Support the Accord*

For the Accord to be agreed to, the left and CPA-aligned unions had to be brought inside the social contract. And for the Accord to be successful, it had to suppress the industrial action of unions characterised by militancy throughout the 1970s and early 1980s. Bringing militant unions inside the Accord required a significant shift in the manner in which these unions approached labour organising; but once inside the Accord, a further shift took place as the union leadership was enwrapped by political society. These shifts represented both an evolution from what came before and a substantial break in the wake of the 1982 recession.

As mentioned previously, the AMWU was the largest and most powerful trade union in Australia, with the fitter's wage rate in the metals industry acting as the benchmark in arbitration of award (wage and condition) rates (G. Campbell 2000; E. Jones 1997, 18–20). The AMWU was at the leading edge of industrial struggle, with the gains it made in shop floor industrial action often flowing onto other segments of the working class. The consent of the AMWU for a social contract was key to ensuring the establishment and implementation of the Accord. As such, analysis of the AMWU provides 'a window on the transformation of the union movement itself over a period of quite pivotal change in Australian labour history' (Scalmer and Irving 1999, 65). Without the sanction and ongoing support of the AMWU over the Accord era, the social contract could not have been cohered (W. Higgins 1987, 221; Singleton 1990b, 61). This shift in the AMWU's approach, from a strategy of rank-and-file mobilisation to a centralised corporatist agreement, was pivotal.

In the early 1970s, the AMWU achieved increased real wages through industrial action (Balnave and Patmore 2013, 25) and this contributed to an increased wage share of national income (Bramble 2001, 8). The AMWU industrial approach, based around 'hot shops', saw campaigns mounted at the best-organised sites with a 'trickle down' effect to the rest of the industry (Bramble 2001, 11). The AMWU was not the only union involved in militant action at this time, and total strike days hit a number of historical peaks in the period from 1973 to 1981 (see Figure 8.1). In the early 1980s the union led a national push for 35-hour working week agreements in large parts of the metals industry (Kahn 1981), and achieved 'a 38-hour week and a $39 per week increase in wages' (Balnave and Patmore 2013, 25). The reduced working week agreements were struck in the midst of the resources boom of the Fraser years (E. Jones 1997, 18).

This militant strategy was undermined from the mid-1970s onwards by recessions—but most particularly by the recessions of the early 1980s—which, up to that time, led to 'the worst labour market conditions since the Depression' (Beggs 2015, 260). The collapse of a short-lived, mining-led economic recovery in 1981 had a dramatic impact on the working class, shifting the AMWU and other CPA-aligned unions behind the Accord for a number of reasons:

1. Mass sackings in manufacturing increasingly undermined the confidence of the union leadership that it could fight at the rank-and-file level, so its focus shifted to the central and national level.
2. There was a significant reassessment of strategy, given the failure of militancy to either beat Fraser decisively or resolve the crisis in the interests of workers. As a result, the union leadership increasingly accepted the

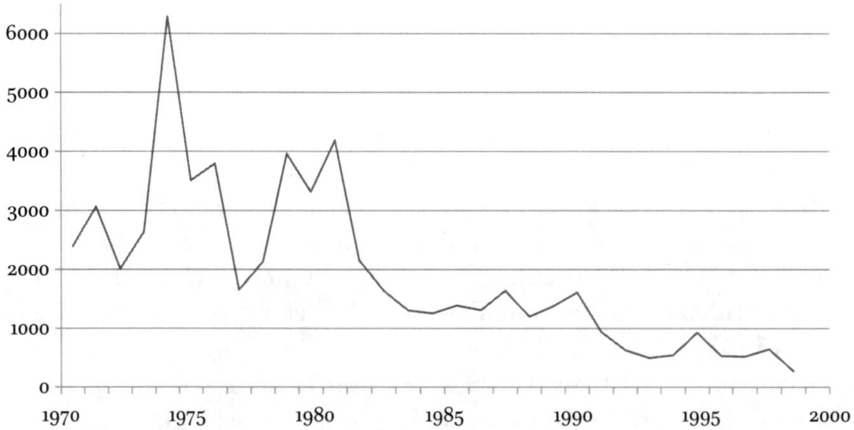

FIGURE 8.1 Number of strike days (000s) in Australia, 1970–2000.
Source: ABS

relevance of indexation as a way to address inflation, encourage growth and increase employment.

3. The leadership increasingly supported improving the efficiency of manufacturing and business competitiveness, in the belief that it would ensure growth and protect or expand employment for members. Union leaders ultimately posited that this would be delivered through the social contract's industry policy.
4. The growing number of unemployed workers (both inside and outside the ranks of the AMWU) drove concern about the inadequacies of welfare state provisions in a high inflation environment. Thus, the social wage had increasing importance for the union's leadership in a period of high unemployment (Bramble 2001, 8; Singleton 1990b, 83).

Australian manufacturing suffered the brunt of the economic collapse in the early 1980s. The 'recession of 1981 destroyed 80,000 jobs in metal manufacturing [but] the upturn later that year and into 1982 restored only 35,000 of them' (Halfpenny 1984a, 3). When the economy collapsed again in 1982, shedding further positions—including 100,000 in the metals and engineering sector alone—it forced the AMWU to significantly rethink its strategy (E. Jones 1997, 18–19). The union leadership believed it could not win back the lost jobs without a coordinated plan across the industry, and that an expanded social wage—including an increase to the level of unemployment benefits—was necessary in the context of escalating job losses. This was the crucial background for the AMWU's decision to support a social contract. This context, moreover, resulted in the social wage gaining an importance it had not enjoyed historically, given the Australia welfare state had been traditionally constructed around the level and conditions of the male wage and full employment. These economic factors occurred alongside a more contingent reason for the shift in the AMWU, involving the impasse of the militant strategy under Fraser and the lack of an alternative approach in that context (Humphrys 2014).

Sean Scalmer and Terry Irving (1999) argued that the CPA-aligned unions were reshaped in more subtle and gradual ways through the 1960s and 1970s, and that this helped to facilitate the more major shift in orientation from the level of the workplace to that of the state through the Accord in the early 1980s. Scalmer and Irving outlined that the number of intellectuals working in the labour movement during the 1960s, usually employed as union researchers, grew significantly. Whitlam's election in 1972 drove attempts to remake the unions in the image of an increasingly technocratic and 'modernised' Labor Party (ibid 1999, 65). The state, under the ALP's auspices, began allocating substantial resources to the union movement to engage in education and to promote 'good industrial relations' (ibid 1999, 65). Under Whitlam the ALP also proposed tripartite (government–business–union) bodies and promoted union structures that were engaged in long-term planning. However, although the AMWU led the way in terms of the expansion of paid union intellectuals, the CPA unions resisted the broader agenda to promote 'good industrial relations' and argued it was problematic when counterposed to union members' self-activity. The CPA unions promoted, instead, 'the expert intellectual as part of an activist "modern union"' (ibid 1999, 65). The CPA vision involved several strategies: a) the formation of industry unions; b) a rejection of arbitration alongside promotion of collective bargaining and industrial action; c) conscious action in response to changes in technology; d) building of union education and research capacities; and e) increased role for the rank and file and the promotion of shop committees (ibid 1999, 65). The original purpose of intellectual projects within the unions was to support rank-and-file activity, so that members could operate effectively in campaigns within their industry.

The growth in size of the union bureaucracy in this period increasingly gave the trade union leadership a base from which to organise union members, in directions it preferred. This later assisted a reorientation from the workplace to the state through the Accord. While union leaders are always in a position of authority, in this period—despite the context of widespread militancy—the union bureaucracy had increasing access to information and resources to sharpen that influence. For example, a '1979 study of meetings in two major unions covering building and metal workers showed that not only did most initiatives come from full-timers, but so did even a sizable proportion of opposing remarks' (Frenkel and Coolican 1983, 168). The expansion of full time staff and union officials altered the way in which unions worked, including the role of rank-and-file workers, in complex (and not always positive) ways.

In order to enter the Accord, the AMWU shifted from being a union with intellectual resources focused on operating relatively independently of political society and the state—strategically using those resources to encourage greater activity of the rank and file and shop committees. The AMWU reconstituted as an organisation that devoted its resources and intellectual capacities to an alliance with a Labor Government—a decision that abnegated those democratic and mobilisational features (Scalmer and Irving 1999). Bramble (2000b, 179) described this change quite directly, stating the AMWU moved from 'being a byword for industrial activism in the late 1960s and early 1970s' to, by the end of the Hawke-Keating era, being 'a mainstream supporter of the ALP establishment [with] its formerly extensive and militant shop steward networks [having] undergone severe corrosion'. The transformation of the AMWU was profound, both structurally and in terms of the political outlook of its leadership.

2.2 *Planning as a Solution to Crisis?*

As the economic crisis persisted throughout the 1970s, the left unions argued state planning was needed to resolve Australia's problems. It was not simply that the industrially weaker unions were looking to the state to resolve the impact of the crisis on their members, but that industrially militant unions increasingly looked to various European countries for models of corporatist alternative economic programs to be implemented by the state (W. Higgins 1980; Kuhn 1986). As mentioned in Chapter 5, various union and ALP members visited Europe to examine planning models and in 1977 the AMWU brought Stuart Holland, author of *The Socialist Challenge* (1975), to Australia (AMWSU 1978). The AMWU leadership had been persuaded by his work—as well as that of intellectuals in the trade union movement, ALP and academia—that the only defence against the ideas of the New Right was a centralised national response in the form of an alternative economic strategy (Langmore 1982; Stilwell 1982).

In the late 1970s and early 1980s, a number of AMWU publications attacked the Fraser government's handling of the crisis and elaborated an alternate economic strategy (Beilharz 1994, 112). The union published *The People's Budget* (AMWSU 1977a), *Australia Up-Rooted* (AMWSU 1977b), *Australia Ripped Off* (AMWSU 1979), and *Australia on the Rack* (AMWSU 1982). These documents provided detailed facts on the state of the economy, emphasising the impact of the crisis and government policy on working people. They highlighted how business was making significant profits in the midst of the crisis, and criticised increasing attacks on labour movement organising. In *Australia Up-Rooted*, the AMWU leadership argued that planning at both the individual firm level and centrally via the state was the only solution to protracted economic stagnation. Similarly, at an ACTU Conference on the Manufacturing Industry in 1978, ACTU Senior Vice-President Cliff Dolan argued in favour of increased state planning involving the unions and criticised both the Fraser and Whitlam Governments for their *ad hoc* approach to the crisis. He stated:

> ... we must include our Labor colleagues in the period 1972–75 in that sort of ad hocery [because of the decision taken] in July 1973 to reduce tariffs by 25 percent across the board. The ACTU Congress has established economic policy, and part of that policy relates to real economic planning over a period of time.
>
> DOLAN and CARMICHAEL 1978

Over time, key militant unions came to accept the argument that the 'old' approach of industrial struggle contributed to social division and price inflation driven by wage pressures, and that there was a shared national interest in managing the crisis cooperatively. The AMWU was, at the same time, shifting from an approach of intervention at the workshop level (a strategy that sought to increase industrial democracy and worker control) to one centred on industry development and tripartite planning at the national level (Scalmer and Irving 1999, 71–74). In a draft paper entitled *A Strategy for the 1980s in the Metal Industry* (1982), published by metal worker members of the CPA, union activists welcomed the possibility of an Accord with an incoming ALP government (Balnave and Patmore 2013, 26). At the 1982 AMWU National Conference, the shift was clear in newly adopted policies stating that:

> Industry plans formed through consultation between capital, labour and the State at a national level, rather than independent union intervention at a workplace level, [were] now the union's primary focus. Rather than workplace intervention being used as a lever to shape investment decisions, it was now quarantined in a separate policy with a reduced focus.
> SCALMER and IRVING 1999, 74

The 'national interest' became progressively more central to the outlook of the labour movement. The focus on planning as a solution to crisis provided fertile ground for those who argued for the Accord, positing it as an alternative economic regime to that embodied in New Right governments in the US and UK. Centralised planning in the national interest was the rhetorical gel that allowed the ALP and a diverse group of unions to develop the social contract.

2.3 *Consultation on, and Support for, the Accord*

The Accord statement was negotiated at a senior level within the labour movement and not through a wider process of open input from unions and their members. Once the document was finalised, there was little consultation with the labour movement prior to its adoption by the ACTU. Jenny Haines, a delegate from the nurses' union in NSW, the single person to vote against the Accord at the 1982 ACTU Special Congress, advised that the only consultation of which she was aware occurred within and between the right and left factions of the Labor Party[1] (Haines 2014). Some senior union officials also expressed frustration about the lack of consultation, with a member of the Western Australian Trades and Labour Council stating that he was asked to adopt the document prior to viewing a final draft (Thompson 1984, 8).

---

1 ALP factions are present not only in the Party, but also within trade unions, many of which are formally affiliated to the ALP.

However, despite the lack of consultation over the specific Accord terms, social contracts were extensively canvassed in the ACTU and unions at a general level from the late 1970s. The 1979 national ALP conference (at which ALP-affiliated unions voted and shaped motions) floated an incomes policy as an alternative anti-inflation policy to the Fraser approach (Ewer, Higgins, and Stephens 1987, 87). By 1981, a national ACTU congress had voted to support an incomes policy under a future Labor government (Bramble and Kuhn 2011, 102) and other key provisions of the Accord were discussed at various times. Mass meetings of the AMWU adopted 'no further claims' provisions limiting industrial activity in the 1981 metals industry agreement, even though such clauses had been continually rejected at AMWU conferences throughout the 1970s. By late 1982, over one million workers were covered by some form of 'no extra claims' provision (Strauss 2013, 52)—and this prepared the ground for the elements of the Accord that suppressed industrial activity. Further, some workplaces debated the Accord after it was endorsed by the ACTU. There was majority support for the Accord at meetings of Victorian railway shunters and Ford Broadmeadows factory delegates in 1983—the latter 'proclaimed "full support" for the government's project of economic recovery through shared responsibility' (ibid 2013, 52).

The AMWU played an important role in winning support for the Accord within rank-and-file networks, both within and outside its ranks. In Victoria, just prior to the 1983 federal election, it organised education sessions on the Accord in local areas. These were pitched internally as well as at members of other unions and their spouses (AMFSU 1983b). The union's Victorian Special Education Sub-Committee proposed a number of topics for study circles including: the Fraser wages freeze; 'the contending forces amongst employers and the Fraser Government'; the role of protection and tariffs; what incomes policy is and is not; and the experience and history of previous wage and price freezes (AMFSU 1983b). The union also printed and distributed copies of the Accord within the labour movement and, after the ALP was elected, distributed speakers' notes to assist with prosecuting arguments in support of it (Halfpenny 1983). In this way, it was the union movement's 'left leaders [from the AMWU and BWIU in particular] who, with the help of an ideological framework supplied by the CPA, did most to win support for the Accord among worker militants' (Bramble and Kuhn 2011, 102).

Support for the Accord among unions was not universal, however, with various state branches of left unions opposing it and small numbers of workers publicly campaigning against it (Rizzo 1991; Strauss 2013). However, dissent was among a minority of workers who were disconnected from each other, and unable to alter the direction of the union movement away from supporting the social contract.

2.4 *Sticking with the Accord*

As noted in the previous chapter, when the Accord was introduced and major components were not implemented, concerns were predominantly expressed privately or in a limited way. The AMWU expressed concerns that the ALP was 'playing down the agreed role of government intervention in market forces' and had reduced the role of the Economic Planning Advisory Council (EPAC)—'from one of direct participation in the economy to that of long-term planning'—but these concerns were kept under a lid (Stewart 1985, 30). The Victorian Branch of the AMWU internally criticised the Economic Summit for parting ways with the letter of the Accord (AMFSU 1983c, 7) and, as early as June 1983, the AMWU reported 'lack of enthusiasm' on the part of the new ALP government for industry policy (AMFSU 1983d, 8). Token efforts at mobilising the AMWU membership around Accord issues—such as the August 1983 wage case when the AMWU organised 200 shop stewards and job delegates to attend the court—were short-lived (AMFSU 1983e, 8). Similarly, although Norm Gallagher, Federal Secretary of the BLF, 'circulated a speech at the April 1983 Economic Summit which was critical of the Accord, [he] did not speak against it at any public forum or at the Summit itself' (Bramble 2000a, 248).

The AMWU did make threats to break with the Accord or to take action against capital to ensure workers did not bear the brunt of austerity, if the agreement was not implemented. Halfpenny stated that there was a:

> … conflict between the insistence that the price workers get [i.e. wages] is to be restrained by a variety of enforcement mechanisms including the Arbitration Commission, yet there is no similar mechanism to ensure that the corporate sector exercise restraint. [However] the existence of this conflict or contradiction need not be damaging to the Accord providing the Trade Union Movement is prepared and able to force restraint onto the corporate sector.
>
> HALFPENNY 1984b, 6–7

But a mobilisation to impose the labour movement's interests—or simply the agreed terms of the Accord—on capital or on the state, never eventuated. This was not simply a result of the context of the economic crisis, but because there was an impasse of left strategy in terms of defining an alternative project to the social contract—which was increasingly apparent as the full Accord failed to be delivered. Thus, despite union protestations about the implementation of the Accord, and in particular industry policy, Jones (1997, 22) has pointed out that the ALP 'never had any intention of taking seriously the underlying spirit of the industry policy section of the Accord'. Many of the Accord's components, such as industry policy and full wage indexation, were viewed simply as a mechanism for drawing the unions inside the Accord process and keeping them there.

In the first few years of the agreement, the trade union leadership was increasingly being drawn inside the corporatist project and tied to the state. The shift to the agency of the state was accompanied by a strengthening of the leadership of trade unions, at the expense of the rank and file. There was a social interest for the trade union leadership in maintaining the Accord, even after it was clear that economic policy was moving against working-class interests overall. This interest of the trade union leadership emerged in response to the weakening of the ground-level civil society organisation based on an active rank and file, and, thus, of the union bureaucracy's social weight. That is, the more that union leaders' entry into high-level and state-centric processes led to the hollowing out of union organisation, the more their own influence rested not on the social power of organised labour but on their ability to manoeuvre within the state and political sphere.

In addition to the widespread collapse of industrial struggle, one example of the decline of rank-and-file weight in the unions was the 1988 AMWU decision to shut down its local branches (against the wishes of some of those associations). Two entries in AMWU minutes books, for the Campbelltown and Coburg local branches, highlight the depth of transformation of the AMWU in the Accord era. It was not the Accord alone that resulted in these shifts, which occurred alongside global shifts in manufacturing and significant technical change, but the transformation of industrial strategy—from the rank and file to one centred on the level of the state—was significant.

On 14 September 1988, the Campbelltown Branch President, Brother B Campbell, 'welcomed members to the final meeting of the branch' given a recent National Conference decision to close local branches. He 'indicated it was with deep regret' that he undertook the responsibility to declare open the final meeting. The final lines of the archived minutes book simply read 'there being no further business, [the] branch President reluctantly adjourned the meeting. 8.30 pm'. The previous month the Coburg Branch, on 9 August 1988 noted, in more critical terms, their 'condemnation of the abrupt closure of the union residential branches without proper notice' or another structure to replace the branch system. The minutes stated that the branch officers would not be attending a forthcoming social function, as a 'protest at the arbitrary action in closing branches which have a long history in the effective operation of the union'. This action was taken 'at the highhanded treatment meted out to loyal union members' and they suggested this was 'unworthy of our union'. Despite the anger of the Coburg Brach at the decision, their history ends simply in the statement:

> Last and final meeting of the AMWU Coburg Branch 321 closed at 9.35pm. Good luck and best wishes to all the loyal members who have attended the branch meetings over the years it has been in existence.

The importance of these entries is not simply that they illustrate anger and disappointment with the national leadership, but that they demonstrate the profound lack of power of these branch members to influence decision-making in a rapidly changing union. Although the branch system had played a key role in union democracy and grassroots education and organising in the past, this function had come to an end. There is a palpable sadness in this fond farewell to members, from the last local leaderships of what were once important organs of the AMWU.

The decision to close the branches was taken because the AMWU leadership believed they were no longer able to fulfill their original purpose, to bring AMWU members together in a locality to discuss union matters and broader political questions. This occurred because of a range of factors including loss of jobs in the metals sector, and the changing nature of the industry and workplace. Crucially, however, the Accord brought about a shift in the locus of labour organisation from one level to another, with profound implications. Clearly, despite the anger at this move in this branch and others, rank and file members felt unable to push back against the AMWU leadership's decision. The hollowing out of the unions was even more clearly evident once enterprise bargaining became entrenched and the ALP lost the 1996 election, as rank-and-file activity could not be reignited (discussed below). The loss of a role in centralised arbitration and government exposed the union leaders' loss of social base.

Stewart (1985, 30) argued that the ACTU leadership stayed within the Accord in the early years because the social contract enhanced the young federation's 'prestige among affiliated unions and help[ed] the ACTU legitimate its role to its base'. This consolidated its role as the centre of the labour movement, after it integrated other union federations in 1981. Stewart argued that the Accord might have been broken if a powerful affiliate had retracted its support, and that (in spite of the central role of the AMWU in backing the social contract) its concerns over the direction of economic policy might spill over into open revolt in the mid-1980s. In retrospect, Stewart underestimated both the level of union leader integration into the Accord process and the lack of any alternative strategy within the left unions. In fact, the CPA-led unions looked to deepen the Accord through industry policy in the *Australia Reconstructed* report (ACTU/TDC 1987), rather than change strategy.

2.5 *Industry Policy and Australia Reconstructed*

The Australian unions best placed to mobilise large numbers of workers were also deeply nationalist, despite being the most politically radical. 'Nationalism provided an important cement for class collaboration, as unions formed alliances with employer groups' and otherwise saw their interests increasingly aligned with capital through the 1970s and 1980s (O'Lincoln 1993, 9). The AMWU and other left union officials:

> ... called for industry plans, reflecting their desire to bolster domestic industry against multinational competition. ... [But over time] hostility to foreign capital, which at least carried some echo of class struggle, was subsumed in the broader notion of national competitiveness which carried none.
>
> KUHN 2005, 6–7

Over the course of the Accord, the unions sought direct engagement with capital to support its profitability and restructuring. So sharply had sections of the labour movement shifted that the *Australia Reconstructed* report called not simply for efforts to ensure the profitability of local capital, but 'a program ... which encourage[d] productive foreign investment' to ensure Australia's competitiveness (quoted in Kuhn 2005, 7).

The original Accord agreed to implement a comprehensive industry development policy with the objective being the 'attainment of full employment' through 'interventionist' planning (ALP & ACTU 1986). Industry planning was a key inclusion to gain the support of the CPA unions and fitted with their broader direction of developing a 'European' model in Australia. In their view, tripartite bodies and industry plans were to be developed and, alongside tariff protection and the use of superannuation funds for national investment, this was to reinvigorate manufacturing and address unemployment.

In the period of the first agreement the government established bodies included the EPAC, the Australian Manufacturing Council (AMC) and the Trade Development Council (TDC)—with such organisations implementing plans in areas including shipping, steel and motor vehicles. However, the plans 'were short-lived and undermined the government's desire for a general reduction in tariffs' (Balnave and Patmore 2013, 29). Industry policy was not implemented in the manner the unions believed the Accord mandated, was ultimately used to achieve ends contrary to those intended by the trade unions that championed it, and often took place with union consent or derisory resistance. As mentioned earlier, clauses related to maintaining tariff protections were ignored, while policy and funding directed at technological adjustment were used to ensure that industries were restructured in the interests of capital in an increasingly less protected environment (Kuhn 2005; Southall 2006; Beeson 1997). Industry planning bodies such as the EPAC and the AMC were in many ways superfluous to government policy development, with economic priorities being set by Treasury and in line with the neoliberal direction of the government (Beeson 1997, 64).

Two of the most successful industry plans rationalised the foreign-owned car and steel industries, shedding tens of thousands of jobs (Kuhn 2005, 7). For example, in the case of the steel plan in Wollongong—a focal point for union militancy in response to the serious effects of unemployment in the midst of the crisis—the government and 'the ACTU accepted BHP's long-term strategy and supported the provision of hundreds of millions of taxpayers' dollars to the company to invest in job-displacing technology' (Southall 2006, 9). The industry plan for steel was intended to restructure the industry in accordance with the wishes of the major employer BHP (Schultz 1985). Thus, when 'Hawke spoke of saving the steel industry, it was the salvation of the balance sheet he was talking about—a balance sheet that made no provision ... for the social impact of the restructuring' (Schultz 1985, 252). Although local unions fought the plan, they were ultimately brought into line by the national union leadership and the threat of mass sackings in a town already ravaged by unemployment (Southall 2006; Schultz 1985). Industry policy was, in practice, a process that placed the unions inside the state's efforts to restructure the economy in the interests of capital.

The left unions often complained that the industry planning elements were not being implemented as per the original Accord statement, or at least not quickly or comprehensively enough. They actively sought to reinvigorate and redeploy the planning elements of the Accord, through the joint ACTU and TDC fact-finding mission to Europe in 1986. The mission arose because it was believed that although the Accord had been adopted and:

> ... set new policy directions, it provided few details to aid policy implementation [and] the economic crisis of late 1985 and 1986 precipitated renewed concern for policy formulation.
>
> DAVIS 1988, 151

In the wake of the visit to Europe, the mission released the *Australia Reconstructed* (ACTU/TDC 1987) report. The document set out recommendations on macroeconomic, incomes and industry policy, as well as a framework of strategic unionism. The AMWU was central to this process and Ted Wilshire, its former national research officer, was Executive Director of the TDC in this period. The mission and report sought to move government policy away from the neoliberal direction of the ALP—i.e. to shift from financial 'deregulation' and towards industry policy—and promoted the curbing of prices and executive salaries (not only wages). It sought the use of superannuation funds to promote 'productive' investment and promoted greater vocational training and industrial democracy (Scott 2006, 3). In many ways, the report echoed the original Accord and highlighted the key components that had not been implemented. The document, and the labour movement more generally, failed to map out a strategy that could see either the Accord or the new recommendations delivered.

The ALP government effectively ignored the recommendations of *Australia Reconstructed* pertaining to industry policy, with few recommendations implemented. John Button, Minister for Industry, Technology and Commerce in the Accord era, highlighted the extent of this in a later interview when he stated: 'I don't think *Australia Reconstructed* got much attention in the Parliamentary Labor Party except from people like myself from whom it had to get some attention' (Bryan 1987, 8).

By 'strategic unionism', the report meant that unions should assume:

> ... greater responsibility for economic conditions in the nation. 'Responsibility' was thought to have two sides: the burden of responsibility, in terms of reducing wage demands as a contribution to a national growth strategy; and the power of responsibility, in terms of increasing union influence on government economic policy.
>
> RAFFERTY 1997, 100

In terms of wages policy, this meant tying increases to 'productivity growth and workplace change (which became known as enterprise bargaining), rather than simply to cost of living rises' (Rafferty 1997, 101). The report argued that 'the creation of wealth is a pre-requisite of its distribution and ... the appreciation of the importance of wealth creation [needs to be developed] *at the workplace*' (ACTU/TDC 1987, 169). The report argued that through 'strategic unionism, trade unions recognise that wealth creation is as important as its distribution' (ibid 1987, 172). The strategic unionism objectives of the report were to be achieved via the 'rationalisation' of union structures, through amalgamations and 'the centralisation of policy control by the ACTU'. The subsequent ACTU (1987b) *Future Strategies* document, together with government legislation and funding, operationalised the strategic unionism and amalgamation recommendations of *Australia Reconstructed* (Rafferty 1997, 99).

In the absence of recommendations around industry policy being adopted, the strategic unionism objectives—and in particular the reorganisation of the trade union movement through union amalgamations—became the key outcome of the mission to Europe. The ACTU believed amalgamation was the way to arrest the decline in union membership. In the first half of the 1990s, the number of unions operating in Australia more than halved, decreasing from 275 in 1991 to 132 by 1996, with more amalgamations occurring in those years than in the previous fifty (Buchanan 2003, 54–56). As Table 8.1 illustrates, the Accord led to a dramatic increase in the number of union mergers. However, despite the magnitude of this effort, the decline of union density was not halted (ibid 2003, 55–58)—as is illustrated in Table 8.2.

One consequence of the amalgamations was the increased centralisation of policy and decision-making in the ACTU and the state-based union federations, further relegating the rank and file of the Australian labour movement. The *Australia Reconstructed* document and its impact on the direction of the ACTU resulted in the:

> ... competitiveness of individual companies increasingly [being] seen as the way to create employment and secure national economic growth—an agenda at odds with the industry planning program of *Australia Reconstructed*. ... In the 1990s competitiveness agenda, it became market forces with union complicity which is the key to profitable industry.
>
> RAFFERTY 1997, 103

TABLE 8.1 Mergers of Australian Unions per Decade, 1905–1996

	Number of mergers
1905–1910	4
1911–1920	28
1921–1930	18
1931–1940	3
1941–1950	14
1951–1960	2
1961–1970	9
1971–1980	9
1981–1990	20
1991–1996	64

Source: Buchanan 2003

TABLE 8.2 Changing Australian Union Density (%), 1905–2015

	Union density
1911	28
1921	47
1931	50
1941	47
1951	60
1961	56
1971	51
1982	50
1990	41
2000	25
2013	17
2015	13.8

Source: Derived from ABS 2013 Cat. No. 6310; Jericho 2015; Buchanan 2003

Ultimately, *Australia Reconstructed* did not effect a break with neoliberalism, but further enwrapped the trade union leadership in the priorities of the state (and therefore capital) in the vanguard neoliberal era.

The *Australia Reconstructed* document was lauded by some as 'the most comprehensive policy manifesto ever published by the mainstream left in Australia' (Scott 2006, 2). Dissenters judged the report to have 'had a brief appearance in the public limelight [but that it was] soon relegated to obscurity in the arena of respectable opinion' (E. Jones 1997, 17). Regardless, the impact of *Australia Reconstructed* was chiefly on 'the internal affairs of the trade union movement' (Stilwell 1997, 43) and on the deepening of the connection between corporatism and neoliberalism in Australia through industry policy. It is not just that the unions were unlikely to succeed in reconstructing industry in Australia 'in circumstances where the leadership of the political and industrial wings of the Australian labour movement were simultaneously conspiring to introduce a panoply of market-oriented reforms' (Beeson 1997, 68), but that by collaborating to maximise the profitability of capital and the productivity of labour this outcome was always the likely one.

The union bureaucracy underwent a 'molecular' transformation during the Accord period, where small quantitative changes to its approach and outlook resulted in a more qualitative change over time. This shift resulted in the AMWU leadership being qualitatively different at the start of the Accord from its middle and later period, despite being populated by predominantly the same people. Gramsci developed his theory:

> ... of molecular transformations, in the first instance, on the political terrain, particularly in relation to absorption of elements of one group by another in the *trasformismo* he saw in the passive revolution of post-Risorgimento Italy.
>
> THOMAS 2009b, 398

However, he also used the term in other contexts to 'describe processes of slow but steady transformation that eventually issue in a dialectical conversion of quantitative into qualitative change' (ibid 2009b, 398)—including in relation to himself while subject to the social circumstances of prison (Gramsci 1975, 137). Gramsci's theory is a useful way in which to understand the transformation of elements of the trade union leadership in the Accord period, demonstrating how—when representatives of subaltern classes become directly incorporated into processes in and around the state—they shift their activities and outlook. At first, modifications can appear barely visible, but over time quantitative becomes qualitative change.

This dramatic shift can perhaps be seen most clearly in the evolution of Laurie Carmichael—Victorian State Secretary, Assistant National Secretary and Research Officer AMWU, and later Assistant Secretary of the ACTU—who was once described as the 'left linchpin in the ALP/ACTU alliance' (Aarons and Murphy 1989). Carmichael argued in the mid-1970s that he would have nothing to do with workers' participation in the running of corporations, because it allowed ordinary workers to rise to higher management only if 'they commit themselves body and soul to profit' (Dare 1974). He would later state, in a publication of a petrochemical company, that 'in the workplace of the future, everyone is a manager' (Kemcor 1993). The contrast between the two positions could not be starker. The CPA union officials entered the Accord on the understanding that it would be used to pursue the interests of the working class and, as late as the 1985 ACTU Congress, Carmichael was arguing that the social contract was 'a transitional program for socialism' (Ross, O'Lincoln, and Willett 1986, 13). Carmichael's change of heart about worker participation in management can be explained as the product of being drawn into a state-centred political project, whereby the participation of workers in business direction became subsumed under a progressive political umbrella. It is not that Carmichael changed his mind about the social priorities of business. Rather, it was because the state and the unions were at the centre of a political project organising industry, and, therefore, Carmichael came to see business imperatives as subordinate to the wider project of the 'national interest' being implemented through the Accord and state (and, thus, no longer simply driven by private capitalist gain).

While it is clear that the Accord was not pursuing a socialist project and that the ALP government was taking an increasingly neoliberal approach to economic policy, a political line like Carmichael's is based on the belief that a 'true Accord' can be implemented if there is the political will. As discussed in Chapters 2 and 3, this position understands the role of the state within corporatism as essentially neutral, when its interests are actually in resolving the crisis of capital accumulation, in the interests of capital, and this is given efficacy through a social contract. The processes of the Accord and *Australia Reconstructed* produced greater and greater assimilation of the trade union movement into state-led economic restructuring. This was concurrent with the widespread containment of industrial militancy through the Accord and the policing of union dissent—including by the ACTU and its leading affiliates.

3 Managing Dissent and Disorganising Labour

The implementation of neoliberalism has typically entailed the defeat of key sections of the labour movement. In the US, this included the 1981 PATCO union dispute, and in the UK the defeat of the 12-month long miners' strike. In Australia, the disorganisation of labour involved both voluntary industrial restraint, and the active policing of workers' industrial action by capital, the state and the organised labour movement itself. Both elements contributed to the process of curbing the militancy of the 1970s and early 1980s.

This section looks at three ways in which industrial activity was suppressed and the labour movement disorganised: (i) through New Right efforts to curb industrial power by targeting strike action; (ii) in the policing of renegade unions by the union movement and/or the holding back of solidarity for unions taking action; and (iii) through the active suppression of industrial struggle by the ALP government. To demonstrate these methods, this section analyses the examples of the 1985 Mudginberri meatworks and Dollar Sweets disputes; the 1986 Robe River dispute; the 1986 deregistration of the BLF; and the defeat of the 1989 pilots' strike.

3.1 *Civil Legal Action against Labour Disputes*

As discussed in Chapter 3, in Australia the arbitration system has historically been charged with overseeing industrial matters and workplace disputes. This fact, however, has not stopped companies and unions from seeking remedies through other legislation. In 1977, Fraser introduced changes to section 45D of the *Trade Practices Act*, based on anti-union legal precedents from the US. These changes prevented 'secondary boycotts', and effectively stopped unionists from taking solidarity action with striking workers—including the act of refusing to cross a picket line or being on a picket line at a company where one did not work (Ericsen 2004). Using this and other trade practices-related legislation, elements of the New Right mobilised in the early years of the Accord to take civil action against various unions. While companies impacted by industrial action officially took the legal remedies, employer organisations underwrote the legal costs and helped coordinate these efforts. In doing this, business 'organisations such as the National Farmers Federation (NFF) and the Melbourne Chamber of Commerce were not merely protecting the interests of their own members, [but] actively trying to reshape the Australian political landscape' (Cahill 2010b, 14). The Accord created openings for these offensives, 'because the officials were determined to avoid a generalised union response [to the New Right attacks] which would in turn undermine the enforced passivity' of the social contract (Griffiths 1989).

The Amalgamated Meat Industry Employees' Union (AMIEU) commenced industrial action at the Mudginberri Abattoir near Darwin in the Northern Territory (NT) in May 1985, imposing a picket to stop the use of contract labour and the requirement that those employees work at a greater pace. The owners of the abattoir took action under the *Trade Practices Act*, with the support of the NFF, as part of a strategy of militant managerialism by the New Right (Cahill 2010b, 10; Brian 1999). The union was found guilty of breaching legal injunctions and, after a $100,000 fine was imposed, it lifted the picket. By the end of the dispute, the total fines and damages ordered against the union were in the range of $2.7 million (Ericsen 2004).

Mudginberri involved the 'first successful use of legal sanctions against a union since the [jailing] of Victorian tramways official Clarrie O'Shea in 1969', when an Australia-wide general strike movement defeated the 'penal powers' under which he was fined and jailed (Brian 1999, 109). After the O'Shea strikes, 'the practice of fining unions for breaches of awards or court orders went into abeyance' (Kitay 2001, 194). Unlike the O'Shea strikes, and in the context of the Accord, Mudginberri resulted in no call from within the trade unions to mount a generalised campaign to defeat the legislation. During the dispute, the ACTU Congress passed a motion calling for support for the workers and a number of unions made donations to the dispute (Bramble 2008, 141). NT waterfront and maritime unions took part in a 24-hour stoppage (Ericsen 2004) and the Transport Workers Union placed bans on exporting meat (Hodgson 1985). However, despite these isolated acts of solidarity, the labour movement and trade union leadership 'failed to get squarely behind the AMIEU'—even though the meatworkers were acting in line with ACTU policy in defying the court orders (Ericsen 2004). The AMIEU stopped short of pulling out 'meatworkers from other sites to put pressure on the company's backers, the Territory Government and the NFF' (Bramble 2008, 141). The support for the dispute that existed was limited and deliberately held back by both the ACTU and the AMIEU.

The legal action at Mudginberri was 'a test case for [the New Right's] strategy of using the courts to break unions' (ibid 2008, 141). Further uses of trade practices legislation included the Dollar Sweets confectionery company dispute in Victoria (see below); the 1985 South-East Queensland Electricity Board (SEQEB) dispute over the privatisation of work previously done by government employees; and the 1986–1987 Sydney Plumbers & Gasfitters Employees Union dispute during a campaign for a $70-a-week wage increase and a nine-day fortnight (Casey 1987).

The Dollar Sweets dispute involved 27 staff represented by the Federated Confectioners' Association (FCA), which was campaigning for a 36-hour week. This was considered outside the terms of the Accord, despite the FCA being one of the unions that refused to sign the social contract. The firm successfully took civil action against a 143-day picket that demanded a reduced working week and the reinstatement of sacked workers. The court ordered an end to the picket and, two years later, ordered that the union pay $175,000 in compensation (O'Malley 2006). The New Right again spearheaded the action. Key actors included Peter Costello, later Treasurer in the Howard government; Michael Kroger, current President of the Victorian Liberal Party; and Andrew Hay. Costello and Kroger represented the company in court. At the time of the dispute, Hay was Deputy President of the Australian Chamber of Commerce and President of the Victorian State Chamber of Commerce and Industry and has been described as the leader of the New Right in that period (Hendy 2006).

The ACTU disciplined the FCA by publicly condemning its actions as 'outside the Accord' and withheld all practical support for the union (Ericsen 2004). During the dispute, there was significant concern within unions about the use of trade practices legislation and many urged the ACTU to take a stronger stance (Galleghan 1985; Hodgson 1985; Barr 1985; McKechnie 1985). However, publicly the ACTU played down the situation, calling it an 'aberration' and 'atypical' (Unknown 1986). The Dollar Sweets dispute and the decision by the ACTU to isolate the workers were used as examples to other unions considering defying the Accord. And, ultimately, the view of the New Right was that the dispute 'rewrote the manual on what are the acceptable limits of industrial action by unions' (Costello 1988).

The 1986 Robe River dispute, at a remote Western Australian mine in the Pilbara Region, saw the ACTU undermine industrial action taken by the Australian Workers Union (AWU) over the sacking of workers who refused changes to over 200 work practices (Bramble 2008, 144). While the dispute gathered more support in the labour movement than Mudginberri or Dollar Sweets, the AWU held back the rest of the company's workforce from striking (ibid 2008, 144). The ACTU and the company eventually struck a deal to resolve the dispute, but some considered the dispute fundamentally a loss given that 400 workers were made redundant and working conditions were driven down (Ross 2014). The importance of highlighting this particular industrial action is that (unlike Mudginberri and Dollar Sweets):

> ... the company at Robe River did not find it necessary to bring its legal action to an ultimate conclusion in the courts [as] ... the mere threat of legal action by the company was sufficient to force the unions to back down and suffer a serious defeat on their own terms.
>
> SMITH and THOMPSON 1987, 297

Socialist critics of the Accord argued that the conditions bargain that resulted from the dispute shaped the Accord process more generally, influencing the 'trade-off of work conditions for CPI rises under the [then] new "two tier" wages system' (Ross 1987, 13).

At the same time as these actions were proceeding the Hawke Government was considering how to deal with trade practices legislation. A 1984 attempt to repeal sections of the *Trade Practices Act* failed. In 1986, the Federal Cabinet decided the scope of sanctions in the industrial relations system would need to be altered, given that a 'system based only on non-monetary penalties would be inadequate, particularly if employers were to be discouraged from seeking alternative statutory or common law remedies' (Murphy 2013). In 1987, legislation that gave effect to the government's amendments lapsed, but by then the use of trade practices law and the Accord more generally had been effective in corralling industrial disputes. Although the ALP government was concerned with the use of the legislation, the solution it entertained involved expanding punitive powers inside the industrial relations system. The ALP proposed a Labour Court that was to have:

> ... the power, if conciliation had failed, to deal with trade union contraventions of sections 45D and 45E of the *Trade Practices Act*', while prohibiting 'access to injunctions under common law to combat industrial action.
>
> ibid 2013

The 1993 changes to legislation around the 'right to strike' removed civil liability for strikes, but only if they occurred in the official enterprise bargaining period and if other requirements (like advance notice) were met. Ericsen (2004) argued that the 'practical thrust of this provision was not to protect unions, but to encourage civil suits against them' and that the provision would not have assisted unions involved in the disputes detailed above.

How the ACTU and leading unions dealt with these early disputes outside the social contract framework shaped union responses for the remainder of the Accord era. The defeats, as well as the failure of the ACTU and leading unions to support the workers involved in the disputes, sent a message to other organisations that any action outside the wages agreement would not be tolerated.

3.2 *Deregistration of the Builders Labourers' Federation*

In the early 1980s, the ALP and ACTU aligned in efforts to deregister one of the most radical and militant unions in the country—the BLF. The union was predominantly Marxist-Leninist aligned and well known for initiating the 'Green Bans' actions in New South Wales, where environmental, social and heritage bans were placed on numerous developments in the 1970s—especially in working class areas (Burgmann and Burgmann 2011). As part of an investigation into union corruption begun in the Fraser era, the union was deregistered federally and in some states in 1986. Many argue that the allegations of union corruption were used as a catalyst for the deregistration, but that the action was also taken for reasons related to the stability of the Accord process (Bramble 2008; Ross 2004; Ericsen 2004; Kaptein 1993). This view is not universal on the left, however, with scholarly accounts such as McQueen's (2009) having argued that deregistration was the result of the conduct of Gallagher (Federal and Victorian State Secretary of the BLF and the person at the centre of the allegations) and his deteriorating relationship with the ALP and ACTU. Nevertheless, McQueen argued that ultimately deregistration resolved the likelihood that the BLF would mount an industrial campaign outside the Accord framework at some point (H. McQueen 2015, pers. comm., 29 September).

The BLF had an ambiguous relationship with the Accord. While initially opposed to the agreement, the union did not vote against it at the Special ACTU Conference where it was adopted. Further, as mentioned above, Gallagher distributed a speech against the Accord at the National Economic Summit, but he did not speak at the forum (Bramble 2000a). Importantly, the union appeared to have little intention of abiding by the agreement and, in 1983, campaigned for a wage claim outside its terms (Bramble 2008, 135). As Liz Ross (2004) notes:

> … on the day of Hawke's National Summit in Canberra, building unions nationwide were striking for the shorter week [and] two days later delegates from seven NSW unions endorsed the national campaign of strikes and bans for a pay rise and 36-hour week [threatening the Summit's] 'spirit of consensus'.

Bob Carr, then a journalist and later NSW ALP Premier, wrote 'that the action presented the ALP and ACTU "with a challenge they must crush"'—given any victory for the BLF might mean the ACTU found 'it impossible to stop flow-ons, first to oil workers, then the metalworkers, ensuring it would spread around the country' (cited in Ross 2004). Carr expressed concern that if the BLF were successful, it would undermine 'the ACTU's ability to police the union movement' (ibid 2004).

While some unions, including those aligned to the ALP Socialist Left faction in Victoria, opposed the deregistration (AMWU 1985), there was no significant union movement action to stop the process. Key deregistration backer, Tom McDonald, an official with the CPA-aligned BWIU (the union that would benefit from recruiting a deregistered BLF's members) argued:

> … the building industry was sliding into anarchy [under Gallagher's influence] undermining support for unionism … and threatening the jobs of building workers by undermining investor confidence.
>
> cited in ROSS 2004

The ALP reneged on its promise to dismantle the Royal Commission into the BLF that Fraser had set up and, ultimately, the union was deregistered. This expelled the BLF from the arbitration system, cancelling the relevant awards for its members and forcing them to seek coverage from other unions (Kaptein 1993, 101–102). Although the BLF continued to organise and fight, it 'could not survive the haemorrhaging of its ranks' (Ericsen 2004). The small and isolated BLF officially ceased to exist as an entity in 1994, when it amalgamated with the Construction, Forestry, Mining and Energy Union (CFMEU).

The ACTU National Executive stated that it opposed legislation such as that which deregistered the BLF, but that:

> … the BLF, not the Trade Union Movement, must be held accountable for that legislation [and that] where the BLF has … adopted codes of normal industrial behaviour it has not lost the support of unions and as such is not threatened by the impact of deregistration.
>
> ACTU 1986, 1–2

The allegations of corruption and concerns about Gallagher were substantive issues in the deregistration, but also provided cover for the ACTU to deal with a potential Accord dissident that had a history of militant struggle within its ranks (Bramble 2008, 136).

3.3 *Pilots' Dispute*

The 1989–1990 pilots' dispute was a key industrial struggle suppressed by the ALP and ACTU, both of which actively disciplined the Australian Federation of Air Pilots (AFAP), in order to maintain union compliance with the Accord. The action took place in the context of enormous changes in the airline industry, which experienced significant growth throughout the 1980s, and the announcement in 1987 that the government intended to re-regulate the sector along neoliberal lines (Sheehan and Jennings 2010, 145–146). The changes included the privatisation of Trans Australia Airlines (later called Australian Airlines) and Qantas.

After six years of real wage suppression, coupled with increasing and record profits in the airline industry in the latter part of the 1980s, the AFAP lodged a 29.47 percent pay claim in May 1989 on behalf of pilots at the government-owned Australian Airlines—simultaneously serving the claim on the privately-owned Ansett, East-West Airlines and IPEC Aviation (Norington 1990, 24). In August, the union announced it would put its first bans in place, with pilots directed to fly only between the hours of 9am and 5pm. The government and ACTU were incensed by the union action and Hawke stated that:

> … the pilots had no right to demand a 30 percent wage increase outside the arbitration system while the rest of the workforce, within it, accepted lower wage increases in the national interest[—and that] giving in to the pilots would spur other militant unions to a wages blow-out that would destroy the economy
>
> cited in SINGLETON 1990b, 188

A key focus of the manoeuvring against the union was to paint them as a wealthy and greedy section of the white-collar workforce, in order to bring left-wing blue-collar unions in behind the attacks on the AFAP.

In August 1989, a hastily convened full bench of the IRC made a unanimous decision to cancel all pilots' awards unless the nine-to-five campaign was called off—a decision supported by the ALP and ACTU. The awards were ultimately annulled and the union deregistered, leading to work bans and further industrial action. The airlines began sacking workers and in an attempt to manoeuvre around trade practices law, and avoid legal action like in the Mudginberri and Dollar Sweets disputes, 1,647 unionised pilots resigned *en masse*. The dispute had a significant impact on airline travel and tourism and the ALP took the decision to use defence force personnel and overseas pilots as strikebreakers, to cover limited domestic airline services. This was only the second time that the Australian military had been used against striking workers; the first being in 1949 when ALP Prime Minister Chifley used armed troops against striking coalminers. The union was roundly defeated, with only a small number of pilots re-employed on individual contracts (as opposed to the old award). The airlines sued the union under civil legislation, with the AFAP ordered to pay $6.3 million in damages (Bramble 2008, 156–157).

The ALP and ACTU believed that if the AFAP were permitted to break out of the Accord framework, other disgruntled unions would follow and undermine the agreement. This conviction galvanised the government's hard line against the pilots (Fellows and Riordan 2000, 33). The ACTU abandoned the union with then ACTU President Simon Crean (later an ALP government minister) stating:

> ... that the ACTU was 'opposed to legal penalties and damages pursued against unions and workers who withdraw their labour', but having chosen 'to go outside the system with its obligations and discipline', the pilots could not expect to enjoy the benefits and protection of that system and of the ACTU.
>
> cited in SINGLETON 1990b, 189

There was little resistance to the ALP and ACTU agenda from the left unions. In the end, delegates voted unanimously at the 1989 ACTU Congress for a motion that backed the ACTU's position. Even when the government stepped up its tactics and used the military to break the strike, leading to increased criticism from the labour movement (Sheehan and Jennings 2010, 174), the ACTU shifted its position only slightly. The ACTU criticised the use of the Royal Australian Air Force but effectively argued there was fault on all sides, rather than swinging its support behind the pilots' union. More broadly, in:

> ... attacking traditions of union struggle and solidarity, the ACTU undermined the fundamental principles on which trade unions could prosper and laid the basis of the membership crisis that was to follow in the 1990s and 2000s.
>
> BRAMBLE 2008, 157

As a delegate in the Victorian Communication Workers Union said, 'the New Right was now glowing with expectation at precedents set and could not believe its luck—all without a whimper from the ACTU' (Singleton 1990b, 189).

The dispute was not without ironies and double standards. The events had exposed increasing frustration in the labour movement with the real wage suppression of the social contract. The ACTU began campaigning in 1990 for enterprise bargaining and direct negotiations with employers, to relieve this pressure within the Accord (discussed below). At the same time as the pilots' dispute was taking place, 'Qantas international pilots ... managed to secure a wage increase of approximately 20 percent, well in excess of the allowable parameters (under the two-tier system) blessed by the IRC' (Fellows and Riordan 2000, 33). Norington notes that, the year after the dispute, 'flight engineers gained a pay rise of 24 percent, remarkably close to the domestic pilots' original claim and [this was] tidily legitimised by the wage system' (Norington 1990, 246–247). The new Accord negotiated at this time further embedded 'limited over-award payments and an end to the "no extra claims" commitment—all with the consent of the Government' (ibid 1990, 247).

That these events occurred so closely together is, in part, explained by the slow shift within the Accord from indexation through two-tier increases to enterprise bargaining—a process in flux at that time—and the desire of the ALP and employers to restructure and privatise elements of the airline industry. Although the AFAP pay claim was outside the Accord (causing difficulties for the ACTU and motivating it to isolate the dispute), the approach of the industry in destroying the union through civil action was 'linked more with the government's planned reorganisation of the industry than the employers' ability to meet the claim' (Green and Wilson 2000, 117).

Further, it was not just when the two-tier system was in place that the ALP and ACTU allowed some unions to go outside the Accord, picking and choosing which unions to tackle in policing industrial activity. When the 1985–1986 Victorian Nurses Dispute for higher pay occurred, the action was not policed by the ACTU. The federation and other left unions effectively backed the strike campaign, with the Victorian arbitration commission ultimately awarding a significant pay rise (Bramble 2008, 136). While the ALP state government threatened to deregister the union, the ACTU backed the nurses' case as an 'anomaly' to the Accord provisions based on gender equity grounds. It effectively argued that the nurses were unlike other unions and therefore an exception. Haines (2014), the lone delegate who voted against the Accord at the ACTU Special Congress, noted that the ACTU treated the nurses differently and more favourably than the BLF despite both unions taking industrial action outside the letter of the agreement. The ACTU judged that, on that occasion, supporting the dispute was the action most likely to ensure the stability of the social contract.

Briggs (1999, 261–262) has outlined the various means by which 'labour market pressures were defused' in the Accord era:

- The use of ACTU internal disciplining procedures.
- Exploiting the ACTU's influence with the tribunals under the Accord to register 'special or extraordinary' agreements and file claims under the anomalies, inequities and work value principle, in hotspots such as building, construction and oil refineries.
- Building and co-ordinating national mobilisations that redefined the boundaries of the political exchange (eg. occupational superannuation campaign 1985–1986, cost-of-living adjustment campaign 1988 and enterprise bargaining campaign 1990–1991).
- ACTU-sanctioned use of state repression against unions isolated by the ACTU within the union movement—for example, Food Preservers Union, Builders Labourers' Federation, Plumbers and Gasfitters Employees Union and the Pilots' Federation.

These various means, illustrated in Chapters 6 and 7, and in this chapter, are pursued further in the discussion of enterprise bargaining in the next section. The disorganisation of labour via the suppression of industrial struggle in Australia occurred as a result of the activity of business and the national government, as it did in other geographic locations where neoliberalism was driven through. However, in Australia it mainly transpired because of the internal policing activities of the trade union movement itself. The ACTU played a leading role in the suppression of key industrial disputes to protect the Accord framework, and actively stopped solidarity from other unions for the same ends. Ted Gnatenko, a former General Motors Holden shop steward and Education Officer with the AMWU, argued that:

> ... the unions' method of dealing with the Hawke Government ... resulted in alienating a large slice of the working population [and that] considerable erosion of their living standards without concerted action to defend them.
>
> cited in BRAMBLE 2008, 155

This resulted in the labour movement almost forgetting how to struggle. The impact of the Accord on grassroots organising was significant, with Australian union leaders 'curbing rank-and-file activism' and the ACTU 'victimising trade unions that *did* want to fight and openly supported efforts by employers and governments to crush such unions' (Bramble 2008, 126).

In outlining the relationship between the Accord and neoliberalism, mainstream journalist George Megalogenis argued it achieved the same ends as Thatcher and Reagan, but through a different mechanism:

> Keating, initially more cautious than Hawke on both the float and the Accord, was able to marry the two initiatives into a powerful political narrative. He told voters that Labor was creating an internationally competitive Australian economy. They believed him while the economy was growing, even though the subtext of the deregulation partnership with the trade unions was that workers would see their real wages fall to allow businesses to improve their own profitability.
>
> The consent of the ACTU allowed Labor to distinguish itself from the American and British models in the 1980s. Reagan and Thatcher played the class warfare card, taking on workers in government-run sectors to establish authority. Reagan defeated America's air traffic controllers in 1981; Thatcher prevailed in the violent dispute with British coal miners in 1984–85. Rupert Murdoch ran a parallel operation against the British printing union in 1986. Australia, on the other hand, saw industrial disputes return to their pre-1970s levels. The number of working days lost per 1000 workers tumbled from nearly 700 at the start of the '80s to less than 200 by 1985. Hawke's reformation was complete. He was no longer settling strikes after the fact, but preventing them from starting in the first place, with the carrot of the Accord.
>
> MEGALOGENIS 2012, 168–169

This shines an unforgiving light on how the Accord integrated the trade union movement into a project similar to those deployed in the paradigmatic cases of vanguard neoliberalism in the US and the UK. It also more keenly articulates this dynamic than much of the scholarly literature, which has tended to emphasise the Accord as a project in opposition to the advance of neoliberalism in Australia's long Labor decade.

4 Enterprise Bargaining and the Antinomies of the Accord

The shift from centralised wage determinations has been presented in some accounts as a response to pressure by New Right business lobbies like the Business Council of Australia. Yet it was not simply introduced by a neoliberal state, but actively campaigned for by the ACTU and key left unions (Bramble 2008, 161; Briggs 2001, 31). Enterprise bargaining was a key element in the neoliberalisation of industrial relations and was, at the same time, both a response to

TABLE 8.3. Real wages by occupation in Australia (%), 1983–1991

Occupation	Real wages
Fitter (Award)	−9.6
Fitter (Market)	−12.4
Drivers	−10.1
Storemen (sic)	−10.7
Shop Assistant (NSW)	−6.8
Public Sector Clerk 2	−6.9

Source: Briggs 2001

the constraints of the Accord and a greater curtailment of workers' organised power. In the wake of the move to enterprise bargaining, 'industrial relations has moved further and further down the path mapped out by "free market deregulationists"' (Briggs 2001, 27).

Enterprise bargaining was first raised during 1985, in a review of arbitration conducted by the Hancock Commission. Based on its recommendations, legislation was changed to allow firms to opt out of arbitration and enter stand-alone agreements with unions. However, this option for employers effectively 'gathered dust' (Bramble 2008, 160–161). By the late 1980s, intense pressures had built up inside unions because of the heavy cost of wage restraint. As detailed earlier, real wages had fallen significantly (see Figure 6.2), but as Table 8.3 shows, the sacrifice was unevenly spread because 'minimum rates adjustments, flat rate increases and social wage benefits moderated the impact of aggregate wage discipline on low-income earners' (Briggs 2001, 32). It was the better-organised, skilled and paid members of key left unions in metals, manufacturing and construction who bore the brunt of real wage cuts—their disciplined adherence to the social contract ironically resulted in them taking the proportionally largest cut in real income (ibid 2001, 32).

Interviewed a decade later, a series of trade union leaders attested to their fears at the time that, without a change to the process of wage setting, there was a real threat of militants leading breakaway unions and undermining the Accord process (ibid 2001, 34). The success of the hegemonic project embodied in the Accord, in increasing the rate of exploitation, had therefore created a reaction that threatened to fragment the relationship between the Labor government and unions—that, through the social contract, had become an instrument of pro-business wages and industry policy. The layers of workers within the unions that had been best organised and more able to mobilise their social power to gain high wages and good working conditions before 1983—and whose social weight had been subordinated to the imperatives of the state-led social contract—were now agitating for a return to a pre-Accord situation, where direct bargaining power would determine pay rates (ibid 2001).

Following the Industrial Relations Commission's 1989 national wage decision, which introduced the SEP and delivered wage increases subject to the delivery of efficiency gains by labour, leading unions and the ACTU began to campaign for enterprise bargaining. In theory, this would allow more strongly organised unions and workplaces to fight for and gain the additional wage increases denied to them under strict centralisation. Accord Mark VI created the conditions for limited wage claims on the basis of bargaining at the individual enterprise level. Rather than seeing this as a regressive step towards decentralised wage setting and union fragmentation, the ACTU and union leaders campaigned throughout 1990 as if they were running a typical over-award campaign to set new wage levels across the board—to the point where the ACTU at one point called the Commission 'irrelevant' (Briggs 1999, 263).

In their push towards enterprise bargaining, the unions found support not just from the government, but from most employer organisations—with the notable exception of the Metal Trades Industry Association, whose members had reaped such benefits from centralised wage restraint by the AMWU and now stood to lose the most from any return to militancy (Bramble 2008, 161). Yet in a surprise ruling, the Commission rejected enterprise bargaining in its April 1991 wage decision, citing a lack of progress on previously-agreed productivity improvements and worries that letting unions off the leash might lead to a wages breakout.

The IRC relented in its October wage decision, allowing enterprise bargaining, but dissociating it from the award system. Under the new system, unions could not 'double-dip' and claim both National Wage Case rises and gains under the new enterprise bargaining provisions (ibid 2008, 162). This meant that wage agreements won on an enterprise-by-enterprise basis could *not* be fed back into the next national award determination, as they had been during wage campaigns of the pre-Accord era with the metal industry's fitters' rate (discussed previously). This made it significantly more difficult to use the bargaining power of stronger workplaces to deliver gains indirectly for weakly organised workers. In this sense, the solidarity implicit in past militancy was broken. As Brett Heino (2017, 146) explains:

> Most important was the historical reversal of the metal trade motive chain; whereas before, the breakthrough in particularly militant 'hot shops' led to improvements for all metal workers (and from thence, many

> other employees), the movement towards award decentralisation promoted a more insular, inward-looking mentality, where, conceptually at least, the weak could be isolated from the gains of the strong.

Strong groups of workers were fighting only for sectional gains. This was a further step in the disorganisation of workers' organised social power, ending their ability to make gains in a class interest beyond a sectional level. The unions accepted the ruling without raising significant criticisms. As Carmichael later argued, this was not a new phase of the old pattern of 'enterprise bargaining—consolidation, enterprise bargaining—consolidation' but 'a new policy ... very much part of economic rationalist policy' (cited in Briggs 2001, 36). It was also the outcome of the slow death of arbitration in Australia, ironically delivered through the deepening of corporatism embodied in the Accord process.

It is possible that this further labour disorganisation could have been defended against, but the push for enterprise bargaining came at a time when unions were least prepared for the new system's negative consequences and least able to take advantage of any possible gains. The previously discussed 1991 recession—the worst since the Great Depression—made wages growth virtually impossible (Kelly 2009, 138–139). Moreover, the Accord's centralising tendencies had led to passivity and decline at the level of workplace and delegate organisation, so that by that point 'one-third of unionised workplaces had no delegate and only in 26 percent of workplaces was there an "active" union presence' (Briggs 2001, 38). In addition, unions had become preoccupied with amalgamations and battles over coverage. They were unable to use enterprise bargaining to their advantage. Finally, unions didn't foresee how much the loss of a legal framework connecting centralised wages rulings and enterprise level bargaining would work against them.

Thus, the early 1990s delivered neither a revival of union fortunes nor a substantial clawing back of lost wages and conditions. There was some recovery of wages for better organised workers who could take most advantage of enterprise bargaining, but the dispersion of wages increased (Peetz 2012, 245)—in part because of the wide variation in enterprise deals, but also because the weakest groups of workers continued to rely on the often sub-inflation award pay rises of subsequent national wage cases (Bramble 2008, 165). This state of affairs was worsened by the 1993 *Industrial Relations Reform Act*, which left awards as a mere 'safety net' for workers who had entered the enterprise bargaining stream. Finally, the introduction of decentralised enterprise bargaining was associated with a sharp drop in the number of strikes, with the agreements limiting industrial action to certain periods and thereby preventing workers from taking advantage of cyclical improvements in economic conditions as had happened under the old centralised system (Hodgkinson and Perera 2004, 455). Rather than enterprise bargaining being a way to reassert workers' organised social weight in their own interests through direct industrial methods, as the ACTU had hoped, it coincided with a further decline in union density (see Table 8.2 on p. 183).

4.1 *Hegemony Unravelling*

The militancy and organisation of the Australian union movement in the 1970s enabled its leaders to push their way into the highest levels of national political and economic decision-making, in the shape of an Accord with the incoming Labor government of 1983. This social contract was central to drawing unionised workers directly into the process of national economic restructuring—what Gramsci (as quoted at the beginning of this chapter) referred to as 'organised consent' for the hegemonic political project being led from the state (Gramsci 2011a, 153–154; Q1 §47). However, the Accord was inseparable from vanguard neoliberal restructuring of economy and society. The cost of this process was the weakening, disorganisation and fragmentation of (in Gramsci's terms), the very 'private organisms' of 'political and trade union associations', which allowed the Accord to be such an effective mechanism for radical reform. Unions suffered from declining membership they could not reverse, decreased activity and organisation at the workplace level, and a necessarily increased focus on local and sectional interests, once enterprise bargaining began to take hold.

The initial consequence of these dynamics was the emerging revolt against the Accord, by sections of the powerful left unions that had been most instrumental in maintaining the discipline of wage restraint and defending the special relationship of the unions with the Labor government. A second consequence was the ongoing decline in the electoral fortunes of the ALP, as it implemented what was effectively a prolonged period of national austerity for the working class through wage suppression and public expenditure restraint—lower than the conservative governments that came before and after it. This was, of course, austerity in the context of professionals and business owners receiving large rises in income and wealth, causing relative inequality to grow.

The resultant strain between the unions and the government meant that things could not continue as before. It was the ACTU which drove the shift to enterprise bargaining—a move that simultaneously saved the Accord, opened the door for it to be undermined, and began the more over neoliberalisation of industrial relations policy. The shift to enterprise bargaining should also be understood, therefore, as an early sign of the unsustainability of the vanguard neoliberal period; even if, in the context of a deep recession and union weakness, the 'solution' ended up being used much more to the advantage of employers and the state than that of to the labour movement. The method of 'educating' consent through the institutions of the labour movement was rapidly breaking down, because of moves aimed at preserving the political influence of the union leadership on government by defending the Accord. This required what turned out to be a further weakening of the organised social weight of labour—a social weight on which the union officials depended to be able to exercise influence in the first instance. By starting with the need to save the Accord at some level—rather than break entirely with it—the ACTU campaigned for conditions that would further hollow out its own social base.

As already canvassed in the periodisation of Australian neoliberalism in Chapter 5, the events of the early 1990s had significant implications for the stability of the neoliberal hegemonic project. It became increasingly unsustainable for the government to try to drive further radical economic reform through centralised agreement with a compliant labour movement. Nevertheless, the disciplining effect of the 1991 recession and chronically-high unemployment meant that at least one of the central factors driving the Accord process—fear of another wages breakout and subsequent stagflation—had been resolved, even if not directly via the Accord itself. It was not that the success of this 'solution' was previously thought unlikely to work—the original Accord did not state brute force wouldn't be effective, only that it was politically unacceptable to 'grind inflation down over an extended period of high unemployment' (Beggs 2015, 263).

The popular reaction to further radical industrial reforms under right-wing neoliberal governments in NZ and the state of Victoria (under the Liberal Party) made it obvious that voters were increasingly sick of the constant cycle of sacrifice and upheaval. As discussed in Chapter 5, when Keating improbably won the 1993 federal election by effectively campaigning against the continuation of the neoliberal agenda he had previously championed, it signalled the end of the vanguard neoliberal period (Kelly 2009, 75–87). There was simply no longer any reliable mechanism through which to keep extracting consent for sacrifice on a national basis. This was emphasised in the deeply unpopular 1993 budget after Keating's re-election, which seemed deliberately targeted at the least well off. Keating faced the most damaging caucus revolt of the 13 years of Labor government (Peake 1993), leading not only to his backing down on key aspects of the budget but to then treasurer Dawkins' resignation (Kelly 2009, 211). The budget was one of a series of increasingly bitter confrontations between the government and the ACTU leadership as the intimate ties of the early Accord years degenerated, especially once centralised wage fixation receded as a key economic policy priority (Briggs 1999, 264; Kelly 2009, 140–141).

Keating's attempts to use both integration with Asia and Australia's transition to a Republic as alternative electoral narratives to the consensus of the Accord fell on deaf ears, as a 'jobless recovery' dragged on up to the March 1996 election—which he lost in a landslide (Jericho 2014b). While overstated for political purposes under the name 'Howard's battlers', a significant share of Labor's blue-collar supporters switched their vote to the Liberal Party in the midst of a crushing swing against the ALP (Kelly 2009, 236–247). Yet the fact that the conservatives had been forced to campaign on the basis of slowing the pace of economic reform was proof of such reform's unpopularity in the electorate—let alone its inadequacy for coalescing society behind its banner. Internal party reports on the reasons the ALP lost the 1996 election, in part based on consultation with party members, noted that the Accord:

> ... [had] turned sour when many unionists felt their living standards were eroding, and they were not consoled by the social safety net and tax reductions, especially in the face of a Government whose political agenda was not seen to be relevant.
>
> ALP 1996, 5

Moreover, 'the impact of economic rationalism on Labor's heartland [was blamed] for their 1996 election defeat' (Johnson 2002, 5; ALP 1996; ALP (NSW) 1996). The national inquiry and report on the election noted that the ALP had lost credibility because it implemented policies such as privatisation. A majority of the submissions to the inquiry centred on economic issues 'and can best be encapsulated as being a collective criticism of Labor's support' for neoliberalism (ALP 1996, 8).

This chapter opened with Gramsci's (2011a, 153–154; Q1 §47) insight:

> Government by consent of the governed, but an organised consent, not the vague and generic kind which is declared at the time of elections: the state has and demands consent, but it also 'educates' this consent through political and trade-union associations which, however, are private organisms, left to the private initiative of the ruling class.

If hegemony is understood as a social group's political leadership of society *within civil society itself*, then the overriding achievement of the Accord was that it won consent for a process of state-led political and economic restructuring at the base of civil society—a process, in practice, that was antithetical to the interests of the very organised workers who were central to its success. Consent for neoliberal restructuring was, ultimately, organised at the level of the workplace through the Accord, where in other circumstances resistance to it would likely have been prepared.

Returning to Gramsci's concept of the integral state, political society enwrapped civil society through the mechanism of a social contract that was 'won' down to the lowest echelons of the union membership. Consent was actively constructed, not just through the arguments and activities of politicians and state managers, but at a much more microscopic level through the way organised workers implemented the state's project—in economic terms, through an increase in the rate of their exploitation and, in broader social terms, through the dismantling of workers' organised weight to contest such change.

Nevertheless, hegemony through such means created its own contradictions. Not only did an increase in the rate of exploitation undermine the social interests of the workers who consented to it, but the disorganisation of a once powerful and militant labour movement undermined the ability of that movement's institutions to maintain consent for restructuring. The picture of how the latter process happened in Australia is more complicated than allowed for by either Panitch's account of corporatism being defeated by open worker revolt (based on his analysis of the UK), or Dabscheck's picture of Australian workers conducting an 'exit-voice' rebellion and simply leaving the unions. As demonstrated in this chapter, the Accord's antinomies provoked a complex set of responses over time. While from 1983–1989 the Accord was accompanied by real membership losses and withdrawal from active participation, by 1989 the left unions that were most central to the implementation and continuation of the corporatist agreement faced growing internal revolt from sections of their memberships—to the point where union leaders believed that dissent could lead to new breakaway unions if not responded to.

The ACTU and union leaders' response was to prevent this outcome by finding a safety valve in the form of decentralised enterprise bargaining for higher wages by better-organised groups of workers. Enterprise bargaining successfully stemmed the threat of the outright destruction of the Accord through open rebellion, but its timing and legal framework meant that the safety valve could not prevent an acceleration of 'exit-voice' union decline (Dabscheck 2000). There was a consequential deterioration of the relationship between the ALP and the ACTU, as both sides found diminishing value in cooperation (Briggs 1999, 263). Whether a sustained pushback by militants forming breakaway unions could have reversed the further decline of worker organisation is impossible to know in retrospect, but it seems likely that the deterioration prior to 1989 had already been sufficient to change the overall balance of forces, and that the shift to enterprise bargaining simply reinforced the downward trajectory of the early 1990s and beyond.

Current ACTU President, Ged Kearney (2013), described the Accord's centralised wage system of the early 1990s as 'a yoke and shackle for unions' and that because of this they 'fought for and won direct collective bargaining'. Kearney (2013) argued that union leaders were aware that the election of a conservative government was inevitable, and that there was a 'need to rejuvenate the capacity of the union movement to organise, to bargain and campaign again'. But this is not what enterprise bargaining delivered in practice. Instead, the labour movement was unable to recover its declining workplace density.

The antinomies of the Accord also point to the improbability of a similar social contract being used to drive radical political economic reform in the future. This is because the social organisations that were central to instituting the Accord were hollowed out in the process of the social contract, so much so they can no longer play the same role—and nor can they be as effective in resisting such reforms as they had been in previous decades. During the Accord years there was a substantial fall in the level of unionisation from 49 to 32.7 percent (Dabscheck 2000, 101–102). In the wake of the Accord, this slumped to 13.8 percent (at its lowest point, in 2015) (Jericho 2015). While there is intense debate about the relationship between the Accord and this decline (Peetz 2000; Kenyon and Lewis 2000; 1992), it is clear that, within the Accord framework and through the ACTU's post-Accord era strategy, there has been no sustained reinvigoration of union activism or organisation across the country.

Despite occasional talk of the need for a new Accord-style agreement between the unions and a Labor government (Emerson 2015; Burke 2014; Howes 2014), the relationship between the two wings of the labour movement has come to be much more defined in terms of: union control over party organisation; pre-selection of candidates and policy; and political career paths for union officials. This is rather than any kind of collaboration that might have a sustained impact on the economy or society. As should be clear from the preceding, the reason for this failure is not lack of will, but a structural impediment—namely, the hollowing out of the organised labour movement. In Gramscian terms, there is no set of civil society institutions and relationships that could play the same role in organising consent for a new hegemonic project—as they did with the Accord.

The changes wrought by the neoliberal period, and through the Accord, have meant that the bourgeoisie exercises hegemony less through those institutions than it did in previous decades. Politics enwraps and overdetermines civil society, but it is also increasingly detached from it. In the context of

Australia, the Accord is the last moment in which political society was able to comprehensively organise consent in civil society through trade union structures. This does not mean that politics has stopped being the 'container' of civil society, given that there is—in the absence of another organised social force—no other institution than the state that can try to organise Australian capitalist society on a national basis. Thus, politics remains the key site of national direction, and while it may still enwrap civil society it is far from 'hegemonic' if the Accord period is used as a measure of successful hegemony building. Thus, capitalist class rule through the state lacks the consciously organised relationships and structures that once gave it stability and force on a national level. Instead, it has to depend much more on what Marx called 'the silent compulsion of economic relations' within civil society (1976, 899) coupled with a labour movement significantly disorganised by the Accord process and wider economic changes in the neoliberal era.

While it is beyond the remit of this book to explore in detail the empirical consequences and implications of this development—that is, the growing detachment of voters from politics, the rise of anti-political sentiment, and the increasing frequency of crisis in political society even in the absence of large-scale social disruptions and struggles—it does have an important bearing on the validity of Gramsci's theorisation of hegemony and the integral state. In this book, Gramsci's approach has been central in coming to a clear analysis of the process by which the labour movement actively incorporated Australian workers into a hegemonic neoliberal political project—even when that project eventuated in a direct attack on workers' social interests. However, the breakdown of organised and institutionalised mechanisms (located within civil society for securing the consent of subaltern classes to the operations of political society and the state) suggests that Gramsci's theory may only be applicable in an increasingly historically-demarcated period in certain advanced capitalist countries like Australia. This might be particularly the case in terms of its applicability to social contracts, given the identified absence of social pacts in more recent years, as a result of declining labour movement social weight and perceived legitimacy—especially in the wake of the 2008 global economic crisis (Culpepper and Regan 2014).

At least in the Australian case that has been explored in this book, the very success of a hegemonic neoliberalism directly and critically undermined the civil society organisation needed for actors in political society to create and maintain hegemony in Gramsci's terms. In the absence of newly invigorated social organisation from below, Australian politics continues to be brittle, unstable and crisis-prone. Indeed, elite commentators regularly decry the inability of the political class to carry out another 'golden age' of economic reform, like that seen to implemented under Hawke and Keating.

During the writing of this book the two national daily newspapers, *The Australian Financial Review* and *The Australian*, called for a National Reform Summit (expressly excluding current politicians from its deliberations) in order to try to come to a reform consensus where successive governments have failed (Patrick 2015). Yet the peak organisations coming together in the Summit suffered from the same deficiency that bedevils parliamentary representatives. That being, they are all marked by the same lack of a social base and absence of deep social roots with which to carry through the kind of reform program that the ALP governments of the vanguard neoliberal era could—something they achieved by incorporating the very social forces which could have been the active opponents of neoliberalism, and turning them into its active constructors.

5 Conclusion

This chapter has explored the role of the trade unions during the Accord, and extended the argument of the previous chapter as to the concord between the social contract and the neoliberal project. It returned to a key element of the dominant narrative, which posits organised labour as chiefly the victim and object of the neoliberal project. It demonstrated the active role of trade unions and labour in the construction of neoliberalism in Australia, through their incorporation into state priorities of restructuring—most particularly through: the adoption of industry policy; curtailing union industrial struggle and rank-and-file organising; and the move to decentralised wages policy in the form of enterprise bargaining.

I concluded by considering some of the contradictions of the Accord and vanguard neoliberalism, including labour disorganisation, antipathy to neoliberal restructuring, and the collapse of trade union density. In reflecting on the implications of these findings related to Gramsci's notions of hegemony and the integral state, the chapter concluded his concepts might be applicable only in a historically demarcated period in locations like Australia. This is because the hollowing out of the civil society institutions analysed in this book, have undermined the social base needed by political society to implement process such as the Accord and neoliberalism.

It has been important to focus on the antagonistic nature of the relationship between the political and social spheres, most specifically as it has related to understanding the relationship between the state and the labour movement.

In the Accord period, the more hegemonic the political society enwrapment and overdetermination of civil society, the more that workers' social interests and organisations were subordinated to the interests of the state and became increasingly disorganised. This meant the labour movement could not exercise its social weight to push back against state-led restructuring and its effects. The hollowing out of the social weight of the labour movement also revealed a political process more obviously detached from labour's interests, which in turn undermined the stability and efficacy of politics in attempting ongoing restructuring of the national political economy. Despite calls in the wake of the recent GFC for a new social contract between the unions and the ALP, a new agreement is not possible given that the efficacy of any future hegemonic project would require it to be built on a social base—and the social base capable of carrying out a revived national corporatism was dismantled by the Accord and neoliberalism.

Vanguard neoliberalism and corporatism, then, were devoured by their own triumph.

CHAPTER 9

A Return to the International

1 Introduction

In every country in which a neoliberal transformation have been implemented, it took place in the context of a class political project to attack the wage and condition claims of the working class and enact a generalised disciplining of the labour movement to ensure reform (Davidson 2010; Harvey 2005). The process was different in every location, but the objective was similar—underlining the fact that neoliberalism is both a national process and a global one. Although the methods of vanguard neoliberal advance in Australia were distinct from the cases informing the dominant narrative, certain 'typical' objectives were still achieved. Through the organisational leadership of the labour movement and the Labor Party within a state-centred project, labour made neoliberalism in Australia—and this vanguard project occurred contemporaneously with the roll out of neoliberalism by the administrations of Thatcher and Reagan. This is in contradistinction to the dominant narrative regarding the rise of neoliberalism, which generalises from the experiences of the UK and US governments and posits that neoliberalism was coercively imposed upon trade unions.

This final chapter reflects on the consequences of the research findings regarding Australia in relation to other locations. The analysis considers whether the claim that 'labour made neoliberalism' has broader applicability. It examines indicative evidence regarding the role of organised labour, and occasions where neoliberalism emerged from within its corporatist 'other'. It asks whether these moments prompt a wider reconsideration of the dominant narrative of neoliberal development and labour's role within it. The chapter focuses on five locations:

- Vanguard neoliberalism in New Zealand, implemented by the Labour Party from 1984–1990.
- The role of the British social contract under the Callaghan and Wilson Labor Governments from 1974–1979, prior to the vanguard neoliberal project of Thatcher.
- The role of labour in the period prior to the vanguard neoliberal project undertaken by Reagan.
- Processes of corporatism and neoliberalism in the New York City Council fiscal crisis from 1975–1981.
- Contemporary neoliberalism in Finland and its relationship to corporatism.

 | DOI:10.1163/9789004383463_010

As noted in the introduction, this way of proceeding follows Gramsci's (2011a, 128–129; Q1 §43) method of seeking to locate 'the real identity underneath the apparent differentiation and contradiction and finding the substantial diversity underneath the apparent identity'. Relatedly, McMichael's (1990) approach of 'incorporating comparison' by bringing together otherwise disparate moments (temporally and geographic) is valuable. He argues that 'in effect the "whole" emerges via comparative analysis of its "parts" as moments of a self-forming whole', and 'give[s] substance to a historical process' (McMichael 1990, 386).

In this chapter, I approach the various locations as complex moments linked by the institutional mutation of social contracts and corporatist arrangements, shaped by the strategic choices of labour, which systematically 'variegates' rather than creates 'varieties of' neoliberalism. Peck's (2012) approach to comparison and relationality in neoliberalism, provides a useful framework in this regard. He argues that in addition to 'the conventional "static" comparison of pairs (or more) of territorially defined economic formations, along with multisite analyses of various kinds', we might:

> More ambitiously, [also] embrace the 'relational' analysis of cases-in-connection, linked by intersecting webs of production, reproductive circuits, institutional mutation, or by shared experiences of restructuring. The promise of probing, comparative research designs here is that they entail a decisive explanatory step beyond the identification of alternative, divergent, idiosyncratic economies, moving on to position these relationally, relative to their others. This way, they become more than free-floating cases, implicitly imagined as exceptions, or spots on an otherwise barely charted landscape. Instead, they would hold the potential of generating new explanatory transects across that landscape, evoking conceptually specified and empirically documented registers of meaningful economic geographical difference.
>
> PECK 2012, 126

Such an approach might avoid the problem of seminal cases (or the dominant narrative) remaining in 'ghostly circulation' by defining exceptions on a 'case-by-case to the singular norm, rather than by establishing variegation, unevenness, or deviation more systematically' (ibid 2012, 126).

In the locations and moments considered in this final chapter, the evidence indicates that the claim that 'labour made neoliberalism' has applicability beyond Australia's shores and in diverse contexts and time periods. Various states have deepened corporatist frameworks and policies in order to manage and control organised labour, while simultaneously advancing neoliberalism. I argue that the agency of labour can also usefully be 'written in' to the narrative of neoliberalism's origins in the US and the UK, to provide a more satisfactory explanation of its development and complexities.

2 A Brief Detour in the Antipodes

Antipodal to Ireland and the UK, Australia and NZ were colonised by the British and capitalist development in those locations has involved a number of common political and economic features. Amongst their shared structures has been their relatively unique systems of centralised labour arbitration and conciliation.

NZ engaged in a synchronous process of vanguard neoliberalisation with Australia, driven by a Labour Party Government (1984–1990) mostly under the leadership of Prime Minister David Lange (Roper 2005; Castles, Gerritsen, and Vowles 1996). Neoliberal reform in NZ was dubbed 'Rogernomics' in a deliberate echo of the term 'Reaganomics', and named after then Finance Minister Roger Douglas. Vanguard neoliberalism in NZ enacted a range of familiar reforms, including the subdual of labour organisation. Jane Kelsey's (1995, 2) *Economic Fundamentalism* carefully documents the wide-ranging effects of these changes—including 'market liberalisation and free trade, limited government, a narrow monetarist policy, a deregulated labour market, and fiscal restraint'—and concludes it resulted in the immiseration (socially and economically) of working people.

In the case of NZ, with parallels to Australia, a spirit of cooperation was encouraged—albeit not within a formal social contract. Maria Humphries (1996, 1, 6) observed that a process of 'compliance rather than force' developed a new approach to the political economy, where 'the emphasis of joint responsibility for economic recovery was established through a discourse of "participation" and "empowerment" of employees'. Unions played a key role in this, as:

> …the reformations of work-place practices…were predicated on a discourse of collective responsibility for economic results, promises of employee participation and empowerment in employment, and predictions of better well-being for all. … Participation, empowerment, and the possibility of collaborating with management were seductive to a number of unions. The old enemy (management) was to be transformed. Together managers and workers (through their unions) would strategise to meet the mutual objective within the parameters of their responsibility to

> meet the company's objectives—which again they may have helped define with the guidance of the necessary information supplied by management. ... [Importantly, the] restructuring of state and private sector organisations were sought not only by managers but also by union representatives.
>
> HUMPHRIES 1996, 9, 8, 3

In Humphries' overview we can identify commonalities with Australia in the same period, including the belief that a discourse of collective responsibly would translate to greater involvement and power of unions in workplace management and national economic matters. The roll out of neoliberalism under NZ Labour was less consensual than in Australia, yet the acquiescence of key unions on various matters, and the curtailing of their power, similarly cultivated the ground for additional reforms once conservatives won government. Chief amongst these changes was the abolition of collective bargaining after Labour lost government to the NZ National Party in 1990–1999, which further weakened workplace organisation.

Kelsey's (2014) more recent work has examined the embeddedness of neoliberalism in Australia and NZ since the GFC. She compares Australia's 'substantive focus on use of institutionalised and systemic mechanisms, more conciliatory political style and cross-party, state-federal consensus', with, NZ's 'ideological and instrumentalist style of neoliberalism, based on legislative fiat and contract' (ibid 2014, 152). Kelsey argues that the examination leads to the 'counter-intuitive conclusion that Australia's style of neoliberalism is more deeply embedded than NZ's' (ibid 2014, 152). She argues that this is because of Australia's focus during implementation on: 1) 'the real economy, productivity and global competitiveness' (ibid 2014, 163); 2) institutionalised frameworks and systemic processes for regulation (ibid 2014, 163); and, 3) a 'commitment to bargained consensus' from the time of the Accord which 'sought to maximise political buy-in from elected governments and the populace' (ibid 2014, 164). Building on this last argument, that the consensus approach resulted in a stronger multi-layered embedding of the neoliberal regime in Australia, as well as the analysis presented in this book, one possible interpretation is that this was the result of the use of the Accord to incorporate civil society organisations—most particularly the unions—to work within the hegemonic project reconstructing the Australian political economy.

While it is clear that the claim 'labour made neoliberalism' has significant purchase in the case of New Zealand, the 'metaphor of the "social laboratory" has periodically been invoked to crystallize Australia's and New Zealand's alleged exceptionalism' in relation to political-economic structures and processes (Cox 2006). Whereas the 19th Century original use of the term social laboratory was used to explain state structures that sought to integrate an increasingly politicised labour force into the state, in order to address concerns about unfettered markets, in the 1980s the metaphor was recast. This later use of the social laboratory described 'experiments [that] played the film of history backwards, embracing markets and rolling back the [arbitration and conciliation structures of] the state' (Cox 2006, 108). Consequently, the case of New Zealand, as a further example to destabilise the dominant narrative, might be attributed to antipodean exceptionalism. Thus, it is essential to locate evidence to substantiate that labour played a role in the development of vanguard neoliberalism in the core capitalist countries of the UK and US, in order for the claim that labour made neoliberalism to function as a useful explanatory framework more widely.

3 The British Social Contract (1974–1979)

The Thatcher era in Britain is one of the key global examples of radical neoliberalism, and was undoubtedly the crucial period of vanguard neoliberalisation in the UK. However, the austerity and wage suppression efforts during the preceding Labour governments of Harold Wilson (1974–1976) and James Callaghan (1976–1979) played an important antecedent role. McIlroy (1995, 192) argues that 'scrutiny of Labour policies [in this era] illustrates the need to see in Thatcherism continuity as well as change'.

The Wilson Government was elected in 1974 into a challenging political-economic situation. Labour faced economic crisis and instability after the end of the post-WWII boom, high inflation (which peaked at 26.9 per cent in the year to August 1975), and the continuing decline in British industry. The context was also shaped by widespread trade union militancy as labour sought to maintain living standards, including through unofficial (wildcat) strikes in some industries. A key factor in Wilson's electoral success was Labour's agreement to implement a social contract with the British Trades Union Congress (TUC). The social contract promised price controls, the repeal of various labour laws and increased social expenditure—in compensation for a 'prompt return to voluntary collective bargaining' (Rogers 2009, 638). However, within a few years of taking office Wilson introduced limits on pay increases, announced widespread public expenditure cuts, and the government's efforts to curb inflation failed.

The British social contract did not include a formal agreement to wage moderation, however in the following years the TUC agreed to wage increases below the level of inflation and failed to seriously challenge decreased public expenditure (Thorpe 1999, 143). Although the TUC was initially opposed to wage suppression and a reduction in fiscal expenditure, the intractability of the economic crisis and concerns over the UK's international competiveness were mobilised in an effort to garner public and union support. Over time, union acquiescence to the state's agenda developed an acceptance for austerity and wage devaluation, and this process 'softened up' support for more widespread neoliberalisation in the Thatcher years (ibid 1999, 147–148).

Public support for the actions of the Labour Government, and the later neoliberalisation under Thatcher, were also facilitated by the prospect of an external financing crisis. In December 1975, the government made application to the IMF for stabilisation funds and this was used 'to mobilise support for further public expenditure cuts' (Rogers 2009, 646). Sections of labour pressed for alternative ways to manage the crisis (Lambie 2013), partly because of concerns that the IMF would require the Labour government to pursue a neoliberal macroeconomic agenda. At the time, the government argued that such funds were essential, and that the IMF conditions tied Labour's hands, but later Callaghan stated that the 'IMF was a useful screen' (Cockerell 1992). This suggests that senior Labour Party figures felt neoliberal measures were desirable, independent of any conditionalities or pressure applied by the IMF (Cockerell, 1992). Lambie recently noted that the IMF austerity program was a:

> ...monumental decision on the part of a major power, to acquiesce to the discipline of what were ultimately private capital interests [in] a defining moment in the development of globalisation and the rise of neoliberalism (2013: 355).

The British social contract, as identified by Panitch and discussed previously, promoted the idea that workers (and their trade unions) shared common national interests with industry and the state. Callaghan argued this to Labour and TUC delegates in 1976, in his speech to the British Labour Party Conference:

> ...industrial relations is not just a matter of avoiding strikes, important though that is. That is a negative approach. Britain's present economic position demands a positive approach: a new spirit of co-operation in industry, yes, co-operation between employers and trade unionists, changes of attitude on both sides. As I go around—and I do this a lot more these days than I used to—I find more and more active trade unionists, not

> theoreticians, but active trade unionists on the shop floor, recognising that they share a joint responsibility in their place of work (1976).

While it was the Labour Party that implemented austerity and wage suppression, it was the trade union leadership that facilitated these efforts. Labour's agency was also essential in efforts to demobilise working class struggle in this period, in an effort to control labour militancy and wage increases. Real wages fell the first three years of the Labour government and this was 'the most sustained and draconian reduction of real wages… in the post-war period' (Panitch 1981, 38). While initial wage suppression held and dissent to public expenditure cuts was muted, the onset of a political crisis was simply delayed (Rogers 2009, 649). From 1977 onwards real wages began to recover when various trade unions broke from the Social Contract. On 22 January 1979, an estimated 1.5 million public sector workers took strike action—the largest single action since the 1926 General Strike—and accelerated the 'Winter of Discontent' (Hay 2009, 545). By 4 May of that year, the Labour Party had lost government to Thatcher.

The 'achievement of the Conservatives and the new right more broadly in 1979 was to define, frame and narrate…the winter of 1978–1979 as a symptom of a more general crisis that required a decisive and systemic response' (Hay 2009, 551). The social contract, and the TUC's role in facilitating austerity and wage restraint, ultimately assisted the implementation of vanguard neoliberalism. The social contract's legacy delivered 'little opposition to the dismantling of the post-war consensus that followed when the Conservatives came to power under Thatcher in 1979' and the 'election of Blair in 1997 marked the success of that project' (Lambie 2013, 357).

The 1974–1979 Labour Government in the UK shares certain features with the Hawke-Keating era in Australia. In both cases labour parties were returned to office on the basis of a 'perceived capacity to work with the union[s] in a way that the Conservatives has long since demonstrated they were unable to do', and on the basis of a 'special relationship' with organised labour which afforded the 'capacity to broker a Social Contract' (Hay 2009, 545). In both cases, the terms of the respective social contracts were ultimately set aside on the basis they could not be delivered in the midst of economic crisis, despite both being specifically developed as an 'alternative economic plan' to address the economic situation. Further, the broader corporatist agreements originally signed between the respective parties and unions were narrowed to be, in effect, an incomes policy (ibid 2009, 546). And finally, in both locations, corporatist frameworks drew organised labour inside the state to enact a project that subordinated the interests of the working class to a projected shared national interest (Panitch 1981). The political overdetermined the social.

However, there were also differences, and a key distinction was the push of organised labour against the Social Contract in Britain as wage suppression took hold. In Australia, the trade unions continued to support the ALP throughout its thirteen years in government despite significant wage suppression (with a few limited exceptions). As discussed in Chapter 3, this was a key moment that informed Panitch's model of corporatism, in which he argued that the constraints of social contracts are ultimately broken by dissent from militant elements within organised labour.

4 The Carter Administration (1977–1981) and Prior

Early antecedent features of neoliberalisation occurred in the US prior to the more radical and widespread policies in the vanguard era. A decade before the election of Reagan, President Richard Nixon announced a 'New Economic Policy' to address the 1970–1971 recession and target unemployment, inflation and international speculation. Nixon (1971) declared the government would suspend temporarily the convertibility of the dollar into gold (effectively a break-up of the Bretton Woods system), apply a surcharge on imports, and implement a wage and price freeze to address inflation. In practice, 'wages were frozen under the control of the wage-price board (assisted by hundreds of thousands of capitalists)' while prices 'were allowed to rise (as no effective mechanism was provided to enforce the mythical freeze…)' (R. Brenner 2016). In the same period an increasingly militant working class engaged in widespread industrial action, including wildcat organising. The US experienced one of its largest strike waves from the late 1960s and into the 1970s, 'during which workers twice set records for the number of strikes in a single year' (A. Brenner 2010, xi).

From the late 1960s and through the 1970s key struggles took place in the public sector (commencing with a quarter of a million post office employees striking in 1970), and across the private sector (where action in the mining and automotive industries was significant). However, union leaderships often found themselves at odds with rank and file radicalism, and sympathetic to the economic pressure on companies in the midst of the economic crisis. On a number of occasions officials isolated struggles, including in 'the summer of 1973 [when] Black workers dramatically seized control of a Detroit Chrysler plant to protest deteriorating conditions, terrible overheating, and racist foremen' (R. Brenner 2016). On that occasion, a socialist union official Doug Fraser 'led more than 1000 UAW staff in smashing physically the picket line outside the occupied plant and dispersing the movement' (R. Brenner 2016). By the end of the decade, trade union leaders were resisting 'the assault from [labour's] ranks on bureaucratic [union] rule and increasingly sided with management in the restoration of workplace-authority and company-competitive priorities' (Moody 2012, 6). Union leaderships moved to concession bargaining, which eroded member's wages and conditions.

Kim Moody (2010, 142) has argued that the arrangements between management and the United Auto Workers' leadership in this period, opened the floodgates for concessionary bargaining during the Carter administration. A crucial point was reached with the 1978–1979 agreement to rescue the Chrysler, made between the US government, company management and the unions. This 'was followed in General Motors (GM) and Ford by a series of give-back deals—supposedly temporary—to tide the companies over the serious recession of 1979–1982' (R. Brenner 2016). However, a later return to record profitability did not see a return to better conditions or transform the approach of the union officials. Moody has argued that the decisions by trade unions in this period were not an inescapable response to the shape of the economic crisis, but are better understood as strategy of 'political choice' by the labour movement leadership (Moody, 2012: 6).

The late 1970s also involved other early policy shifts towards neoliberalism, in the re-regulation of various industries and sectors of the economy. One of the first significant changes occurred in the airline industry, when the *Airline Deregulation Act 1978* 'removed all controls over pricing, route structure, and entry into the industry' (Avent-Holt 2012, 1). This was followed by the re-regulation of railroads, trucking, finance, and telecommunications, and reform reshaping electric utilities and other industries to facilitate market competition. By the election of Reagan in 1981, 'the notion that the state should withdraw itself from economic life was the backdrop to virtually all political discourse' (ibid 2012, 1). Further, it was President Carter who appointed Paul Volcker as the Chairman of the US Federal Reserve in 1979, and he who dramatically shifted to an 'inflation first' monetary policy regardless of the consequences for unemployment (Harvey 2005, 1). By this time Thatcher was in power in the UK, and Harvey has argued that together they (Volcker and Thatcher) had 'plucked from the shadows of relative obscurity a particular doctrine that went under the name of "neoliberalism" and transformed it into the central guiding principle of economic thought and management' (ibid 2005, 2).

In considering whether labour built neoliberalism in the US, it is noted that the US Democratic Party is not a party of labour and there is no party of labour in the US (Eidlin 2016), However, the 'New Deal landslide victory of 1936 marked, for the first time, the supersession of the traditional ethno-religious patterning of the Northern electorate by a clear polarisation of workers and capitalists between the Democratic and Republican parties' (Davis 1980, 55). Since that time the working class vote and the backing of organised labour has predominantly followed the Democratic Party. Although on the former there was a temporary shift of white unionised workers to Reagan and Bush in the 1980–1988 period, and some white working-class voters have broken to the Republic Party through the candidacies of Mitt Romney (who lost to Barack Obama in 2012) and Donald Trump. Although organised labour has never had formal representation within the Democratic Party in a manner similar to the trade unions within the UK and Australia, it has deep roots.

While the role of Carter and the Democratic Party does not wholly evidence that 'labour made neoliberalism', what is certain is that the US trade unions were actively involved in facilitating policies and processes that were part of the US neoliberal path. Concessions to employers helped facilitate the move to lean production and granted 'management greater prerogatives over the labour process, a hallmark of the neoliberal era, as well as contributing to working class austerity' (Humphrys and Cahill 2017, 680). These shifts aided in a revival of accumulation in 1982 predicated on the 'basis of a continued fall in real wages, and productivity-growth through the intensification of work'—'a downward trend in the value of labour-power (Moody 2012, 4, 23). Although this was clearly a defeat of (and imposition on) the working class, fought in various ways and locations, organised labour helped implement workplace neoliberalisation. This process included the undermining of worker's wildcat and unauthorised industrial actions 'in the interests of maintaining or re-securing the power and control of trade union leaders within and over the institutions of organised labour' (Humphrys and Cahill 2017, 680). As such, it is too simple to view the unions as the victims of coercive neoliberal economic and political developments. As Moody (2012, 24) has argued:

> ...the strategies of retreat that have characterised the decisions and practices of most US union-leaders since the late 1970s have failed. Chief among these were labour-management cooperation or 'partnership', the near abandonment of the strike as a weapon, the mergers so common in the 1990s, and bureaucratic re-organisation [of unions themselves].

Despite significant institutional, economic and political differences, there are certain underlying parallels in the options pursued by the US and Australian union leaderships from the 1970s onwards—with co-operation, concessional bargaining, and labour de-mobilisation pursued by choice.

It is important to reflect on the fact that the events described in this section occurred prior to the set piece and coercive defeat of the PATCO air traffic controllers by the Reagan government—which is most often singled-out as the key labour defeat in the rise of neoliberalism in the US. In a situation suggestive of the isolation of disputes by the ACTU in Australia, which would occur only few years later, in 1981 the US national trade union federation the AFL-CIO failed to mobilise behind the PATCO employees when Reagan fired over 11,000 striking union members. In refusing to widen the strike, and with members of the International Association of Machinists crossing the picket lines of the sacked workers, the AFL-CIO and leading unions failed to display 'the kind of strike solidarity necessary to meet Reagan's existential threat' (Early 2012). There are clear lines of continuity in the approach of trade unions both before and after the election of Reagan.

5 New York City Council Fiscal Crisis (1975–1981)

In the 1970s and 1980s New York experienced a significant debt crisis, in the midst of the global economic downturn. The fiscal crisis was bought on by a loan default in 1974 and the subsequent refusal of Washington to assist the municipality with financial relief (Tabb 1982). Between 1975 and 1981 New York City shed 60,000 jobs, closed health and public services, and ended free higher education. This led to declining living standards, and reduced the wages and conditions of public employees (Krinsky 2011, 382–383; Harvey 2005, 45). It is often argued that these events were the first neoliberal restructuring to take place in democratic conditions, and the 'inaugural event in the history of domestic neoliberal policy making in the United States' (Krinsky 2011, 400).

Harvey (2005, 52) has stated that the location was a pioneering attempt to force labour and labour organisation to conform to a new social order through the disciplining of powerful municipal unions. Harvey's approach emphasises the coercive aspects of the New York City Council Fiscal Crisis, but other authors point to a more complex interplay of force, pressure and cooperation. Moody (2007, 42) states that the events during the fiscal crisis could not have taken place without the cooperation of the municipal unions:

> While the unions lacked the power to direct matters, they had the power to disrupt and, thereby, influence them. At times they used that power, but for the most part they, or at least their leaders, accepted the policy and institutional framework proposed by business and implemented by the state as the crisis regime.

Krinsky has detailed how trade unions became enmeshed in the crisis response in a number of ways. Firstly, and importantly, the unions backed away from their militant approach to job losses and protecting living standards, and signalled to the rank and file engaged in wildcat strikes that they would not be supported (Krinsky 2011, 399). Secondly, organised labour invested more than $2.5 billion of union managed pension funds in council issued bonds to prop up fiscal viability and the ability of council to meet its payroll, ensuring that the long-term health of union pensions was 'entwined with concern for the long-term health of the city's finances' (ibid 2011, 399). Thirdly, the unions agreed to the establishment of an appointed financial control body—consisting of elected officials, bureaucrats, and members from financial and nonfinancial businesses—which had the power to 'approve or reject municipal budgets and to approve or reject collective bargaining agreements with the city's unions' (ibid 2011, 399–400). Fourthly, the Municipal Assistance Corporation Act required the council to balance their budget within three years, by 1978, and unions acquiesced to this inclusion in law. Fifthly, in 1976 the unions and council agreed to 'agency shop', meaning all employees had to pay the equivalent of union dues, regardless of membership, and this:

> ...increased the unions' treasuries at a time when they were depleted by layoffs and attrition, and it reduced the need for union staff to collect dues. This also meant that union staff spent less time in the field and had less contact with the rank and file, which had been the wellspring of public-worker militancy.
>
> ibid 2011, 400

Krinsky has argued that the advance of neoliberalism should be understood as a concurrent extension of corporatism. Shifts in corporatist arrangements and relationships in the period from the 1950s to the 1970s 'steadily detached union leaders from their membership by disempowering them, providing the groundwork for union cooperation in and victimisation through neoliberal policies' (Johnson 2011, 329). Corporatist arrangements established in the 1950s were recast in the crisis of the 1970s—alongside neoliberalism—resulting in their being undermined while laying the groundwork for further neoliberalisation from the 1990s onwards. Corporatism and neoliberalism were 'facets or dialectical moments in the same process', where addressing the crisis 'preserved and indeed deepened the institutional outlines of pre-crisis corporatism even as it recontextualised it' (Krinsky 2011, 411–412).

Krinsky has argued against the idea that the response to the fiscal crisis was a singular event, but, rather, that there were strong continuities from the pre-crisis period. This continuity included the survival of the previous framework for collective bargaining and the reinforcement of the corporatism of the previous twenty years. Thus,

> ...if anything, the fiscal crisis deepened the corporatism that initially took shape...but it also changed it by locating it among a set of assumptions different from those that drove the expansion of local and national welfare states in the post-World War II period'.
>
> KRINSKY 2011, 401

The process in New York resembles the later process in Australia in some important features, in which corporatist and neoliberal features must be considered as part of a coterminal process:

1. The development of the Accord was earlier characterised as corporatism within corporatism, in that it deepened corporatism and re-integrated the leadership of the union movement in to the state after its exclusion in the Fraser years. In New York, the self-activity of the labour movement was party managed by the incorporation of the unions into decision making and continuing their rights to collective bargaining.
2. In Australia, the introduction of compulsory superannuation created a significant private sector capital fund, and the majority of worker's money was placed in funds that directly involved the trade union leadership in management. In NYC during the fiscal crisis, labour was incorporated into the new neoliberal direction through the tying of workers' pension funds to the solvency of the council. In both cases, in different ways, the maintenance of worker's pensions was tied directly by unions into securing new rounds of accumulation.
3. Similar to earlier findings regarding Australia, during the NYC fiscal crisis 'the local labour movement centralised significantly' and through such centralisation and bureaucratisation made 'the threat of strike action increasingly remote' (ibid 2011, 401). During the Hawke-Keating crisis era, the amalgamation of unions and the centralisation of industrial strategy limited the possibility of strikes and hobbled rank and file networks.

However, the processes were also dissimilar given the nature of the crisis, the limited location of the changes within one city, and that the process involved public sector workers only. Further, the shift in Australia was achieved through the Accord operating on more direct formal and informal levels, operationalised through the historic relationship between the labour party and the trade unions. Despite these differences, the usefulness of comparing the fiscal crisis in New York City to the Accord is in identifying the ability of both governments to use corporatist institutional features (neoliberalism's 'others') in order to implement a new regime. The eventual undermining of corporatism in New York, once it had outlived its usefulness, demonstrates how the use of non-neoliberal tools was able to set the city on a path to a broader neoliberal adjustment. An initial deepening of corporatism shifted over time to be, in Krinksy's (2011) terms, a neoliberal repertoire of governance.

Tabb argued that the response to the New York Council fiscal crisis was not fixed, and mirrored other locations where 'conscious political decisions favouring the wealthy and more powerful' restructured cities (1982, 119). Although Tabb argued this largely in relation to the action and decisions of elites, in is useful to reflect on the relevance of Moody's claim that union decisions in this era are best understood as a strategy of 'political choice' by labour leaders. In considering the wider relevance of the claim that labour made neoliberalism, an account of the fiscal crisis attentive to the action and strategic choices of the unions destabilises the dominant narrative—despite this location being a touchstone in constructing the neoliberal origin story. Through this lens, the widely acknowledged 'inaugural' democratic event of neoliberalism was not a situation of crisis used in some simple sense by elites to impose neoliberal policies, but a far more complex and longer-term shift to neoliberalism involving (in part) the incorporation of the unions into that shift through an already existing corporatist framework.

6 Contemporary Finland

The Nordic model was constructed in Finland from the late 1950s onwards, culminating in the late 1980s. It involved the 'scaling of the state around the "national" as the primary scale of political action, social life, state development policies and political virtue' through a corporatist focus on growth (Ahlqvist and Moisio 2014, 27). The welfare policies of the Finnish Nordic model were also attentive to growth, and their development involved 'a high degree of consensus among capital, unions and the leading political forces about the need for a redistributive state' (ibid 2014, 28). Although the model was appreciably redistributive, and embedded in processes of central planning, it was also tolerant of private enterprise and efforts to nationalise industry were not significant. Between 1968 and 2008 social contacts were central to economic management, and the industrial relations system was a corporatist regime involving widespread collective bargaining (Adkins et al. 2017, 3). Incomes policy agreements were centrally managed, and covered both wage rates and the social wage. Although the last incomes agreement concluded in 2006, collective agreements still cover the majority of workers and 'the social partners (trade union confederations and employers' associations) are present in virtually all labour market policy processes' (ibid 2017, 3).

Neoliberalisation in Finland began in the early 1990s, when ideas of competition were instituted into state structures and replaced those focused on central, national planning (Ahlqvist and Moisio 2014, 29; Kantola and Kananen 2013). In the early 2000s there was a strengthening of critiques of the national welfare model, and more recently a new government led by Prime Minister Juha Sipilä has actively pursued an agenda of austerity and more intensive neoliberal reforms. The new right-wing coalition government took office in May 2015, led by the Centre Party (and involving the National Coalition Party and the populist Finns Party). The recent neoliberal intensification has utilised established corporatist processes to advance key policy transformations, in part because (despite the neoliberalisation processes of the 1990s and 2000s) trade unions have continued to play an influential role in shaping and contesting macroeconomic policy. The neoliberal move under Sipilä has more directly confronted the question of wage levels, and in seeking their suppression drawn the trade unions into a project of national restructuring and wage devaluation (Adkins et al. 2017, 2).

In 2015 a new social contract was proposed as a central feature to the reform agenda of the new Sipilä government, and sought to supress labour costs by a minimum of 5 per cent (Adkins et al. 2017, 2). Early negotiations with the unions in May, June and December 2015 failed, as the trade unions would not agree to the regressive wage and working conditions proposed. However, in early 2016 the unions agreed to re-enter discussions and by February there was a draft agreement—which was renamed the Competitiveness Pact. By September 2016 unions covering 90 per cent of workers had signed on to the social contract. The Competitiveness Pact included:

- A wage freeze in 2017
- An annual increase in working hours by 24, without compensation
- Reduced pay for public sector employees
- A part transfer of unemployment insurance and social security contributions from employers to employees
- A decrease in employers' health insurance contributions (Adkins et al. 2017; Savolainen 2016).

Lisa Adkins et al. (2017) have emphasised that the current state-led social contact is not one where wages are being reduced through liberation from heavy regulation, as has tended to be the characterisation, but takes the form of an organised devaluation implemented by (and enabled through reform of) the state. Of course, as Panitch and this book have argued, wage suppression is the inherent nature of social contracts more generally.

In return for agreeing to the Pact, the unions will be 'compensated' by taxation cuts of €415 million and some other minor gains. The European Foundation for the Improvement of Living and Working Conditions has argued that the 'Competitiveness Pact is exceptional in both national and international comparisons, as it is thought there has never before been a negotiated solution that weakens employee working conditions to this extent' (Savolainen 2016). Unions acquiesced to government demands with very little in return, on the basis that they believed they would achieve a better outcome inside the reform process as opposed to fighting it—partly arguing that if they were outside the process elements of collective bargaining may have been under threat. As in Australia and NYC, the process has involved an initial mobilisation of corporatist processes and later an undermining of these structures as a new neoliberalised agenda is rolled out. In the context of Peck's articulation of variegation, we can appreciate how neoliberalism emerging through its corporatist 'other' unfolds in diffuse and systematically uneven ways.

7 Conclusion

Krinsky (2011, 382) asked: 'if paths to neoliberalism are not always sudden and are populated by policies that are not necessarily driven by neoliberal assumptions', how should we understand neoliberalism's content and development? This question, in light of complexities over time and geography, remains a crucial one confronting scholars.

In analysing neoliberalism, we need to be attentive not only to the historical 'break' that took place with the election of particular governments, but the level of continuity with efforts prior to its rise. The British Labour Party and TUC social contract under Callaghan and Wilson in the UK, and trade union strategy of concession bargaining and undermining workers' self-activity during the Carter era and prior, cannot be seen as wholly separate from the later attacks on labour by Thatcher and Reagan. Similarly, Australia is not the only location where corporatism has been entwined with neoliberalism as it advanced, as the New York City Council fiscal crisis and the current wave of neoliberalisation in Finland demonstrate. Corporatist structures have been key to integrating labour into neoliberal structural adjustment on a number of occasions, and each time it has been path-dependent.

In examining geographically and temporally specific instances of neoliberalisation, important similarities as to the role of labour have emerged. Clearly these processes have differed, but in each instance labour movements or labour parties—and on occasion both—have been active in the advance of neoliberalism. As an analytical frame, the claim that 'labour made neoliberalism' has validity beyond Australia. This prompts a re-evaluation of the forces involved in constructing neoliberalism, to highlight locations and agents hitherto obscured. By bringing together geographies of exception to the dominant narrative (Australia, NZ and Finland) together with exemplars of it (the UK and US), new dimensions to the 'origins of neoliberalisation processes in the wake of the systemic crisis of the Keynesian geoinstitutional order' can be revealed (Brenner, Peck and Theodore 2010: 217).

By subjecting the dominant narrative to critique for foreclosing the range of possible experience of vanguard neoliberal restructuring, this book has also been able to identify a series of potentially less essential features of neoliberalism that have been given much weight in the literature—in particular the *necessity* of New Right parties and the 'neoliberal thought collective' (Mirowski and Plehwe 2009) to implementation. Further, outcomes common to both the 'dominant narrative' and Australian case examples can be accounted for, despite the more superficial divergences between them. The common inner logic of case examples has been drawn out and shown to underpin: widely variable details regarding the political positioning of neoliberal reformers; a mix of features imported from elsewhere and developed within a geographic location; a differing balance between coercive and consensual methods; the use of integrative versus exclusionary approaches to trade unions; and, importantly, that neoliberalism was a global process from the start.

Disrupting the dominant origin story of neoliberalism's development with the detailed case study of Australia, and the indicative evidence regarding NZ, the UK, the US and Finland, invites further consideration of the usefulness or otherwise of the prevailing account. And, in disconnecting vanguard neoliberalism's advance from a necessary attachment to the election of New Right parties seeking open confrontation with labour, we are prompted to question and investigate the role of the trade union movement and its officials in the longer-term development of the neoliberal project. This opens up the possibility of 'writing in' the more complex and diffuse ways in which in the advance of neoliberalism has occurred—in other words, its variegation.

CHAPTER 10

Conclusion: Neoliberalism at Dusk

The neoliberal era was a defeat for labour in Australia, as it similarly was in other advanced capitalist countries. There are important consequences, however, in the strategic choices made in a period of setback. The failure to break with the Accord, and with the state-led neoliberal transformation implemented under successive Labor Governments, has had deep consequences. The effects are even more important to recognise given, thirty years after it was implemented, the social contract remains lionised within large sections of the labour movement and the academy despite its failure. We must ask why many still assume the Accord process to be positive, given it was central to incorporating labour into neoliberal restructuring.

The examination undertaken in this book has revealed that most analysis has used inadequate conceptual tools, which limit consideration to only the external relations between corporatism and neoliberal restructuring. There has also been a failure to be attentive to the antinomies and residues of the Accord in the contemporary moment. In the twilight of neoliberalism, we can furthermore reflect on the current crises of trade unions and workplace organisation. Understanding the complexities of neoliberalism's origins and advance is not simply a matter of scholarly interest; clarity on organised labour's relationship to neoliberalism is necessary to inform action in the here and now.

1 Internal Relations

This book commenced by reconsidering Marx's theoretical writings on the state and politics in light of Gramsci's concept of the integral state. The seeming tension between Marx's emphasis on the separation and antagonism between the state and civil society, and Gramsci's emphasis on their dialectical unity (where civil society is integrated under the leadership of political society), is bridged when the integral state is understood as being always necessarily unstable. Civil society enwrapment is never fully realised because a state based on an atomistic and internally divided civil society can never fully overcome the logic of the fundamental social relations that produce those contradictions.

In combining Marx and Gramsci's insights with Panitch's understanding of corporatism, the state and political interests can be placed at the heart of

 | DOI:10.1163/9789004383463_011

understanding the Accord. Gramsci's concept of the integral state both supports and extends Panitch's analysis of corporatism, highlighting the dynamic way in which corporatism is a distinct and concrete expression (alongside social democracy) of how politics acts to contain initiatives from civil society. In light of the Australian case study's divergence from Panitch's account of corporatism, the concept of the integral state highlights how the social contract could be used as the key method of incorporating the trade unions into a hegemonic neoliberal project. Corporatism was used within vanguard neoliberalism to overcome, partially and temporarily, state-civil society separation and antagonism during a lengthy period of wage devaluation.

Gramsci's concept of the integral state, as a process of political society enwrapping and overdetermining civil society, usefully illuminates the relationship between the state, the Australian Labor Party, and the labour movement. This clarifies the process of trade union incorporation into a hegemonic neoliberal project, by highlighting how the social contract was a key element of integral state class rule in the period. Thus, Gramsci's theorisation can help to locate how civil society was brought under the leadership of political society in a particular instance of vanguard neoliberalism.

In reflection, we must ask: Why is the Accord still feted by many involved in the ALP and trade unions? Why do most scholars assume the Accord process to be positive, given it was central to incorporating labour into neoliberal restructuring? And why does analysis often emphasise the social contract and neoliberalism as contradictory and counterposed sets of ideas, policies and processes, when they were in concord?

These problems arise because analysis tends to rest on inadequate conceptual tools, which focus on the external relations between politics and economics—on the external relations between corporatism and neoliberalism. In order to comprehend the complexity involved in the process of neoliberalisation in Australia, and labour's role within it, we must grasp the internal relations of this moment and how the Accord functioned to enwrap civil society (including the economy) in a state-led political economic transformation. As William I Robinson (2004, 96) argues:

> In the historical-materialist conception, the economic and the political are distinct moments of the same totality; that is, they enjoy an internal relation. An internal relation is one in which each part is constituted in its relation to the other, so that one cannot exist without the other and only has meaning when seen within the relation, whereas an external relation is one in which each part has an existence independent of its relation to each other.

Thus, the relations between the economy and states, 'as sets of institutionalised class relations that adhere to those production relations', is internal (ibid 2004, 96). As a consequence—and applicable to most analysis of the relationship between politics and economics as it relates to the Accord and vanguard neoliberalism—'the relations that come together to make up the whole get expressed in what are taken to be its parts' (Ollman cited in Bieler and Morton 2008, 116).

The theoretical and conceptual underpinning developed in this book assists us to break through the appearance of the relationship between the Accord and neoliberalism as exogenous, and to realise the internal connection.

2 Antinomies and Residues

This book has been, in part, an examination of labour movement strategy in the midst of the economic crisis that ended the long boom. The concrete examination of the Accord—and the analysis of the choices made by trade unions, the labour leadership and rank-and-file activists—contributes to debates about: the impasse of left strategy in the early 1980s; the strategic choice made to engage in corporatist structures; the strategic choice made to not effect a break with the Accord for fear of destabilising the ALP government; and, the trajectory of the labour movement after the ALP lost power. This research continues the process of problematising corporatist arrangements on a Marxist basis, begun by Panitch and others, concluding that the question of how the state acted through the Accord—incorporating key sections of civil society into a new hegemonic project and one that was intended to shift the balance of class forces against labour—should give the labour movement cause for reconsideration of the corporatist paradigm and strategy.

The process of *simultaneously deepening corporatism and advancing neoliberalism* resulted in a number of contradictions. The Accord could only be constructed because of the centrality and strength of Australian trade unions in social and political life, but neoliberalism—as implemented through the social contract—contributed to their hollowing out and the retreat of the social forces involved. The Accord disorganised the working class and the labour movement, to the point where unions have manifestly been unable to reorganise. The diminution of the strength and relevance of trade unions means that a corporatist project, similar to that of the Accord and capable of implementing major political and economic changes, cannot in all probability be constructed again—despite persistent calls in recent years for just such a state–civil society initiative.

Worryingly, calls for a new Accord—or more broadly for Keynesian-style corporatist arrangements—are usually made by those dissenting from neoliberalism and austerity, and they suggest such a 'new' arrangement would be an alternative to it. This has included pleas for a 'New New Deal' in the US, and for 'radical' co-operative action in Australia (Larkin and Goldhammer 2015; Cazdyn and Szeman 2011; Klein and Smith 2008; Harvey 2003). Bill Shorten, current leader of the ALP, recently addressed the John Curtin Research Centre gala dinner to argue that:

> We need business and unions and policymakers and leaders and the Parliament to do something drastic, something radical, something profoundly different that we haven't seen since the 1980s: we need to co-operate.
>
> SHORTEN 2017

The analysis presented here demonstrates the problem of seeing state/political society interests and civil society interests (especially those of trade unions) as aligned. Similarly, those who argue 'the Accord model should not be written off for all time because it failed in inauspicious conditions' in the midst of economic crisis (Beggs 2015, 275), might be urged to reflect on not only the limitations of a social contract in the midst of crisis, but also the inherent class nature of corporatism more generally.

Further research needs to be done on corporatist-neoliberal moments, as commenced in the previous chapter, as well as on how state-led neoliberal restructuring created political uncertainty and engendered disharmony and dissent in civil society (Fairbrother, Svensen, and Teicher 1997, 22–23). While this was only raised in the briefest of terms in the introduction to this book, it seems likely that neoliberal restructuring may have contributed to 'anti-politics'. Anti-politics is the 'prevailing popular mood of detachment from and hostility to politicians and politics, including radical politics' (Humphrys and Tietze 2015, 22). While the phenomenon of anti-politics predates the rise of neoliberalism, the era of restructuring accelerated the process (Mair 2013; Hay 2007). In regards to Australia specifically, further inquiry is necessary to be clear about: potential lines of causation between the economic changes after 1983; the process of hollowing out of support for the major political parties and civil society groups, including trade unions; and the growth of sentiment against politicians and political society.

One potentially fruitful line of investigation opened up by the conceptual framework developed in this book, is how neoliberal reforms may have accelerated the end of the era of mass politics and revealed, once more, the tensions of the state-civil society relationship. The contemporary crisis of politics and rise of anti-politics may represent not a contingent break from stable politics undergirded by deep (mass politics) roots in society, but a return to the norm in modern capitalist society. Gramsci showed how mass participation of civil society individuals and groups in political activities can foster their consensual integration and subordination under state-led national projects. But this process of 'hegemony' is weakened when organic links between political society and the state, on the one hand, and civil society on the other (i.e. the social bases of politics), break down. In considering the antinomies of neoliberalism, the period resolved one political-economic crisis only to deliver capitalism into another through the form of that solution.

The contemporary period also allows us to appreciate complicated residues of the Accord. The Australian labour movement has not ended up in an entirely different place to the movements of other advanced capitalist countries in certain ways (Baccaro and Howell 2011), but certain consequences specific to that location are clear. The coterminal nature of the Accord and neoliberalism, and the active involvement of labour, has embedded neoliberalism deeply in the Australia political economy. Ideas of productivity and efficiency are rarely challenged, even rhetorically, by labour leaders. Financialised pensions in the form of superannuation have directly tied the trade union leadership, who sit on the managing boards of the largest funds, into state and capital efforts to secure new rounds of accumulation. And despite the deeply problematic consequences of the Accord for trade unions, many in the labour leadership remains deeply embedded in, and committed to, the ALP at a time when greater trade union independence appears essential.

3 Neoliberalism at Dusk

'The owl of Minerva', wrote Hegel (1967, 13) 'spreads its wings only with the falling of the dusk'. A metaphor for philosophy and understanding, it posited that wisdom was destined to arrive only as a historical moment recedes and night gathers. In the twilight of neoliberalism, perhaps it is only now that many involved in the implementation and defence of the project realise their promise of a stable economy, together with increasing security for those at the bottom of society, was a mirage. For orthodox economists, 'the mid-2000s were an occasion to celebrate economic dynamism and stability on one hand, and the achievements of economics on the other' (Boyer 2013, 1). Yet, the 2008 global crisis and its long tail have revealed the profoundly tenuous nature of the project.

Although people's experience of neoliberalism made them cognisant of its harmful impacts as these were being wrought (Davidson 2010), the content and trajectory of economic transformation since the end of the long boom has also been opaque (Plehwe 2009, 1). Some might also invoke Hegel's adage to argue it is only now that we can distinguish clearly the complex nature of neoliberalism, and its diverse geographical paths. The question 'what is (or was) neoliberalism?' has proven difficult to answer. This is the case for the Antipodes, as it is for the core capitalist economies that constructed the dominant narrative. It is my hope that this book has advanced understandings of the role of labour in the construction of neoliberalism, including in Australia as a distinct national spatial outcome that is both 'original' and '(in a certain sense) unique' (Gramsci 1971, 240; Q14 §68).

The emphasis of the preceding analysis has necessarily fallen on the question of labour involvement in, acquiescence to, and active construction of neoliberalism. This is not to say that labour was the only, or even at times the central, actor in constructing neoliberalism. Rather, it repositions our lens of analysis to ensure we are focussed on the complexities of structural adjustment since the end of the long boom. A focus on how labour made neoliberalism is also attentive to the impressive adaptability and longevity of neoliberalism. This book is not the end of the story on the question of labour and neoliberalism, even in relation to Australia, but a starting point for understanding its processes and residues. Far from simply urging criticism of organised labour, I hope to open up discussion—in particular amongst those active in the labour movement—as to how we deal with a central consequence of neoliberalism: the profound disorganisation of trade unions and the working class and labour's role within that.

Appendices

Appendix A: List of Australian Governments

1972–1975	Whitlam Government (Labor Party)
1975–1983	Fraser Government (Liberal-Country Coalition)
1983–1996	Hawke and Keating Governments (Labor Party)
1996–2007	Howard Government (Liberal-National Coalition)
2007–2013	Rudd and Gillard Governments (Labor Party)
2013–	Abbott, Turnbull and Morrison Governments (Liberal-National Coalition)

Appendix B: Timeline of Predecessors to the AMWU

	Union Name	Notes
1852/1905	Amalgamated Society of Engineers (Branch of the British Union)	First meeting of Sydney Branch, on the immigrant vessel *Frances Walker*, in Sydney Harbour in October 1852. Registered for the first time in 1905, under Commonwealth law.
1921	Amalgamated Engineering Union (Australian Section) (AEU AUS)	Name change to more accurately reflect its association with the British AEU.
1938	Amalgamated Engineering Union (Australian Section) (AEU AUS)	Deregistered February 1938 but another union, with the same name, formed later that year.
1969	Amalgamated Engineering Union (AEU)	Separation from the British organisation
1972/1973	Amalgamated Metal Workers' Union (AMWU)	Amalgamation of the Australian Engineering Union, the Sheet Metal Workers' Union (q.v.), the Boilermakers' and Blacksmiths' Society (q.v.), Federated Jewellers' Watchmakers' & Allied Trades Union of Australia.
1976	Amalgamated Metal Workers' & Shipwrights' Union (AMWSU)	Amalgamation of AMWU and the Federated Shipwrights & Ship Constructors Association of Australia.

	Union Name	Notes
1983	Amalgamated Metals Foundry and Shipwrights' Union (AMFSU)	Amalgamation of AMSWU and Federated Moulders' (Metals) Union of Aust. (q.v.).
1985	Reverted to the name Amalgamated Metal Workers' Union (AMWU)	
1991	Metals & Engineering Workers' Union (MEWU)	Amalgamation with Association of Draughting Supervisory & Technical Employees (ADSTE)
1993	Automotive Metals and Engineering Union (AMEU)	Amalgamation with Vehicle Builders' Employees Federation of Australia (VBEF)
1994	Automotive, Food, Metals & Engineering Union (AFMEU)	Amalgamation with Confectionery Workers' & Food Preservers' Union (CFPWU)
	Automotive, Food, Metals, Engineering, Printing and Kindred Industries Union (AFMEPKIU)	Amalgamation with the Printing and Kindred Industries Union (PKIU)
1995	Australian Manufacturing Workers' Union (AMWU)	Metal and Engineering Division

Note: Amalgamations other than those listed have occurred. This simplified version focuses on key amalgamations from 1972 onwards.
Source: Constructed from materials at the Noel Butlin Archives.

References

Aarons, Brian, and Peter Murphy. 1989. "Labor's Five Years: Counsel for the Defence. An Interview with Laurie Carmichael." *Australian Left Review* 109:21–25.

ABS. 2013. "Employee Earnings, Benefits and Trade Union Membership, Australia." Cat No 6310.0. Canberra: Australian Bureau of Statistics. http://www.justlabour.yorku.ca/volume2/pdfs/buchanan.pdf.

ACTU. 1983. "Statement by President (Cliff Dolan), Special Unions Conference 21st February, on Prices and Incomes Accord." ACTU. Z282A, Box 286. Noel Butlin Archive.

ACTU. 1986. "ACTU Executive Decisions May 26–30 1986." 2010.0048, Box 428. Melbourne University Archive.

ACTU. 1987a. "BWIU, Seamans' Union and ACOA Motions on the 'New Right' to ACTU Congress." ACTU. 2010.0048, Box 463. University of Melbourne Archive.

ACTU. 1987b. *Future Strategies for the Trade Union Movement*. Melbourne: ACTU.

ACTU/TDC. 1987. "Australia Reconstructed: ACTU/TDC Mission to Western Europe." Canberra: ACTU/TDC Mission to Western Europe.

Adkins, Lisa, Matti Kortesoja, Mona Mannevuo, and Hanna Ylöstalo. 2017. "Experimenting with Price: Crafting the New Social Contract in Finland." *Critical Sociology* online before print:1–14.

Ahlquist, John S. 2011. "Navigating Institutional Change: The Accord, Rogernomics, and the Politics of Adjustment in Australia and New Zealand." *Comparative Political Studies* 44:127–155.

Ahlqvist, Toni, and Sami Moisio. 2014. "Neoliberalisation in a Nordic State: From Cartel Polity towards a Corporate Polity in Finland." *New Political Economy* 19 (1):21–55.

ALAC. 1981. "Basis of Discussion: Incomes-Prices Policy." Australian Labor Advisory Committee. Z282A, Box 287, 1982–1984 ALAC Folio. Noel Butlin Archive.

Albo, Greg. 2002. "Neoliberalism, the State, and the Left: A Canadian Perspective." *Monthly Review* 54 (1):46–55.

Albo, Greg. 2009. "The Crisis of Neoliberalism and the Impasse of the Union Movement." *Development Dialogue* 51:119–31.

ALP. 1996. "Report by the National Consultative Review Committee to the ALP National Executive Committee."

ALP & ACTU. 1986. "Accord Mark I: 1983–84." In *The Accord … and Beyond*, edited by Frank Stilwell, 159–176. Leichhardt: Pluto Press Australia.

ALP & ACTU. 2000a. "Accord Mark II: 1985–87." In *Australia in Accord: An Evaluation of the Prices and Incomes Accord in the Hawke-Keating Years*, edited by Kenneth Wilson, Joanne Bradford, and Maree Fitzpatrick, 307–317. Footscray: South Pacific Publishing.

ALP & ACTU. 2000b. "Accord Mark III: 1987–88." In *Australia in Accord: An Evaluation of the Prices and Incomes Accord in the Hawke-Keating Years*, edited by Kenneth Wilson, Joanne Bradford, and Maree Fitzpatrick, 319–329. Footscray: South Pacific Publishing.

ALP & ACTU 2000c. "Accord Mark VI: 1990–93 (November)." In *Australia in Accord: An Evaluation of the Prices and Incomes Accord in the Hawke-Keating Years*, edited by Kenneth Wilson, Joanne Bradford, and Maree Fitzpatrick, 347–354. Footscray: South Pacific Publishing.

ALP & ACTU, Bill. 2000. "Accord Mark VIII: 1995–1996." In *Australia in Accord: An Evaluation of the Prices and Incomes Accord in the Hawke-Keating Years*, edited by Kenneth Wilson, Joanne Bradford, and Maree Fitzpatrick, 381–406. Footscray: South Pacific Publishing.

ALP (NSW). 1996. "Federal Campaign Consultative Panel, Draft Report." ALP (NSW).

Althusser, Louis. 2005. *For Marx*. London: Verso.

AMA. 2014. "Anniversary of the 1984 NSW Doctors' Dispute—30 Years On." *The NSW Doctor (Australian Medical Association NSW)*, April 2014.

AMFSU. 1983a. "National Council Minutes 12–17 December 1983." Amalgamated Metals Foundry and Shipwrights' Union. Z102, Box 571. Noel Butlin Archive.

AMFSU. 1983b. "Victorian State Council Minutes 2 February 1983." Amalgamated Metals Foundry and Shipwrights' Union. Z102, Box 515. Noel Butlin Archive.

AMFSU. 1983c. "Victorian State Council Minutes 16 May 1983." Amalgamated Metals Foundry and Shipwrights' Union. Z102, Box 515. Noel Butlin Archive.

AMFSU. 1983d. "Victorian State Council Minutes 20 June 1983." Amalgamated Metals Foundry and Shipwrights' Union. Z102, Box 515. Noel Butlin Archive.

AMFSU. 1983e. "Victorian State Council Minutes 22 August 1983." Amalgamated Metals Foundry and Shipwrights' Union. Z102, Box 515. Noel Butlin Archive.

AMFSU. 1984a. "Victorian State Council Minutes 16 April 1984." Amalgamated Metals Foundry and Shipwrights' Union. Z102, Box 515. Noel Butlin Archive.

AMFSU. 1984b. "AMWU Speaker's Notes on the Accord." Amalgamated Metals Foundry and Shipwrights' Union. Z102, Box 620. Noel Butlin Archive.

AMFSU and others. 1984. "Combined Trade Unions' Statement to 1984 ALP National Conference."

AMWSU. 1977a. "A People's Economic Program." Amalgamated Metal Workers' & Shipwrights' Union.

AMWSU. 1977b. "Australia Up-Rooted." Amalgamated Metal Workers' & Shipwrights' Union.

AMWSU. 1978. "Dr Stuart Holland ABC Radio Interview, 8 August 1977." Amalgamated Metal Workers' & Shipwrights' Union. 1995.0096, Box 56. University of Melbourne Archive.

AMWSU. 1979. "Australia Ripped Off." Amalgamated Metal Workers' & Shipwrights' Union.

AMWSU. 1980. "Consolidated Decisions of Biennial National Conferences 1973–1980." Amalgamated Metal Workers' & Shipwrights' Union. 1995.0096, Box 56. University of Melbourne Archive.

AMWSU. 1982. "Australia on the Rack." Amalgamated Metal Workers' & Shipwrights' Union.

AMWU. 1985. "Victorian State Council Minutes 5 August 1985." Amalgamated Metal Workers' Union. Z102, Box 515. Noel Butlin Archive.

AMWU. 1986a. "National Conference Minutes 13–18 July 1986." Amalgamated Metal Workers' Union. 1995.0096 (unlisted), Box 82. University of Melbourne Archive.

AMWU. 1986b. "'Death Wish': Free Market Policies Strain Accord." *The Metal Worker*, April 3, 1986. Collection 2006.0006, Box 2. Melbourne University Archive.

AMWU. 1987. "Who's Who on the New Right." *The Metal Worker*, April 1987. Collection 2006.0006, Box 2. Melbourne University Archive.

AMWU and others. 1989. "Progressive Unions' Wage/Tax Report." AMWU, BWIU, FEDFA, Miscellaneous Workers, ACOA, Seamen's Union, and Australian Teachers Federation. 2006.0006, Box 19. Melbourne University Archive.

Anderson, Tim. 1999. "The Meaning of Deregulation." *Journal of Australian Political Economy* 45 (December):5–21.

APRA. 2013. "Annual Superannuation Bulletin 2013." http://www.apra.gov.au/Super/Publications/Documents/Revised%202013%20Annual%20Superannuation%20Bulletin%2005-02-14.pdf.

Armstrong, Philip, Andrew Glyn, and John Harrison. 1984. *Capitalism Since World War II: The Making and Breakup of the Great Boom*. London: Fontana Paperbacks.

ASFA. 2017. "Superannuation Statistics." Association of Superannuation Funds of Australia (ASFA). June 2017. https://www.superannuation.asn.au/resources/superannuation-statistics.

Ashbolt, Allan. 1976. "Threats to Democracy." *Australian Left Review* 1 (55):19–24.

Ashman, Sam, and Alex Callinicos. 2006. "Capital Accumulation and the State System: Assessing David Harvey's 'The New Imperialism.'" *Historical Materialism* 14 (4):107–131.

Avent-Holt, Dustin Robert. 2012. "Organizing Markets: The Structuring of Neoliberalism in the US Airline Industry." PhD, Amherst: University of Massachusetts. http://scholarworks.umass.edu/cgi/viewcontent.cgi?article=1612&context=open_access_dissertations.

Baccaro, Lucio, and Chris Howell. 2011. "A Common Neoliberal Trajectory: The Transformation of Industrial Relations in Advanced Capitalism." *Politics & Society* 39 (4):521–563.

Balakrishnan, Gopal. 2014. "The Abolitionist I." *New Left Review* 90:101–136.

Balakrishnan, Gopal. 2015. "The Abolitionist II." *New Left Review* 91:69–100.

Balnave, Nikki, and Greg Patmore. 2013. "The AMWU: Politics and Industrial Relations, 1852–2012." In *Organise, Educate, Control: The AMWU in Australia 1852–2012*, 3–33. Melbourne: Melbourne University Press.

Banaji, Jairus. 2010. *Theory as History: Essays on Modes of Production and Exploitation*. Historical Materialism Book Series. Chicago: Haymarket Books.

Barker, Colin. 1978. "A Note on the Theory of Capitalist States." *Capital & Class* 4:118–126.

Barr, Gill A. 1985. "Letter to Bill Kelty, ACTU." Australian Workers Union. Z282A, Box 272, Mudginberri Folder. Noel Butlin Archive.

Barry, Michael, and Pat Walsh. 2007. "State Intervention and Trade Unions in New Zealand." *Labor Studies Journal* 31:55–78.

Battellino, Ric. 2007. "Australia's Experience with Financial Deregulation, Speech by Deputy Governor of the Reserve Bank of Australia." presented at the China Australia Governance Program, Melbourne, July 16. http://www.rba.gov.au/speeches/2007/sp-dg-160707.html.

Beeson, Mark. 1997. "Organised Labour in an Era of Global Transformation: Australia Reconstructed Revisited." *Journal of Australian Political Economy* 39:55–71.

Beeson, Mark, and Ann Firth. 1998. "Neoliberalism as a Political Rationality Australian Public Policy Since the 1980s." *Journal of Sociology* 34 (3):215–231.

Beggs, Michael. 2015. *Inflation and the Making of Australian Macroeconomic Policy, 1945–85*. Basingstoke: Palgrave MacMillan.

Beilharz, Peter. 1985. "The Australian Left: Beyond Labourism?" *The Socialist Register* 22:210–232.

Beilharz, Peter. 1994. *Transforming Labor: Labour Tradition and the Labor Decade in Australia*. Melbourne: Cambridge University Press.

Beilharz, Peter. 2009. *Socialism and Modernity*. Minneapolis: University of Minnesota Press.

Beilharz, Peter, and Rob Watts. 1983. "The Discovery of Corporatism." *Australian Society*, November, 27–30.

Bentley, Philip. 1974. "Australian Trade Unionism 1973–74." *Journal of Industrial Relations* 16:374–387.

Berry, Peter. 1977. "The Wage-Price Freeze." *Journal of Australian Political Economy* 1:78–82.

Bieler, Andreas. 2007. "Co-Option or Resistance? Trade Unions and Neoliberal Restructuring in Europe." *Capital & Class* 93:111–124.

Bieler, Andreas, and Adam David Morton. 2008. "The Deficits of Discourse in IPE: Turning Base Metal into Gold?" *International Studies Quarterly* 52:103–128.

Bieler, Andreas, Ian Bruff, and Adam David Morton. 2010. "Acorns and Fruit: From Totalization to Periodization in the Critique of Capitalism." *Capital & Class* 34 (1):25–37.

Biggs, Amanda. 2003. "Medicare—Background Brief." Parliamentary Library, Parliament of Australia. http://www.aph.gov.au/About_Parliament/Parliamentary_Departments/Parliamentary_Library/Publications_Archive/archive/medicare.

Birch, Kean. 2015. "Neoliberalism: The Whys and Wherefores ... and Future Directions." *Sociology Compass* 9 (7):571–584.

Body, Radford, and James Crotty. 1976. "Wages, Prices, and the Profit Squeeze." *Review of Radical Political Economics* 8 (2):63–67.

Boothman, David. 2007. "Critique and Semantic Modification in Gramsci's Approach to Paradigmatic Translation." *Italian Culture* 24 (1):115–143.

Boxall, Anne-marie, and James A Gillespie. 2013. *Making Medicare: The Politics of Universal Health Care in Australia*. Sydney: New South Publishing.

Boyer, Robert. 2013. "The Present Crisis. A Trump for a Renewed Political Economy." *Review of Political Economy* 25 (1):1–38.

Boyle, Peter. 1991. "Factional Warfare in Victorian ALP." *Green Left Weekly*, June 26, 1991. https://www.greenleft.org.au/node/1121.

Bramble, Tom. 1992. "Conflict, Coercion and Co-Option: The Role of Full-Time Officials in the South Australian Branch of the Vehicle Builders Employees' Federation, 1967–80." *Labour History* 63:135–154.

Bramble, Tom. 1994. "Interventionist Industry Policy: A Marxist Critique." *Journal of Australian Political Economy* 33:65–89.

Bramble, Tom. 2000a. "Social Democracy and the 'Failure' of the Accord." In *Australia in Accord: An Evaluation of the Prices and Incomes Accord in the Hawke-Keating Years*, edited by Kenneth Wilson, Joanne Bradford, and Maree Fitzpatrick, 243–264. Footscray: South Pacific Publishing.

Bramble, Tom. 2000b. "'The Rise of the Modern Labour Technocrat': Response." *Labour History* 79:179–184.

Bramble, Tom. 2001. "Australian Union Strategies Since 1945." *Labour & Industry* 11 (3):1–25.

Bramble, Tom. 2008. *Trade Unionism in Australia: A History from Flood to Ebb Tide*. Melbourne: Cambridge University Press.

Bramble, Tom. 2014. "Australian Capitalism in the Neoliberal Age." *Marxist Left Review* 7. http://marxistleftreview.org/index.php/no7-summer-2014/98-australian-capitalism-in-the-neoliberal-age.

Bramble, Tom, and Rick Kuhn. 1999. "Social Democracy After the Long Boom: Economic Restructuring Under Australian Labor, 1983 to 1996." In *The State and Globalization: Comparative Studies of Labour and Capital in National Economies*, edited by Martin Upchurch, 20–55. London: Mansell Publishing.

Bramble, Tom, and Rick Kuhn. 2010. "Making Capitalism Acceptable: The Economic Policy of Australian Social Democracy Since the 1970s." *Marxism 21* 20:306–337.

Bramble, Tom, and Rick Kuhn. 2011. *Labor's Conflict: Big Business, Workers and the Politics of Class*. Port Melbourne: Cambridge University Press.

Brenner, Aaron. 2010. "Preface." In *Rebel Rank and File: Labor Militancy and Revolt from Below During the Long 1970s*, edited by Aaron Brenner, Robert Brenner, and Cal Winslow, xi–xix. New York: Verso.

Brenner, Robert. 2006. *The Economics of Global Turbulence: The Advanced Capitalist Economies from Long Boom to Long Downturn, 1945–2005*. London: Verso.

Brenner, Robert. 2016. "The Paradox of Social Democracy: The American Case." *Verso Books Blog*, February 26, 2016. https://www.versobooks.com/blogs/2517-the-paradox-of-social-democracy-the-american-case-part-two.

Brenner, Neil, and Nik Theodore. 2002a. "Chapter 1." In *Spaces of Neoliberalism: Urban Restructuring in North America and Western Europe*. Malden: Blackwell.

Brenner, Neil, and Nik Theodore. 2002b. "Cities and the Geographies of 'Actually Existing Neoliberalism.'" *Antipode* 34 (3):349–379.

Brenner, Neil, Jamie Peck, and Nik Theodore. 2010. "Variegated Neoliberalisation: Geographies, Modalities, Pathways." *Global Networks* 10 (2):182–222.

Brent, Peter. 1991. "The 'No's Have It: The Politics of Australian Constitutional Referendums." Honours, University of Sydney.

Brett, Judith. 1998. "Representing the Unrepresented: One Nation and the Formation of the Labor Party." In *Two Nations: The Causes and Effects of the Rise on the One Nation Party*, 26–37. Melbourne: Bookman Press.

Brian, Bernie. 1999. "The Mudginberri Abattoir Dispute of 1985." *Labour History* 76: 107–124.

Briggs, Chris. 1999. "The Transition and Decline of the ACTU During the 1990s: From a 'Governing Institution' to a 'Servicing Organisation.'" *New Zealand Journal of Industrial Relations* 24 (3):257–289.

Briggs, Chris. 2001. "Australian Exceptionalism: The Role of Trade Unions in the Emergence of Enterprise Bargaining." *The Journal of Industrial Relations* 43 (1):27–43.

Brogan, Peter. 2013. "Neoliberalisation and the Matrix of Action: In Conversation with Neil Brenner, Jamie Peck and Nik Theodore." *Alternate Routes: A Journal of Critical Social Research* 24:183–197.

Bryan, Dick. 1987. "Interview with John Button." *Journal of Australian Political Economy* 39:7–16.

Bryan, Dick. 1991. "Australian Economic Nationalism: Old and New." *Australian Economic Papers* 30:290–309.

Bryan, Dick. 1995. "International Competitiveness: National and Class Agendas." *Journal of Australian Political Economy* 35:1–23.

Bryan, Dick. 2004. "Superannuation: The Ricardian Crisis." *Journal of Australian Political Economy* 53:100–115.

Buchanan, John. 2003. "Union Amalgamations as a Basis for Union Renewal in Australia: Insights from Unfinished Business." *Just Labour* 2:54–63.

Buchanan, John, Damian Oliver, and Chris Briggs. 2014. "Solidarity Reconstructed: The Impact of the Accord on Relations Within the Australian Union Movement." *Journal of Industrial Relations* 56 (2):288–307.

Burford, Mark. 1983. "Prices & Incomes Policies and Socialist Politics." *Journal of Australian Political Economy* 14:7–32.

Burgmann, Meredith, and Verity Burgmann. 2011. "Green Bans Movement." Dictionary of Sydney. http://www.dictionaryofsydney.org/entry/green_bans_movement.

Burke, Latika. 2014. "Paul Howes Calls For End to 'Industrial Warfare' over Workplace Relations; Abbott Distances Himself from Penalty Rates Review." *ABC News Online*, February 6, 2014. http://www.abc.net.au/news/2014-02-05/howes-grand-accord-industrial-relations-grand-compact-accord/5240710.

Butlin, Matthew, Robert Dixon, and Peter J Lloyd. 2014. "Statistical Appendix: Selected Data Series,1800–2010." In *The Cambridge Economic History of Australia*, edited by Simon Ville and Glenn Withers, 555–594. Cambridge: Cambridge University Press.

Buttigieg, Joseph A. 2011. "Introduction." In *Prison Notebooks (Vol 1)*, edited by Joseph A Buttigieg, translated by Joseph A Buttigieg and Antonio Callari. New York: Columbia University Press.

Cahill, Damien. 2007. "The Contours of Neoliberal Hegemony in Australia." *Rethinking Marxism* 19 (2):221–233.

Cahill, Damien. 2008. "Labo(u)r, the Boom and the Prospects for an Alternative to Neo-Liberalism." *Journal of Australian Political Economy* 61:321–335.

Cahill, Damien. 2010a. "'Actually Existing Neoliberalism' and the Global Economic Crisis." *Labour & Industry* 20 (3):298–316.

Cahill, Damien. 2010b. "Business Mobilisation, the New Right and Australian Labor Governments in the 1980s." *Labour History* 98:7–24.

Cahill, Damien. 2013. "Ideas-Centred Explanations of the Rise of Neoliberalism: A Critique." *Australian Journal of Political Science* 48 (1):71–84.

Cahill, Damien. 2014. *The End of Laissez Faire?: On the Durability of Embedded Neoliberalism*. Cheltenham: Edward Elgar.

Cairns, Jim F. 1975. "'Change, Planning, the System, and Inflation', Speech to the 31st Federal Conference of the Australian Labor Party." Z102, Box 50. Noel Butlin Archive.

Callaghan, James. 1976. "James Callaghan: Leader's Speech." presented at the British Labour Party Conference, Blackpool. http://www.britishpoliticalspeech.org/speech-archive.htm?speech=174.

Campbell, George. 2000. "A Union View of The Accord." In *Australia in Accord: An Evaluation of the Prices and Incomes Accord in the Hawke-Keating Years*, edited by Kenneth Wilson, Joanne Bradford, and Maree Fitzpatrick, 49–50. Footscray: South Pacific Publishing.

Campbell, James Keith. 1979. "The Australian Financial System Inquiry (Campbell Report)." Canberra: Commonwealth of Australia.

Carmichael, Laurie. 1983a. "Letter to New Zealand Engineering Union." Amalgamated Metals Foundry and Shipwrights' Union. Z102, Box 562, AMWU Collection, New Zealand General Correspondence Folio. Noel Butlin Archive.

Carmichael, Laurie. 1983b. "Letter to New Zealand Engineering Union." Amalgamated Metals Foundry and Shipwrights' Union. Z102, Box 562, AMWU Collection, New Zealand General Correspondence Folio. Noel Butlin Archive.

Carney, Shaun. 2002. "The Tale of Two Budgets." *The Age*, May 25, 2002. http://www.theage.com.au/articles/2002/05/24/1022038477070.html.

Casey, Andrew. 1987. "Plumbers' Union Faces Court Battle With Bosses." *Sydney Morning Herald*, February 7, 1987.

Castles, Francis, Rolf Gerritsen, and Jack Vowles, eds. 1996. *The Great Experiment: Labour Parties and Public Policy Transformation in Australia and New Zealand.* St Leonards: Allen & Unwin.

Catley, Bob. 2005. "The Technocratic Labor Thesis Revisited." *Thesis Eleven* 82 (August):97–108.

Catley, Bob, and Bruce McFarlane. 1974. *From Tweedledum To Tweedledee: The New Labor Government in Australia.* Artarmon: Australia & New Zealand Book Company.

Cazdyn, Eric, and Imre Szeman. 2011. *After Globalisation.* Malden: Wiley-Blackwell.

Chapman, Bruce. 2000. "The Accord as a Macroeconomic Policy Instrument: Influences and Changes." In *Australia in Accord: An Evaluation of the Prices and Incomes Accord in the Hawke-Keating Years*, edited by Kenneth Wilson, Joanne Bradford, and Maree Fitzpatrick, 231–242. Footscray: South Pacific Publishing.

Clancy, Peter. 1996. "The New Zealand Experiment: A Canadian Perspective." *EJROT: Electronic Journal of Radical Organisational Theory* 2 (1):1–12.

Clark, Andrew. 2015. "John Hewson Reveals the Real Hero of Australia's Economic Reform." *Australian Financial Review*, September 5, 2015. http://www.afr.com/leadership/john-hewson-on-australias-heroes-and-villains-of-economic-reform-20150902-gjd7fi.

Coates, Nick, Sacha Vidler, and Frank Stilwell. 2004. "Editor's Introduction." *Journal of Australian Political Economy* 53:3–8.

Cockerell, Michael. 1992. *Labour's Last Premier.* BBC. https://www.youtube.com/watch?v=QOn69eukaDU.

Cohen, G A. 1978. *Karl Marx's Theory of History.* Oxford: Claredon Press.

Colletti, Lucio. 1973. *From Rousseau to Lenin: Studies in Ideology and Society.* New York: Monthly Review Press.

Colletti, Lucio. 1975. "Introduction." In *Early Writings*, edited by Karl Marx, 7–56. Harmondsworth: Penguin Books.

Collett, John. 2014. "Australia's 2014 Federal Budget Forces Rethink of Retirement Plans." *Sydney Morning Herald*, May 20, 2014. http://m.smh.com.au/money/australias-2014-federal-budget-forces-rethink-of-retirement-plans-20140515-zre2h.html.

Combet, Greg. 2004. "Superannuation: Past, Present and Future. An Interview with Greg Combet, Secretary of the ACTU." *Journal of Australian Political Economy* 53:17–26.

Commonwealth of Australia. 1983. "National Economic Summit Conference Communiqué." Canberra: Commonwealth of Australia.

Commonwealth of Australia. 2014. "Australia-New Zealand Closer Economic Relations Trade Agreement." Department of Foreign Affairs and Trade. November 2014. http://dfat.gov.au/trade/agreements/anzcerta/Pages/australia-new-zealand-closer-economic-relations-trade-agreement.aspx.

Commonwealth Parliamentary Debates. 1974. "Hansard." House of Representatives.

Connell, Raewyn, and Nour Dados. 2014. "Where in the World Does Neoliberalism Come From?" *Theory and Society* 43:117–138.

Cooper, Melinda. 2008. *Life as Surplus: Biotechnology and Capitalism in the Neoliberal Era*. Seattle: University of Washington Press.

Cooper, Rae, and Bradon Ellem. 2008. "The Neoliberal State, Trade Unions and Collective Bargaining in Australia." *British Journal of Industrial Relations* 46 (3):532–554.

Cooper, Rae, and Greg Patmore. 2002. "Trade Union Organising and Labour History." *Labour History* 83 (November):3–18.

Costello, Peter. 1988. "The Dollar Sweets Story." In *In Search of the Magic Pudding*. Vol. 5. Lorne: H R Nicholls Society. http://archive.hrnicholls.com.au/archives/vol5/vol5-5.php.

Cottle, Drew, and Joe Collins. 2010. "Labor Neoliberals or Pragmatic Neo-Laborists? The Hawke and Keating Labor Governments in Office, 1983–96." *Labour History* 98 (May):25–37.

Cottle, Drew, and Joseph Collins. 2008. "WorkChoices: Ruling Class Mobilisation in Contemporary Australia." *Journal of Economic and Social Policy* 12:1–14.

Cowgill, Matt. 2013. "The Inadequacy of Newstart." *We Are All Dead* (blog). July 1, 2013. https://mattcowgill.wordpress.com/2013/07/01/the-inadequacy-of-newstart/.

Cox, Lloyd. 2006. "The Antipodean Social Laboratory, Labour and the Transformation of the Welfare State." *Journal of Sociology* 42 (2):107–124.

CPA. 1974. "The Socialist Alternative: Documents of CPA National Congress 1974." Red Pen Publications.

CPA. 1982. "A Strategy for the 1980s in the Metal Industry." Communist Party of Australia.

Crean, Simon. 1986. "Letter from ACTU President to the Minister Responsible for the Prices Surveillance Authority." Australian Council of Trade Unions. Z282A, Box 296. Noel Butlin Archive.

Crouch, Colin. 2011. *The Strange Non-Death of Neo-Liberalism*. Cambridge: Polity Press.

Culpepper, Pepper D, and Aidan Regan. 2014. "Why Don't Governments Need Trade Unions Anymore? The Death of Social Pacts in Ireland and Italy." *Socio-Economic Review* 12 (4):723–745.

Czada, Roland. 2011. "Corporativism (Corporatism)." Edited by Bertrand Badie and Dirk Berg-Schlosser. *International Encyclopedia of Political Science*. London: SAGE.

Dabscheck, Braham. 1989. *Australian Industrial Relations in the 1980s*. Melbourne: Oxford University Press.

Dabscheck, Braham. 2000. "The Accord: Corporatism Visits Australia." In *Australia in Accord: An Evaluation of the Prices and Incomes Accord in the Hawke-Keating Years*, edited by Kenneth Wilson, Joanne Bradford, and Maree Fitzpatrick, 93–104. Footscray: South Pacific Publishing.

Dabscheck, Braham, and Jim Kitay. 1991. "Malcolm Fraser's (Unsuccessful) 1977 Voluntary Wages and Prices Freeze." *The Journal of Industrial Relations* 33 (2):249–264.

Dare, Tim. 1974. "Join In? But Nobody Wants to Know." *The Australian*, February 1, 1974.

David, Uren. 2012. "Super Funds' Losses Among Worst in World." *The Australian*, June 13, 2012.

Davidson, Neil. 2009. "Shock and Awe." *International Socialism Journal* 124:159–178.

Davidson, Neil. 2010. "What Was Neoliberalism?" In *Neoliberal Scotland: Class and Society in a Stateless Nation*, edited by Neil Davidson, Patricia McCafferty, and David Miller, 1–92. Newcastle Upon Tyne: Cambridge Scholars Publishing.

Davidson, Neil. 2013. "The Neoliberal Era in Britain: Historical Developments and Current Perspectives." *International Socialism Journal* 139:171–223.

Davidson, Neil. 2015. "The New Middle Class and the Changing Social Base of Neoliberalism: A First Approximation." *Oxford Left Review* 14:4–10.

Davidson, Neil. 2017. "Crisis Neoliberalism and Regimes of Permanent Exception." *Critical Sociology* 43 (4–5):615–634.

Davis, Edward M. 1988. "Australia Reconstructed: A Symposium; Australia Reconstructed: An Ambitious Report." *Prometheus: Critical Studies in Innovation* 6 (1):150–158.

Davis, Mike. 1980. "The Barren Marriage of American Labour and the Democratic Party." *New Left Review* 1 (124):43–84.

Dettmer, Andrew. 2013. "Laurie Carmichael Talks to Andrew Dettmer." In *Organise, Educate, Control: The AMWU in Australia 1852–2012*, edited by Andrew Dettmer and Andrew Reeves, 173–190. Melbourne: Melbourne University Press.

Dibley-Maher, Paul. 2012. "Friend or Foe? The Impact of the Hawke/Keating Neoliberal Reforms on Australian Workers and the Australian Public Sector." Master of Arts (Research), Queensland University of Technology.

Dolan, Cliff. 1984. "'Welcome Address', Speech to Conference on Industrial Relations and the Accord, Macquarie University." ACTU. Z282A, Box 262. Noel Butlin Archive.

Dolan, Cliff, and Laurie Carmichael. 1978. "ACTU Conference on Manufacturing Industry (cassette Recording)." Z282A, Box 701, Tape 3, Side A. Noel Butlin Archive.

Duménil, Gérard, and Dominique Lévy. 2005. "The Neoliberal (Counter-)Revolution." In *Neoliberalism: A Critical Reader*, edited by Alfredo Saad-Filho and Deborah Johnson, 9–19. London: Pluto Press.

Duménil, Gérard, and Dominique Lévy. 2011. *The Crisis of Neoliberalism*. Cambridge, MA: Harvard University Press.

Duménil, Gérard, and Dominique Lévy. 2012. "The Crisis of Neoliberalism as a Stepwise Process: From the Great Contraction to the Crisis of Sovereign Debts." In *Neoliberalism: Beyond the Free Market*, edited by Damien Cahill, Lindy Edwards, and Frank Stilwell, 31–53. Cheltenham: Edward Elgar.

Dunn, Bill. 2015. "Down With Neoliberalism...as a Concept!" Historical Materialism Australasia Conference, University of Sydney.

Early, Steve. 2012. "Reviving the Strike in the Shadow of PATCO." *Monthly Review*, 2012. https://monthlyreview.org/2012/03/01/reviving-the-strike-in-the-shadow-of-patco/.

Easson, Michael, and Tom Forrest. 1994. "Good While It Lasted: The Position and Prospects of Australian Unions in 1993." *The Economic and Labour Relations Review* 5 (1):117–136.

Eidlin, Barry. 2016. "Why Is There No Labor Party in the United States? Political Articulation and the Canadian Comparison, 1932 to 1948." *American Sociological Review* 81 (3):488–516.

Emerson, Craig. 2015. "Summit Will Build Consensus for Economic Reform." *Australian Financial Review*, July 14, 2015.

Ericsen, Peter. 2004. "From the Plague to Reith: The Legal Antecedents of the Workplace Relations Act." Marxist Interventions. http://www.anu.edu.au/polsci/marx/interventions/law.htm.

Ewer, Peter, Winton Higgins, and Annette Stephens. 1987. *Unions and the Future of Australian Manufacturing*. North Sydney: Allen & Unwin.

Fairbrother, Peter, Stuart Svensen, and Julian Teicher. 1997. "The Withering Away of the Australian State: Privatisation and Its Implications for Labour." *Labour & Industry* 8 (2):1–29.

Fellows, Julia, and Joe Riordan. 2000. "Sentimental Reflections on Industrial Relations Practitioners." In *Australia in Accord: An Evaluation of the Prices and Incomes Accord in the Hawke-Keating Years*, edited by Kenneth Wilson, Joanne Bradford, and Maree Fitzpatrick, 36–44. Footscray: South Pacific Publishing.

Fiori, Giuseppe. 1973. *Antonio Gramsci: Life of a Revolutionary*. London: New Left Books.

Fletcher, Paul. 2013. "Superannuation's Role in Advancing the Power and Economic Influence of the Union Movement." presented at the HR Nicholls Society, July 8. http://www.paulfletcher.com.au/speeches/other-speeches/item/953-superannuation-s-role-in-advancing-the-power-and-economic-influence-of-the-union-movement-speech-to-hr-nicholls-society.html.

Flew, Terry. 2014. "Six Theories of Neoliberalism." *Thesis Eleven* 122 (1):49–71.

Foster, RA. 1996. *Australian Economic Statistics: 1949/50 to 1994/95*. Sydney: Reserve Bank of Australia.

Foucault, Michel. 2004. *The Birth of Biopolitics: Lectures at the Collège de France, 1978–79*. Translated by Graham Burchell. Hampshire: Palgrave Macmillan.

Frankel, Boris. 1993. "Picking Up the Pieces: The ACTU in the 1990s." *Arena Magazine* 7:4–5.

Frankel, Boris. 1997. "Beyond Labourism and Socialism: How the Australian Labor Party Developed the Model of 'New Labour.'" *New Left Review* 221:3–33.

Frenkel, Stephen, and Alice Coolican. 1983. "Union Organisation and Decision Making." In *Australian Unions: An Industrial Relations Perspective*, edited by Bill Ford and David Plowman. Macmillan.

Friedman, Milton. 1962. *Capitalism and Freedom*. Chicago: University of Chicago Press.

Frijters, Paul, and Robert Gregory. 2006. "From Golden Age to Golden Age: Australia's 'Great Leap Forward'?" *The Economic Record* 82 (257):207–224.

Gahan, Peter. 1996. "Did Arbitration Make for Dependent Unionism? Evidence from Historical Case Studies." *Journal of Industrial Relations* 38 (4):648–698.

Galleghan, R. 1985. "Telegram to Bill Kelty, ACTU." Ship Painters and Dockers Union. Z282A, Box 272, Mudginberri Folder. Noel Butlin Archive.

Gallery, Natalie, Kerry Brown, and Gerry Gallery. 1996. "Privatising the Pension." *Journal of Australian Political Economy* 38:98–124.

Garnaut, Ross. 2002. "Australia: A Case Study of Unilateral Trade Liberalisation." In *Going Alone: The Case for Relaxed Reciprocity in Freeing Trade*, edited by Jagdish Bhagwati, 139–166. Massachusetts Institute of Technology.

Gibson, Steve. 1984. "Another View of the Prices & Incomes Accord." *Locomotive Journal (Publication of the Australian Federated Union of Locomotive Employees)* September/October:5.

Glyn, Andrew, and Bob Sutcliffe. 1972. *British Capitalism, Workers and the Profit Squeeze*. London: Penguin.

Grahl, John, and Paul Teague. 1997. "Is the European Social Model Fragmenting?" *New Political Economy* 2 (3):405–426.

Gramsci, Antonio. 1971. *Selections from the Prison Notebooks of Antonio Gramsci*. London: Lawrence and Wishart.

Gramsci, Antonio. 1975. *Letters From Prison*. Translated by Lynne Lawner. London: Jonathon Cape.

Gramsci, Antonio. 1995. *Further Selections from the Prison Notebooks*. Edited by David Boothman. Minneapolis: University of Minnesota Press.

Gramsci, Antonio. 2011a. *Prison Notebooks (Vol 1)*. Edited by Joseph A Buttigieg. Translated by Joseph A Buttigieg and Antonio Callari. New York: Columbia University Press.

Gramsci, Antonio. 2011b. *Prison Notebooks (Vol 3)*. Edited by Joseph A Buttigieg. Translated by Joseph A Buttigieg and Antonio Callari. New York: Columbia University Press.

Greber, Jacob. 2017. "Workers Must Demand Greater Share of Pie, Says RBA Governor Philip Lowe." *Australian Financial Review*, June 19, 2017. http://www.afr.com/news/

economy/workers-must-demand-greater-share-of-pie-says-rba-governor-philip-lowe-20170619-gwtxht.

Green, Roy, and Andrew Wilson. 2000. "The Accord and Industrial Relations: Lessons for Political Strategy." In *Australia in Accord: An Evaluation of the Prices and Incomes Accord in the Hawke-Keating Years*, 105–121. Footscray: South Pacific Publishing.

Griffin, Gerard, and Vincent Giuca. 1986. "One Union Peak Council: The Merger of ACSPA and CAGEO with the ACTU." *Journal of Industrial Relations* 28 (4):483–503.

Griffiths, Phil. 1989. "The Social Roots of the Labor Tradition." *The Socialist*, December 1989.

Griffiths, Phil. 1997. "Strike Fraser Out! The Labour Movement Campaign Against the Blocking of Supply and the Sacking of the Whitlam Government, October-December 1975." Marxist Interventions. http://www.anu.edu.au/polsci/marx/interventions/sacked.htm.

Gruen, David. 2000. "Introduction." In *The Australian Economy in the 1990s*, edited by David Gruen and Sona Shrestha, 1–7. H.C. Coombs Centre for Financial Studies, Kirribilli: Economic Group, Reserve Bank of Australia.

Gruen, David, and Glenn Stevens. 2000. "Australian Macroeconomic Performance and Policies in the 1990s." In *The Australian Economy in the 1990s*, edited by David Gruen and Sona Shrestha, 32–72. H.C. Coombs Centre for Financial Studies, Kirribilli: Economic Group, Reserve Bank of Australia.

Hagan, Jim, and Rob Castle. 1986. "The Accord: No Alternatives in Sight." *National Outlook*, April, 12–13.

Haines, Jenny. 2014. "ALP and ACTU Accord (Personal Correspondence)," February 27, 2014.

Halfpenny, John. 1983. "Briefing Notes: The Accord, The Summit, Wages, Prices and Industry Policies." Amalgamated Metals Foundry and Shipwrights' Union. Z102 Box 990, Document NRC-F-M692-0048. Noel Butlin Archive.

Halfpenny, John. 1984a. "Victorian State Conference State Secretary's Report 1984." Amalgamated Metals Foundry and Shipwrights' Union. 1989.0054, Box 3/3. Melbourne University Archive.

Halfpenny, John. 1984b. "For Adequate Promotion, Implementation and Development of the Accord: Prices Surveillance (Joint Union Seminar Briefing Paper)." Amalgamated Metals Foundry and Shipwrights' Union. Z102, Box 620, Folio "Economy and the Accord." Noel Butlin Archive.

Hampson, Ian. 1996. "The Accord: A Post-Mortem." *Labour & Industry* 7 (2):55–77.

Hampson, Ian. 1997. "The End of the Experiment: Corporatism Collapses in Australia." *Economic and Industrial Democracy* 18:539–566.

Hancock, Keith. 1999. "Labour Market Deregulation in Australia." In *Reshaping the Labour Market: Regulation, Efficiency and Equality in Australia*, edited by Sue Richardson, 38–85. Cambridge: Cambridge University Press.

Hancock, Keith. 2014. "The Accord, the Labour Market and the Economy." *Journal of Industrial Relations* 56 (2):273–287.

Harcourt, Tim. 2013. "Lessons of the Hawke-Keating Years Mean There's Only One Choice in Labor's Leadership Ballot." *Business Review Weekly*, October 3, 2013. http://www.brw.com.au/p/business/choice_harcourt_lessons_leadership_kZ8VVW20KrGqivAGLYfk7L.

Harding, Neil. 2009. *Lenin's Political Thought: Theory and Practice in the Democratic and Socialist Revolutions*. Chicago: Haymarket Books.

Hardt, Michael, and Antonio Negri. 2000. *Empire*. Cambridge: Harvard University Press.

Harvey, David. 2003a. *The New Imperialism*. Oxford: Oxford University Press.

Harvey, David. 2003b. "David Harvey: It's About a New Deal." Discussion List. *Marxism* (blog). November 30, 2003. http://greenhouse.economics.utah.edu/pipermail/marxism/2003-November/007240.html.

Harvey, David. 2005. *A Brief History of Neoliberalism*. Oxford: Oxford University Press.

Harvey, David. 2007. "Neoliberalism as Creative Destruction." *Annals of the American Academy of Political and Social Science* 610:22–44.

Hawke, Robert JL. 1979. *The Resolution of Conflict* (*Boyer Lectures*). Sydney: The Australian Broadcasting Commission.

Hawke, Robert JL. 1983a. "Cabinet Submission 72—National Economic Summit Conference (NESC)—Report and Further Action—Decision 204/M." Commonwealth of Australia. National Archives, A13977, 31405672. http://recordsearch.naa.gov.au/SearchNRetrieve/Interface/DetailsReports/ItemDetail.aspx?Barcode=31405672&isAv=N.

Hawke, Robert JL. 1983b. "Speech by the Prime Minister." presented at the Financial Review Dinner, Sydney, August 24. http://pmtranscripts.dpmc.gov.au/browse.php?did=6185.

Hawke, Robert JL. 1986. "Address to the Nation on the Economic Situation." Canberra, June 11. http://pmtranscripts.dpmc.gov.au/browse.php?did=6950.

Hawke, Robert JL. 1987. "Hawke On The Issues: Address to ACTU Congress." *ETU News*, September 2, 1987. 2006.0006, Box 11. University of Melbourne Archive.

Hay, Colin. 1999. "Marxism and the State." In *Marxism and Social Science*, edited by Andrew Gamble, David Marsh, and Tony Tant, 152–174. Urbana: University of Illinois Press.

Hay, Colin. 2007. *Why We Hate Politics*. London: Polity.

Hay, Colin. 2009. "The Winter of Discontent Thirty Years On." *The Political Quarterly* 80 (4):545–552.

Hegel, Georg Wilhelm Friedrich. 1967. *Philosophy of Right*. Translated by TM Knox. Oxford: Oxford University Press.

Heino, Brett. 2017. *Regulation Theory and Australian Capitalism: Rethinking Social Justice and Labour Law*. London: Rowman & Littlefield.

Held, David. 1983. "Introduction: Central Perspectives on the Modern State." In *States and Society*, edited by David Held, James Anderson, Bram Gieben, Stuart Hall, Laurence Harris, Paul Lewis, Noel Parker, and Ben Turok. Oxford: Martin Robertson.

Hendy, Peter. 2006. "Changes in Employer Organisations 1985–2005." In *Let's Start All Over Again*. Vol. 27. Sydney: H R Nicholls Society. http://archive.hrnicholls.com.au/archives/vol27/vol27-5.php.

Higgins, Henry Bournes. 1915. "A New Province for Law and Order: Industrial Peace through Minimum Wage and Arbitration." *Harvard Law Review* 29 (1):13–39.

Higgins, Winton. 1980. "Class Mobilization and Socialism in Sweden: Lessons from Afar." In *Work and Inequality*, by Geoff Dow and Paul Boreham, 1:153–154. South Melbourne: Macmillan.

Higgins, Winton. 1987. "Unions as Bearers of Industrial Regeneration: Reflections on the Australian Case." *Economic and Industrial Democracy* 8:213–236.

Hilmer, Fred. 1993. "National Competition Policy Review (Hilmer Report)." Commonwealth of Australia.

Hobbes, Thomas. 1997. *Leviathan*. New York: Touchstone.

Hodgkinson, Ann, and Nelson Perera. 2004. "Strike Activity Under Enterprise Bargaining: Economics or Politics?" *Australian Journal of Labour Economics* 7 (4): 439–457.

Hodgson, I. 1985. "Telegram to ACTU." Transport Workers' Union of Australia. Z282A, Box 272, Mudginberri Folder. Noel Butlin Archive.

Holland, Stuart. 1975. *The Socialist Challenge*. London: Quartet Books.

Holland, Stuart. 1977. "ABC Radio Interview." Amalgamated Metal Workers and Shipwrights Union. Collection 1995.0096 (unlisted collection), Box 56. Melbourne University Archive.

Holloway, John. 2002. *Change the World Without Taking Power: The Meaning of Revolution Today*. London: Pluto Press.

Holloway, John, and Alex Callinicos. 2005. "Can We Change the World Without Taking Power: A Debate." *International Socialism Journal* 2 (106):112–134.

Horne, Donald. 1975. *Death of the Lucky Country*. Ringwood: Penguin Books Australia.

Howard, WA (Bill). 1977. "Australian Trade Unions in the Context of Union Theory." *Journal of Industrial Relations* 19:255–273.

Howard, Michael C, and John E King. 2004. "The Rise of Neo-Liberalism in Advanced Capitalist Economies: Towards a Materialist Explanation." In *The Rise of the Market: Critical Essays on the Political Economy of Neo-Liberalism*, edited by Philip Arestis and Malcolm Sawyer. Cheltenham: Edward Elgar.

Howard, Michael C, and John E King. 2008. *The Rise of Neoliberalism in Advanced Capitalist Economies: A Materialist Analysis*. Hampshire: Palgrave Macmillan.

Howes, Paul. 2014. "Speech by Australian Workers' Union." presented at the National Press Club, Canberra, February 5. http://www.awu.net.au/opinions/paul-howes-address-national-press-club-5214.

Hughes, Barry. 1979. "The Economy." In *From Whitlam to Fraser: Reform and Reaction in Australian Politics*, edited by Allan Patience and Brian Head, 9–49. Melbourne: Oxford University Press.

Humphries, Maria. 1996. "The Political Economy of Organisational Discourse and Control in New Zealand's Liberalised Economy." *EJROT: Electronic Journal of Radical Organisational Theory* 2 (1):1–12.

Humphrys, Elizabeth. 2014. "The Primacy of Politics: Stilwell, the Accord and the Critique of the State." In *Challenging the Orthodoxy. Reflections on Frank Stilwell's Contribution to Political Economy*, edited by Susan Schroeder and Lynne Chester, 151–172. Berlin: Springer-Verlag.

Humphrys, Elizabeth, and Damien Cahill. 2017. "How Labour Made Neoliberalism." *Critical Sociology* 43 (4/5). https://doi.org/10.1177/0896920516655859.

Humphrys, Elizabeth, and Tad Tietze. 2015. "Anti-Politics and the Illusions of Neoliberalism." *Oxford Left Review* 14:20–27.

James, Estelle, and Sarah Brooks. 2001. "The Political Economy of Structural Pension Reform." In *New Ideas About Old Age Security*, edited by Robert Holzmann and Joseph Stiglitz, 133–170. Washington DC: World Bank.

Jericho, Greg. 2014a. "Cabinet Papers Show Paul Keating Had a 'Budget Emergency' of His Own." *The Guardian*, January 1, 2014. http://www.theguardian.com/world/2013/dec/31/cabinet-papers-show-paul-keating-had-a-budget-emergency-of-his-own.

Jericho, Greg. 2014b. "Why Australian Voters Care More about Jobs than Fixing the Budget." *The Guardian*, July 14, 2014. http://www.theguardian.com/business/grogonomics/2014/jul/14/why-australian-voters-care-more-about-jobs.

Jericho, Greg. 2015. "Union Membership Figures Plunge. And the Future Looks Worse." *The Drum Opinion*, October 28, 2015. http://www.theguardian.com/commentisfree/2015/oct/28/union-membership-figures-plunge-and-thats-the-good-news.

Jessop, Bob. 1979. "Corporatism, Parliamentarism and Social Democracy." In *Trends Toward Corporatism Intermediation*, edited by Philippe C Schmitter and Gerhard Lehmbruch, 185–212. London: SAGE Publications.

Jessop, Bob. 1982. *The Capitalist State: Marxist Theories and Methods*. Oxford: Martin Robertson & Company.

Jessop, Bob. 1990. *State Theory: Putting the Capitalist State in Its Place*. University Park: Penn State University Press.

Jessop, Bob. 2001. "What Follows Fordism? On the Periodization of Capitalism and Its Regulation." In *Phases of Capitalist Development: Booms, Crises, and Globalization*, edited by Robert Albritton, Makoto Itoh, Richard Westra, and Alan Zuege, 283–299. Basingstoke: Palgrave.

Jessop, Bob. 2002. "Liberalism, Neoliberalism, and Urban Governance: A State-Theoretical Perspective." *Antipode* 34 (3):452–472.

Johnson, Carol. 1989. *The Labor Legacy: Curtain, Chifley, Whitlam, Hawke*. North Sydney: Allen & Unwin.

Johnson, Carol. 2002. "Australian Political Science and the Study of Discourse." Australasian Political Studies Association Conference, Australian National University, Canberra.

Johnson, Val Marie. 2011. "Introduction." *Social Science History* 35 (3):323–336.

Johnson, Carol, and Fran Tonkiss. 2002. "The Third Influence: The Blair Government and Australian Labor." *Policy & Politics* 30 (1):5–18.

Jones, Barry. 2006. *A Thinking Reed*. Crows Nest: Allen & Unwin.

Jones, Evan. 1979. "Fraser and the Social Wage." *Journal of Australian Political Economy* 5:33–48.

Jones, Evan. 1997. "The Background to Australia Reconstructed." *Journal of Australian Political Economy* 39:17–38.

Kahn, Alec. 1981. "The Fraser Years." *International Socialist* 11:3–16.

Kantola, Anu, and Johannes Kananen. 2013. "Seize the Moment: Financial Crisis and the Making of the Finnish Competition State." *New Political Economy* 18 (6):811–826.

Kaptein, Ed. 1993. "Neo-Liberalism and the Dismantling of Corporatism in Australia." In *Restructuring Hegemony in the Global Political Economy: The Rise of Transnational Neoliberalism in the 1980s*, edited by Henk W Overbeek, 79–109. London: Routledge.

Kasper, Wolfgang, Richard Blandy, and John Freebairn. 1980. *Australia at the Crossroads: Our Choices to the Year 2000*. Sydney: Harcourt Brace Jovanovich Group.

Keane, Bernard. 2014. "How the Government Bumbled into a Budget Disaster." *Crikey*, May 23, 2014. http://www.crikey.com.au/2014/05/23/keane-how-the-government-bumbled-into-a-budget-disaster.

Kearney, Ged. 2013. "Address to 'The Accord 30 Years On' Symposium." presented at the The Accord 30 Years On, Macquarie University Sydney Campus, May 31. http://www.actu.org.au/Media/Speechesandopinion/GedKearneyaddresstoTheAccord30YearsOnsymposium31May2013.aspx.

Keating, Paul. 1992. *One Nation: Statement*. Canberra: Australian Government Publishing Service.

Keating, Paul. 1993a. "Investing in the Nation." Canberra: Australian Government Publishing Service.

Keating, Paul. 1993b. "1993 Federal Election Acceptance Speech." Bankstown Sports Club Sydney, March 13. http://www.keating.org.au/shop/item/victory-speech-true-believers---13-march-1993.

Keating, Paul. 1993c. "National Competition Policy Review." Commonwealth of Australia. http://pmtranscripts.dpmc.gov.au/transcripts/00008945.pdf.

Keating, Paul. 2007. Paul Keating on the Lead-Up to the Federal Election Interview by Tony Jones. Lateline, ABC. http://www.abc.net.au/lateline/content/2007/s1945485.htm.

Keating, Paul. 2012. "Paul Keating Address to ACTU Congress 2012 Dinner, on Bill Kelty." presented at the 2012 ACTU Congress Dinner. http://www.actu.org.au/Media/Speechesandopinion/PaulKeatingaddresstoACTUCongress2012dinneronBillKelty.aspx.

Kelly, Paul. 1976. *The Unmaking of Gough*. Sydney: Angus & Robertson.

Kelly, Paul. 1992. *The End of Certainty: The Story of the 1980s*. St Leonards: Allen & Unwin.

Kelly, Paul. 1995. *November 1975: The Inside Story of Australia's Greatest Political Crisis*. St Leonards: Allen & Unwin.

Kelly, Paul. 2009. *The March of Patriots: The Struggle for Modern Australia*. Carlton: Melbourne University Press.

Kelly, Paul. 2011. "The Birth of a Modern Era." *The Australian*, January 1, 2011.

Kelsey, Jane. 1995. *Economic Fundamentalism*. London: Pluto Press.

Kelsey, Jane. 2014. "The Neoliberal Emperor Has No Clothes: Long Live the Emperor." In *Challenging the Orthodoxy. Reflections on Frank Stilwell's Contribution to Political Economy*, edited by Susan Schroeder and Lynne Chester, 151–172. Berlin: Springer-Verlag.

Kelty, Bill. 2012. "Keynote Address." presented at the 2012 ACTU Congress Dinner. http://www.actu.org.au/Media/Speechesandopinion/BillKeltyaddresstoACTUCongress2012dinner.aspx.

Kemcor. 1993. "Work Training Forum Comes to Kemcor." Kemcor.

Kenyon, Peter, and Philip ET Lewis. 1992. "Trade Union Membership and the Accord." *Australian Economic Papers* 31 (59):325–345.

Kenyon, Peter, and Philip ET Lewis. 2000. "The Decline in Trade Union Membership: What Role Did the Accord Play?" In *Australia in Accord: An Evaluation of the Prices and Incomes Accord in the Hawke-Keating Years*, edited by Kenneth Wilson, Joanne Bradford, and Maree Fitzpatrick, 159–174. Footscray: South Pacific Publishing.

Kitay, Jim. 2001. "'The Mudginberri Abattoir Dispute of 1985': Response." *Labour History* 80:191–196.

Klein, Naomi. 2007. *The Shock Doctrine*. Camberwell: Penguin Books.

Klein, Naomi, and Neil Smith. 2008. "The Shock Doctrine: A Discussion." *Environment and Planning D: Society and Space* 26 (4):582–595.

Konings, Martijn. 2014. "Hoodwinked by Hayek." *Journal of Cultural Economy* 7 (4):527–531.

Kriesler, Peter, and Joseph Halevi. 1997. "Australia Deconstructed." *Journal of Australian Political Economy* 39:107–121.

Krinsky, John. 2011. "Neoliberal Times: Intersecting Temporalities and the Neoliberalisation of New York City's Public-Sector Labor Relations." *Social Science History* 35 (3):381–422.

Kuhn, Rick. 1986. *Militancy Uprooted: Labour Movement Economics 1974–1986*. Melbourne: Socialist Action.

Kuhn, Rick. 1993. "The Limits of Social Democratic Policy in Australia." *Capital & Class* 51:17–52.

Kuhn, Rick. 2005. "The History of Class Analysis in Australia." 2005. http://www.anu.edu.au/polsci/marx/interventions/clan.pdf.

Kuhn, Rick, and Tom O'Lincoln. 1989. "Profitability and the Economic Crisis." *Journal of Australian Political Economy* 25:44–69.

Lambie, George. 2013. "Globalisation Before the Crash: The City of London and UK Economic Strategy." *Contemporary Politics* 19 (3):339–360.

Langmore, John. 1982. "An Economic Strategy for a Labor Government." *Journal of Australian Political Economy* 12/13:20–39.

Langmore, John. 2000a. "Some Background Context to the Origins of The Accord." In *Australia in Accord: An Evaluation of the Prices and Incomes Accord in the Hawke-Keating Years*, edited by Kenneth Wilson, Joanne Bradford, and Maree Fitzpatrick, 19–25. Footscray: South Pacific Publishing.

Langmore, John. 2000b. "The Political Economy of Incomes Policy: 1978." In *Australia in Accord: An Evaluation of the Prices and Incomes Accord in the Hawke-Keating Years*, edited by Kenneth Wilson, Joanne Bradford, and Maree Fitzpatrick, 26–28. Footscray: South Pacific Publishing.

Lapavitsas, Costas. 2011. "Theorising Financialisation." *Work, Employment and Society* 25:611–626.

Larkin, James M, and Zach Goldhammer. 2015. "Is It Time for a New New Deal?" *The Nation*, September 30, 2015.

Laurie, Kirsty, and Jason McDonald. 2008. "A Perspective on Trends in Australian Government Spending." Economic Roundup. Australian Government, The Treasury. http://archive.treasury.gov.au/documents/1352/HTML/docshell.asp?URL=03_spending_growth.asp.

Lavelle, Ashley. 2005. "Social Democrats and Neo-Liberalism: A Case Study of the Australian Labor Party." *Political Studies* 53:753–771.

Lavelle, Ashley. 2010. "The Ties That Unwind? Social Democratic Parties and Unions in Australia and Britain." *Labour History* 98 (May):55–75.

Law, Alex, and Gerry Mooney. 2007. "Beyond New Labour: Work and Resistance in the 'New' Welfare State." In *New Labour/Hard Labour?: Restructuring and Resistance Inside the Welfare Industry*, edited by Alex Law and Gerry Mooney, 263–286.

Leard, John. 1983. "Letter to Prime Minister Bob Hawke." Australian National Industries. Z282A, Box 241. Noel Butlin Archive.

Lehmbruch, Gerhard. 1977. "Liberal Corporatism and Party Government." *Comparative Political Studies* 10:91–126.

Leigh, Andrew. 2002. "Trade Liberalisation and the Australian Labour Party." *Australian Journal of Politics and History* 48 (4):487–508.

Leigh, Andrew. 2005. "Deriving Long-Run Inequality Series from Tax Data." *The Economic Record* 81 (255):S58–70.

Loewenstein, Antony. 2015. *Disaster Capitalism: Making a Killing out of Catastrophe*. London: Verso.

Lucarelli, Bill. 2003. "Deindustrialisation Under Labor: 1983–1996." *Journal of Australian Political Economy* 51:77–102.

Lucas, Clay. 2012. "Keating Pays Tribute to Former ACTU Boss Kelty." *Sydney Morning Herald*, May 17, 2012. http://www.smh.com.au/national/keating-pays-tribute-to-former-actu-boss-kelty-20120517-1yrqb.html#ixzz29tRIzxSK.

Mair, Peter. 2013. *Ruling the Void: The Hollowing of Western Democracy*. London: Verso.

Maniatis, Thanasis. 2014. "Does the State Benefit Labor? A Cross-Country Comparison of the Net Social Wage." *Review of Radical Political Economics* 46 (1):15–34.

Markey, Ray. 2002. "Explaining Union Mobilisation in the 1880s and Early 1900s." Working Paper, Faculty of Business, University of Wollongong. http://ro.uow.edu.au/cgi/viewcontent.cgi?article=1606&context=commpapers.

Markey, Ray. 2013. The Accord "Saved us from Thatcherism"ABC Radio National. http://www.abc.net.au/radionational/programs/breakfast/30th-anniversary-of-prices-and-incomes-accord/4725066.

Martin, Peter. 2014. "Super System Expensive and Inefficient, Says Treasury." *Sydney Morning Herald*, April 7, 2014.

Marx, Karl. 1973. *Grundrisse*. London: Penguin.

Marx, Karl. 1975a. "Critical Notes on the Article 'The King of Prussia and Social Reform. By a Prussian' (1844)." In *Early Writings*, edited by Karl Marx, 401–420. Harmondsworth: Penguin Books.

Marx, Karl. 1975b. "Critique of Hegel's Doctrine of the State (1843)." In *Early Writings*, edited by Karl Marx, 57–198. Harmondsworth: Penguin Books.

Marx, Karl. 1975c. *Marx: Early Writings* (*The Contribution to a Critique of Hegel's Philosophy of Right*). London: Penguin.

Marx, Karl. 1975d. "On the Jewish Question (1843)." In *Early Writings*, edited by Karl Marx, 211–242. Harmondsworth: Penguin Books.

Marx, Karl. 1975e. "Preface (to 'A Contribution to the Critique of Political Economy')." In *Early Writings*, edited by Karl Marx, 424–428. Harmondsworth: Penguin Books.

Marx, Karl. 1976. *Capital I: A Critique of Political Economy*. London: Penguin.

Marx, Karl. 1991. *Capital III*. London: Penguin.

Marx, Karl, and Frederick Engels. 1976. *The German Ideology*. Moscow: Progress Publishers.

Marx, Karl, and Frederick Engels. 1998. *The Communist Manifesto: A Modern Edition*. London: Verso.

Matthews, Trevor. 1994. "Employers' Associations, Corporatism and the Accord: The Politics of Industrial Relations." In *State, Economy and Public Policy in Australia*, edited by Stephen Bell and Brian Head, 194–224. Oxford: Oxford University Press.

McDonald, Daren. 1984. "The Accord and the Working Class: Political Gimmick or Viable Strategy?" Honours, University of New South Wales.

McEachern, Doug. 1986. "Corporatism and Business Responses to the Hawke Government." *Politics* 21 (1):19–27.

McFarlane, Ian. 2006. "The Recession of 1990 and Its Legacy (Boyer Lecture)." http://www.abc.net.au/radionational/programs/boyerlectures/lecture-4-the-recession-of-1990-and-its-legacy/3353124.

McGarvie, R E. 1976. "Wage Indexation and the Impact of the 1975 National Wage Cases." *Monash University Law Review* 2:153–165.

McIlroy, John. 1995. *Trade Unions in Britain Today*. 2nd ed. Manchester: Manchester University Press.

McKechnie, A. 1985. "Letter to Bill Kelty, ACTU." Waterside Workers' Federation of Australia (Port Adelaide Branch). Z282A, Box 272, Mudginberri Folder. Noel Butlin Archive.

McKinnon, Ken. 1990. "The New Agenda for Higher Education." *Journal of Tertiary Education Administration* 12 (1):235–241.

McLelland, Alison. 2000. "A Welfare Perspective on the Accord." In *Australia in Accord: An Evaluation of the Prices and Incomes Accord in the Hawke-Keating Years*, edited by Kenneth Wilson, Joanne Bradford, and Maree Fitzpatrick, 51–54. Footscray: South Pacific Publishing.

McMichael, Philip. 1990. "Incorporating Comparison within a World-Historical Perspective: An Alternative Comparative Method." *American Sociological Review* 55 (3):385–397.

McQueen, Humphrey. 2009. *Framework of Flesh: Builders' Labourers Battle for Health and Safety*. Canberra: Ginninderra Press.

Megalogenis, George. 2006. *The Longest Decade*. Carlton North: Scribe Publications.

Megalogenis, George. 2012. *The Australian Moment: How We Were Made for These Times*. Camberwell: Viking.

Millmow, Alex. 2004. "Niemeyer, Scullin and the Australian Economists." *Australian Economic History Review* 44 (2):142–160.

Minns, John. 1989. *The Hawke Government: Class Struggle and the Left*. Melbourne: International Socialists.

Mirowski, Philip. 2013. *Never Let a Serious Crisis Go to Waste: How Neoliberalism Survived the Financial Meltdown*. London: Verso.

Mirowski, Philip, and Dieter Plehwe. 2009. *The Road from Mont Pèlerin: The Making of the Neoliberal Thought Collective*. Cambridge, MA: Harvard University Press.

Mitchell, Bill. 2000a. "Accord Mark III: 1987–88—Summary Outcomes." In *Australia in Accord: An Evaluation of the Prices and Incomes Accord in the Hawke-Keating Years*, edited by Kenneth Wilson, Joanne Bradford, and Maree Fitzpatrick, 319. Footscray: South Pacific Publishing.

Mitchell, Bill. 2000b. "Accord Mark IV: 1988–89—Summary Outcomes." In*Australia in Accord: An Evaluation of the Prices and Incomes Accord in the Hawke-Keating Years*, edited by Kenneth Wilson, Joanne Bradford, and Maree Fitzpatrick, 331. Footscray: South Pacific Publishing.

Mitchell, Bill. 2000c. "Accord Mark V: 1989–90—Summary Outcomes." In *Australia in Accord: An Evaluation of the Prices and Incomes Accord in the Hawke-Keating Years*, edited by Kenneth Wilson, Joanne Bradford, and Maree Fitzpatrick, 335. Footscray: South Pacific Publishing.

Mitchell, Bill. 2000d. "Accord Mark VI: 1990–93—Summary Outcomes." In *Australia in Accord: An Evaluation of the Prices and Incomes Accord in the Hawke-Keating Years*, edited by Kenneth Wilson, Joanne Bradford, and Maree Fitzpatrick, 341. Footscray: South Pacific Publishing.

Mitchell, Bill. 2000e. "Accord Mark VII: 1993–1996—Summary Outcomes." In *Australia in Accord: An Evaluation of the Prices and Incomes Accord in the Hawke-Keating Years*, edited by Kenneth Wilson, Joanne Bradford, and Maree Fitzpatrick, 355. Footscray: South Pacific Publishing.

Mohun, Simon. 2003. "The Australian Rate of Profit 1965–2001." *Journal of Australian Political Economy* 52:83–112.

Molina, Oscar, and Martin Rhodes. 2002. "Corporatism: The Past, Present, and Future of a Concept." *Annual Review of Political Science* 5:305–331.

Moody, Kim. 2007. *From Welfare State to Real Estate: Regime Change in New York City, 1974 to Present*. New York: The New Press.

Moody, Kim. 2010. "Understanding the Rank-and-File Rebellion in the Long 1970s." In *Rebel Rank and File: Labor Militancy and Revolt from Below During the Long 1970s*, edited by Aaron Brenner, Robert Brenner, and Cal Winslow, 105–146. New York: Verso.

Moody, Kim. 2012. "Contextualising Organised Labour in Expansion and Crisis: The Case of the US." *Historical Materialism* 20 (1):3–30.

Moore, Des. 1998. "Why The Labour Market Should Be Deregulated." In *MUA—Here to Stay ... Today!* Vol. 19. Melbourne: H R Nicholls Society. http://archive.hrnicholls.com.au/archives/vol19/vol19-2.php.

Morton, Adam David. 2007. *Unravelling Gramsci: Hegemony and Passive Revolution in the Global Political Economy*. London: Pluto Press.

Moss, Jim. 1985. *Sound of Trumpets: History of the Labour Movement in South Australia*. Netley, SA: Wakefield Press.

Murphy, Damien. 2013. "Cabinet Papers 1986–87: The Struggle for Indigenous Land Rights." *Sydney Morning Herald*, December 28, 2013. http://www.smh.com.au/

federal-politics/political-news/cabinet-papers-198687-the-struggle-for-indigenous-land-rights-20131228-3017r.html.

National Archives of Australia. 2014. "Robert Hawke." National Archives of Australia, Commonwealth of Australia. Australia's Prime Ministers. 2014. http://primeministers.naa.gov.au/primeministers/hawke/.

Nixon, Richard. 1971. "Address to the Nation Outlining a New Economic Policy: The Challenge of Peace." Oval Office, White House, August 15. http://www.presidency.ucsb.edu/ws/?pid=3115.

Nolan, Peter. 1979. "'The Challenge of the 80s', Speech to the Employers' Federation of NSW, 23rd Annual Industrial Relations Conference." Amalgamated Metals Foundry and Shipwrights' Union. Z282A, Box 395. Noel Butlin Archive.

Norington, Brad. 1990. *Sky Pirates: The Pilots' Strike That Grounded Australia*. Crows Nest: Australian Broadcasting Corporation.

Oakes, Laurie. 1976. *Crash Through Or Crash: The Unmaking of a Prime Minister*. Richmond: Drummond.

O'Brien, Martin, and John Burgess. 2004. "Workforce Developments Affecting the Adequacy of Superannuation." *Journal of Australian Political Economy* 53:179–190.

O'Connor, James. 1973. *The Fiscal Crisis of the State*. London: St. Martin's Press.

O'Connor, John. 2010. "Marxism and the Three Movements of Neoliberalism." *Critical Sociology* 36 (5):691–715.

Odom, Frederick. 1992. "Pressures, Shifts, Trade Offs and Renegotiations: Limits of the ALP-ACTU Accord." Master of Public Policy, Armidale: University of New England.

OECD. n.d. "Quarterly National Accounts: Quarterly Growth Rates of Real GDP, Change Over Previous Quarter." Organisation for Economic Co-operation and Development. Accessed November 20, 2015. https://stats.oecd.org.

O'Lincoln, Tom. 1993. *Years of Rage: Social Conflicts in the Fraser Years*. Melbourne: Bookmarks Australia.

Oliver, Pam, and Janet Collins. 1993. "Labor in Power." Sydney: Australian Broadcasting Corporation.

Olsberg, Diana. 2004. "Women and Superannuation: Still Ms … ing Out." *Journal of Australian Political Economy* 53:161–178.

O'Malley, Nick. 2006. "The Sweets of a Famous Victory." *Sydney Morning Herald*, July 26, 2006. http://www.smh.com.au/news/national/the-sweets-of-a-famous-victory/2006/07/25/1153816182414.html.

Panitch, Leo. 1976. *Social Democracy and Industrial Militancy: The Labour Party, the Trade Unions and Incomes Policy, 1945–1974*. Cambridge: Cambridge University Press.

Panitch, Leo. 1977. "The Development of Corporatism in Liberal Democracies." *Comparative Political Studies* 10 (1):61–90.

Panitch, Leo. 1980. "Recent Theorisations of Corporatism: Reflections on a Growth Industry." *The British Journal of Sociology* 31 (2):159–187.

Panitch, Leo. 1981. "Trade Unions and the Capitalist State." *New Left Review* 1 (125):21–43.

Panitch, Leo. 1986. "The Tripartite Experience." In *The State and Economic Interests*, edited by Keith Banting, 37–119. Toronto: University of Toronto Press.

Panitch, Leo. 1999. "The Impoverishment of State Theory." *Socialism and Democracy* 13:19–35.

Panitch, Leo, and Sam Gindin. 2012. *The Making of Global Capitalism: The Political Economy of American Empire*. London: Verso.

Parker, Jean. 2012. "Labor's Accord: How Hawke and Keating Began a Neoliberal Revolution." *Solidarity*, October 12, 2012. http://www.solidarity.net.au/mag/back/2012/50/labors-accord-how-hawke-and-keating-began-a-neo-liberal-revolution/.

Parker, Jean. 2013. "Saving Neoliberalism: Rudd Labor's Response to the 2008 Global Economic Crisis." PhD, Sydney: University of Technology Sydney.

Patrick, Aaron. 2015. "Newspaper Truce for a Summit to Fix Australia." *Australian Financial Review*, July 18, 2015.

Peake, Ross. 1993. "Caucus in Budget Boilover." *The Canberra Times*, August 31, 1993.

Peck, Jamie. 2012. "Economic Geography: Island Life." *Dialogues in Human Geography* 2 (2):113–133.

Peck, Jamie, and Adam Tickell. 2002. "Neoliberalizing Space." *Antipode* 34 (3):380–404.

Peck, Jamie, Nik Theodore, and Neil Brenner. 2009. "Neoliberal Urbanism: Models, Moments, Mutations." *SAIS Review of International Affairs* 29 (1):49–66.

Peck, Jamie, Nik Theodore, and Neil Brenner. 2010. "Postneoliberalism and Its Malcontents." *Antipode* 41 (s1):94–116.

Peetz, David. 2000. "The Accord and the Paradigm Shift in Union Membership." In *Australia in Accord: An Evaluation of the Prices and Incomes Accord in the Hawke-Keating Years*, edited by Kenneth Wilson, Joanne Bradford, and Maree Fitzpatrick, 141–158. Footscray: South Pacific Publishing.

Peetz, David. 2012. "The Impacts and Non-Impacts on Unions of Enterprise Bargaining." *Labour & Industry* 22 (3):237–254.

Peetz, David. 2013. "The Lessons of the Accord for Modern Times: Think Outside the Box." *The Conversation*, June 10, 2013. https://theconversation.com/the-lessons-of-the-accord-for-modern-times-think-outside-the-box-14985.

Peters, Michael A. 2011. *Neoliberalism and After: Education, Social Policy, and the Crisis of Western Capitalism*. New York: Peter Lang Publishing.

Pierson, Chris. 2002. "'Social Democracy on the Back Foot': The ALP and the 'New' Australian Model." *New Political Economy* 7:179–197.

Pierson, Chris, and Francis Castles. 2002. "Australian Antecedents of the Third Way." *Political Studies* 50 (4):683–702.

Plehwe, Dieter. 2009. "Introduction." In *The Road from Mont Pèlerin: The Making of the Neoliberal Thought Collective*, edited by Philip Mirowski and Dieter Plehwe, 1–42. Cambridge, MA: Harvard University Press.

Poulantzas, Nicos. 2001. *State, Power, Socialism*. London: Verso.

Prasad, Monica. 2006. *The Politics of Free Markets: The Rise of Neoliberal Economic Policies in Britain, France, Germany, and the United States*. Chicago: The University of Chicago Press.

Pusey, Michael. 1991. *Economic Rationalism in Canberra: A Nation Building State Changes Its Mind*. Cambridge: University of Cambridge.

Quiggin, John. 1995. "Does Privatisation Pay?" *The Australian Economic Review* 2nd quarter:23–42.

Quiggin, John. 1998. "Social Democracy and Market Reform in Australia and New Zealand." *Oxford Review of Economic Policy* 14 (1):76–95.

Quiggin, John. 2001. "Social Democracy and Market Reform in Australia and New Zealand." In *Social Democracy in Neoliberal Times: The Left and Economic Policy since 1980*, edited by Andrew Glyn, 80–109. Oxford: Oxford University Press.

Quiggin, John. 2010. "Risk Shifts in Australia: Implications of the Financial Crisis." In *Risk, Welfare and Work*, edited by Greg Marston, Jeremy Moss, and John Quiggin. Melbourne: Melbourne University Press.

Rafferty, Mike. 1997. "Union Amalgamation: The Enduring Legacy of Australia Reconstructed." *Journal of Australian Political Economy* 39:99–105.

Rafferty, Mike. 2011. "Global Economic Shakeout: The Cracks in Australia's Superannuation Nest Egg." *The Conversation*, August 10, 2011. http://theconversation.com/global-economic-shakeout-the-cracks-in-australias-superannuation-nest-egg-2783.

Ramsay, Tony. 2004. "The Socialisation of Investment in a Contemporary Setting." *Journal of Australian Political Economy* 53:116–131.

Ramsay, Tony, and Tim Battin. 2005. "Labor Party Ideology in the Early 1990s: Working Nation and Paths Not Taken." *Journal of Economic and Social Policy* 9 (2):1–13.

Rizzo, Michael. 1991. "The Left and the Accord." Master of Arts (Research), Bundoora: La Trobe University.

Roberts, Michael. 2012. "A World Rate of Profit." In. http://thenextrecession.files.wordpress.com/2012/07/roberts_michael-a_world_rate_of_profit.pdf.

Robinson, William I. 2004. *A Theory of Global Capitalism: Production, Class, and State in a Transnational World*. Baltimore: The Johns Hopkins University Press.

Rogers, Chris. 2009. "From Social Contract to 'Social Contrick': The Depoliticisation of Economic Policy-Making under Harold Wilson, 1974–75." *The British Journal of Politics and International Relations* 11 (4):634–651.

Roper, Brian S. 2005. *Prosperity for All? Economic, Social and Political Change in New Zealand Since 1935*. Southbank Victoria: Thompson.

Ross, Liz. 1987. "How We Lost at Robe River—and Why." *Socialist Action*, May 19, 1987.

Ross, Liz. 2004. *Dare to Struggle, Dare to Win!: Builders Labourers Fight Deregistration 1981–94*. Carlton North: Vulgar Press.

Ross, Liz. 2014. "Rank and File Rebellion at Robe River Dispute." *Red Flag*, November 10, 2014. https://redflag.org.au/article/rank-and-file-rebellion-robe-river-dispute.

Ross, Liz, Tom O'Lincoln, and Graham Willett. 1986. "Labor's Accord: Why It's a Fraud." Socialist Action.

Rudd, Kevin. 2009. "The Global Financial Crisis." *The Monthly*, 2009.

Rydon, Joan. 1974. "Prices and Incomes Referendum 1973: The Pattern of Failure." *Australian Journal of Political Science* 9 (1):22–30.

Saad-Filho, Alfredo. 2010. "Crisis in Neoliberalism or Crisis of Neoliberalism?" *Socialist Register* 47:242–259.

Saunders, Peter. 1993. "Longer Run Changes in the Distribution of Income in Australia." *The Economic Record* 69 (207):353–366.

Savolainen, Anna. 2016. "Finland: Tripartite Competitiveness Pact Signed." EuroFound. September 2, 2016. https://www.eurofound.europa.eu/observatories/eurwork/articles/working-conditions-industrial-relations-business/finland-tripartite-competitiveness-pact-signed.

Scalmer, Sean, and Terry Irving. 1999. "The Rise of the Modern Labour Technocrat: Intellectual Labour and the Transformation of the Amalgamated Metal Workers' Union, 1973–85." *Labour History* 77:64–82.

Schmitter, Philippe C. 1974. "Still the Century of Corporatism?" *The Review of Politics* 36 (1):85–131.

Schmitter, Philippe C. 1979. "Still the Century of Corporatism?" In *Trends Toward Corporatism Intermediation*, edited by Philippe C Schmitter and Gerhard Lehmbruch, 7–52. London: SAGE Publications.

Schulman, Jason. 2015. *Neoliberal Labour Goverments and the Union Response: The Politics of the End of Labourism*. Basingstoke: Palgrave MacMillan.

Schultz, Julianne. 1985. *Steel City Blues: The Human Cost of Industrial Crisis*. Melbourne: Penguin.

Scott, Andrew. 2000. *Running on Empty*. Annandale: Pluto Press Australia.

Scott, Andrew. 2006. "Social Democracy in Northern Europe: Its Relevance for Australia." *Australian Review of Public Affairs* 7 (1):1–17.

Selwyn, Ben, and Satoshi Miyamura. 2014. "Class Struggle or Embedded Markets? Marx, Polanyi and the Meanings and Possibilities of Social Transformation." *New Political Economy* 19 (5):639–661.

Sheehan, Mary, and Sonia Jennings. 2010. *A Federation of Pilots: The Story of an Australian Air Pilots' Union*. Melbourne: Melbourne University Press.

Shorten, Bill. 2017. "Bill Shorton Address to John Curtin Research Centre Gala Dinner." presented at the 2017 John Curtin Research Centre Gala Dinner, October 11.

Siemensma, Nick. 2012. "Australian Stalinist Academics Face the 1980s." *Churls Gone Wild* (blog). February 25, 2012. http://churlsgonewild.wordpress.com/2012/02/25/what-me-worry/.

Singleton, Gwynneth. 1990a. "Corporatism or Labourism?: The Australian Labour Movement in Accord." *The Journal of Commonwealth & Comparative Politics* 28:162–182.

Singleton, Gwynneth. 1990b. *The Accord and the Australian Labour Movement*. Carlton: Melbourne University Press.

Singleton, Gwynneth. 2000. "The Accord in Retrospect: A Marriage of Convenience." In *Australia in Accord: An Evaluation of the Prices and Incomes Accord in the Hawke-Keating Years*, edited by Kenneth Wilson, Joanne Bradford, and Maree Fitzpatrick, 83–92. Footscray: South Pacific Publishing.

Smith, Howard, and Herb Thompson. 1987. "Industrial Relations and the Law: A Case Study of Robe River." *The Australian Quarterly* 59 (3/4):297–304.

Sonder, Larry. 1984. "The Accord, the Communiqué and the Budget." *The Australian Quarterly* 56 (2):153–162.

Souter, H J. 1974. "Letter from ACTU Secretary to Prime Minister and Cabinet Regarding National Wage Case." Australian Council of Trade Unions. Z282A, Box 466. Noel Butlin Archive.

Southall, Nick. 2006. "Working for the Class: The Praxis of the Wollongong Out of Workers' Union." Honours, Wollongong: University of Wollongong.

Spies-Butcher, Ben. 2012. "Markets with Equity? Lessons from Australia's Third Way Response to Neoliberalism." In *Neoliberalism: Beyond the Free Market*, edited by Damien Cahill, Lindy Edwards, and Frank Stilwell, 204–227. Cheltenham: Edward Elgar.

Spies-Butcher, Ben. 2014. "Welfare Reform." In *Australian Public Policy: : Progressive Ideas in the Neo-Liberal Ascendency*. Bristol: Policy Press.

Stewart, Randal G. 1985. "The Politics of the Accord. Does Corporatism Explain It?" *Australian Journal of Political Science* 20 (1):26–35.

Stilwell, Frank. 1982. "Towards an Alternative Economic Strategy." *Journal of Australian Political Economy* 12–13:40–59.

Stilwell, Frank. 1986. *The Accord ... and Beyond*. Leichhardt: Pluto Press Australia.

Stilwell, Frank. 1993. "Wages Policy and the Accord." In *The Australian Economy Under Labor*, edited by Greg Mahony, 65–84. St Leonards: Allen & Unwin.

Stilwell, Frank. 1997. "Australia Reconstructed: Oops, Missed the Turning." *Journal of Australian Political Economy* 39:39–47.

Stilwell, Frank. 2000. "The Accord: Contemporary Capitalist Contradictions." In *Australia in Accord: An Evaluation of the Prices and Incomes Accord in the Hawke-Keating*

Years, edited by Kenneth Wilson, Joanne Bradford, and Maree Fitzpatrick, 265–281. Footscray: South Pacific Publishing.

Strauss, Jonathan. 2013. "Opposition to the Accord as a Social Contract in the 1980s." *Labour History* 105:47–62.

Tabb, William K. 1982. *The Long Default: New York City and the Urban Fiscal Crisis*. New York: Monthly Review Press.

Teeple, Gary. 1984. *Marx's Critique of Politics: 1842–1847*. Toronto: University of Toronto Press.

Teeple, Gary. 2000. *Globalisation and the Decline of Social Reform: Into the Twenty-First Century*. Aurora: Garamond Press.

Thomas, Peter. 2009a. "Gramsci and the Political: From the State as 'Metaphysical Event' to Hegemony as 'Philosophical Fact.'" *Radical Philosophy* 153:27–36.

Thomas, Peter. 2009b. *The Gramscian Moment*. Historical Materialism Book Series. Leiden: Brill.

Thompson, Herb. 1984. "The Accord: Raising Profit at Workers' Expense." *Australian Left Review* 89:8–16.

Thornthwaite, Louise, and Peter Sheldon. 1996. "The Metal Trades Industry Association, Bargaining Structures and the Accord." *Industrials Relations & Labor* 38 (2):171–195.

Thorpe, Andrew. 1999. "The Labour Party and the Trade Unions." In *British Trade Unions and Industrial Prolitics: Volume Two—The High Tide of Trade Unionism, 1964–79*, edited by John McIlroy, Nina Fishman, and Alan Campbell, 133–150. Aldershot: Ashgate.

Tickell, Adam, and Jamie Peck. 2003. "Making Global Rules: Globalisation or Neoliberalisation?" In *Remaking the Global Economy*, edited by Jamie Peck and Henry Wai-chung Yeung. London: SAGE.

Timmerman, Frans. 2013. "The Accord and the Pledge (Personal Correspondence)," July 21, 2013.

Unknown. 1974. "Whitlam Pleads with Unions." *The Age*, August 6, 1974.

Unknown. 1986. "Kelty Plays Down the Mudginberri Payout." *The Age*, July 28, 1986.

Upchurch, Martin, Graham Taylor, and Andrew Mathers. 2016. *The Crisis of Social Democratic Trade Unionism in Western Europe: The Search for Alternatives*. Oxon: Routledge.

Urban, Hans-Jurgen. 2012. "Crisis Corporatism and Trade Union Revitalisation in Europe." In *A Triumph of Failed Ideas: European Models of Capitalism in the Crisis*, edited by Steffen Lehndorff, 219–241. Brussels: European Trade Union Institute.

Valenzuela, MA Rebecca, Hooi Hooi Lean, and George Athanasopoulos. 2014. "Economic Inequality in Australia between 1983 and 2010: A Stochastic Dominance Analysis." *The Economic Record* 90 (288):49–62.

Venugopal, Rajesh. 2015. "Neoliberalism as Concept." *Economy and Society* 44 (2): 165–187.

Vidler, Sacha, and Nick Coates. 2004. "Superannuation Policy: Commentary on an Interview with Paul Keating, Former Prime Minister." *Journal of Australian Political Economy* 53:9–16.

Ville, Simon, and Glenn Withers. 2014. *The Cambridge Economic History of Australia.* Cambridge: Cambridge University Press.

Wacquant, Loïc. 2012. "Three Steps to a Historical Anthropology of Actually Existing Neoliberalism." *Social Anthropology* 20 (1):66–79.

Walker, Bob, and Betty Con Walker. 2006. *Privatisation: Sell Off or Sell Out? The Australian Experience.* Sydney: Australian Broadcasting Corporation.

Weisskopf, Thomas E. 1979. "Marxian Crisis Theory and the Rate of Profit in the Postwar U.S. Economy." *Cambridge Journal of Economics* 3:341–378.

Weller, Sally, and Phillip O'Neill. 2014. "An Argument with Neoliberalism: Australia's Place in a Global Imaginary." *Dialogues in Human Geography* 4 (2):105–130.

West, Jonathan. 1982. *Labor's Social Contract: Workers Ripped Off!* Sydney: Pathfinder Press.

Whiteford, Peter. 2014. "Income and Wealth Inequality: How Is Australia Faring?" *The Conversation*, March 5, 2014. http://theconversation.com/income-and-wealth-inequality-how-is-australia-faring-23483.

Whitlam, EG. 1975. "Keynote." Address by the Prime Minister presented at the 31st Federal Conference of the Australian Labor Party, Terrigal NSW, February 5.

Whitlam, EG. 2006. *The Truth of the Matter.* Melbourne: Melbourne University Press.

Willis, Ralph. 1979. "The Case for a Co-Operative Prices and Incomes Policy Under a Labor Government." Z282A, Box 287. Noel Butlin Archive.

Willis, Ralph, and Kenneth Wilson. 2000. "Introduction." In *Australia in Accord: An Evaluation of the Prices and Incomes Accord in the Hawke-Keating Years*, edited by Kenneth Wilson, Joanne Bradford, and Maree Fitzpatrick, 1–18. Footscray: South Pacific Publishing.

Wilson, Frank L. 1983. "Interest Groups and Politics in Western Europe: The Neo-Corporatist Approach." *Comparative Politics* 16 (1):105–123.

Yates, Charlotte. 1996. "Neo-Liberalism and the Working Girl: The Dilemmas of Women and the Australian Union Movement." *Economic and Industrial Democracy* 17:627–665.

Yeatman, Anna. 1990. *Bureaucrats, Technocrats, Femocrats: Essays on the Contemporary Australian State.* St Leonards: Allen & Unwin.

Index